The School of Moses

Program in Judaic Studies
Brown University
BROWN JUDAIC STUDIES

Edited by
Shaye J. D. Cohen, Calvin Goldscheider

Editor for *Studia Philonica*
Shaye J. D. Cohen

Number 304
Studia Philonica Monographs 1
The School of Moses
Studies in Philo and Hellenistic Religion
In Memory of Horst R. Moehring

edited by
John Peter Kenney

The School of Moses
Studies in Philo and Hellenistic Religion

In Memory of Horst R. Moehring

edited by

John Peter Kenney

Scholars Press
Atlanta, Georgia

The School of Moses
Studies in Philo and Hellenistic Religion

In Memory of Horst R. Moehring

Library of Congress Cataloging-in-Publication Data
The school of Moses : studies in Philo and Hellenistic religion : in
  memory of Horst R. Moehring / edited by John Peter Kenney.
      p.   cm. — (Brown Judaic studies ; no. 304)   (Studia Philonica
  monographs ; 1)
    Includes bibliographical references and index.
    ISBN 0-7885-0162-3 (cloth : alk. paper)
    1. Philo, of Alexandria. 2. Hellenism. 3. Judaism—Relations—
  Greek. 4. Platonists—Egypt—Alexandria. 5. Ontology—History.
  I. Moehring, Horst R., 1927–1986. II. Kenney, John Peter.
  III. Series. IV. Series: Studia Philonica monographs ; 1.
  B689.Z7S37   1995
  181'.06—dc20   95-37978
                                         CIP

Printed in the United States of America
on acid-free paper

STUDIA PHILONICA MONOGRAPHS

STUDIES IN HELLENISTIC JUDAISM

EDITOR
David M. Hay, *Coe College, Cedar Rapids*

ADVISORY BOARD

Like *The Studia Philonica Annual*, the Studia Philonica Monographs series accepts monographs in the area of Hellenistic Judaism, with special emphasis on Philo and his *Umwelt*. Proposals for books to be published in the Monograph series should be sent to Prof. David M. Hay, Coe College, Cedar Rapids, IA 52402, U.S.A.

Article-length contributions should be sent to the Editor of *The Studia Philonica Annual,* Prof. David T. Runia, Rijnsburgerweg 116, 2333 AE Leiden, The Netherlands. Books for review in the Annual should be sent to the Book Review Editor, Prof. Gregory E. Sterling, Dept. of Theology, University of Notre Dame, Notre Dame, IN 46556, U.S.A.

Horst R. Moehring
1927–1986

CONTENTS

INTRODUCTION

This collection of essays is dedicated to the memory of Horst Rudolph Moehring by his colleagues and friends. Professor Emeritus of Religious Studies at Brown University, Horst was a respected scholar and teacher, whose life showed a special concern for his students. Each paper in this volume is intended as a contribution to Philonic studies; together they represent an acknowledgement of Horst's legacy in the study of Hellenistic religions.

Born in Goerlitz, Germany in 1927, Horst studied Oriental Philology at the University of Heidelberg from 1947–50. He then came to the United States, reading Classics at the University of Minnesota and the University of Illinois, where he took a Masters degree in 1954. He moved next to the new program in New Testament and Early Christian Literature at The University of Chicago, completing his Ph.D under Allen Wikgren and Ralph Marcus in 1957. His dissertation examined novelistic elements in Flavius Josephus. From the beginning his scholarly interests were clearly marked by a concern to locate ancient Christian literature within the context of Hellenistic Judaism and, more broadly, within the wider sphere of Greco-Roman culture. Perhaps this was the most salient aspect of Horst's scholarship, his interest in the entire spectrum of the religions of the Hellenistic and Roman world and his lucid perspective on nascent Christianity.

This capacious vision was characteristic of Horst; he brought to his scholarship an enlightenment conviction about the value of education. For him, the scholar's project was meant to provide balance and judiciousness, qualities that applied both to one's research and to the understanding one achieved through this process. What was at stake was clear to all who worked with him: that humane learning should be the central value of our academic culture. It was certainly so in his life, for he evinced in both attitude and bearing the lineaments of this old European approach to the humanities, whose roots lay in the ancient period he studied.

Brown was the seat of this intellectual endeavor and the center of his life for over a quarter of a century. He came to Providence from Chicago in1957 as an instructor in Religious Studies and he remained there until ill health forced his early retirement as Emeritus Professor in the summer of 1985. He died in March,1986. During his years at the university he served for a term as chairman of the department of Religious Studies and was its director of graduate studies for many years. He was also the architect of Brown's graduate program in History of Religion: Early

Christianity, directing its progress from its inception until his retirement. This program bears the distintive mark of his scholarship, expanding as it does the horizon in the study of ancient Christianity to encompass Greco-Roman culture and formative Judaism.

Horst Moehring also participated in national and international scholarly organizations and was especially active in various sections of the Society of Biblical Literature. In the years immediately prior to his death, his professional responsibilities included service as chairman of the SBL Group on Hellenistic Judaism, chairman of the SBL Philo Seminar, co-chairman of the Claremont Philo Research Team, and President of the New England Region of the SBL, among others.

One aspect of Horst Moehring's life bears special mention: his concern for his students, both graduate and undergraduate. He invested in them an enormous amount of energy and attention. He invited them into his project of understanding ancient religion and demanded of them a serious commitment to his standards. He sought to impart to them his own devotion to learning, love of the humanities, and commitment to the vocation of teaching. He was always instructing them and advising them. He shared their anxieties amidst the vicissitudes of the academic world and he was genuinely delighted by their successes. He continued to express this singular devotion to his students, even to the day of his death.

This volume is dedicated to his memory by his scholarly associates and students; it includes the last major project which he completed, a study in Philonic arithmology. It gives me great pleasure that it is the first volume in a new subseries within the Brown Judaic Series. The new subseries is entitled Studia Philonica Monographs: Studies in Hellenistic Judaism. I think Horst would also have been pleased.

John Peter Kenney
Reed College

Selected Bibliography of Horst R. Moehring

"Novelistic Elements in the Writings of Flavius Josephus." Ph.D. Dissertation: University of Chicago, 1957.

"The Verb AKOYEIN in Acts 9:7 and 22:9." *Novum Testamentum* 3 (1959): 80–99.

"The Persecution of the Jews and the Adherents of the Isis Cult at Rome A.D. 19." *Novum Testamentum* 3 (1959): 293–304.

"Josephus and the Marriage Customs of the Essenes." In *Early Christian Origins* , edited by Allen P. Wikgren, 120–127. Chicago: Quandrangle Books, 1961.

"Some Remarks on SARX in Philippians 3." In *Studia Evangelica IV* (*Texte und Untersuchungen zur Geschichte der altchristlichen Literatur* 102), edited by F. L. Cross, 432–36. Berlin: Akadmie-Verlag, 1968.

"Catacombs." *Encyclopedia Americana.*

"On Josephus." *Judaism* 15 (1966): 226–28.

"The Census in Luke as an Apologetic Device." In *Studies in New Testament and Early Christian Literature* (Supplements to *Novum Testamentum* XXXIII), edited by David E. Aune, 144–60. Leiden: E. J. Brill, 1972.

"Rationalization of Miracles in the Writings of Flavius Josephus." In *Studia Evangelica VI* (*Texte und Untersuchungen zur Geschichte der altchristlichen Literatur* 112), edited by E. A. Livingston, 376–83. Berlin: Akademie-Verlag, 1973.

"The *Acta pro Judaeis* in the *Antiquities* of Flavius Josephus." In *Christianity, Judaism and Other Greco-Roman Cults* III (*Studies in Judaism in Late Antiquity* XII), edited by J. Neusner, 124–58. Leiden: E. J. Brill, 1975.

"Moses and Pythagoras: Arithmology as an Exegetical Tool in Philo." *Journal for the Study of the Old Testament,* Supplemental Series 11, 205–08. Sheffield, 1979.

"Arithmology As An Exegetical Tool In The Writings Of Philo Of Alexandria." Society Of Biblical Literature 1978 Seminar Papers, Vol. I, edited by Paul J. Achtemeier (Seminar Papers Series,13), Missoula: Scholars Press, 1978. Reprinted in this volume, 141–176.

English translation of *Der Gott der Makkabaeer* by Elias Bickermann. *The God of the Maccabees: Studies on the meaning and origin of the Maccabean revolt (Studies in Judaism in Late Antiquity XXXII*). Leiden: E.J. Brill, 1979.

"Josephus ben Matthia and Flavius Josephus- The Jewish Prophet and Roman Historian." In *Aufstieg und Niedergang der roemischen Welt* II. 21.2, edited by Wolfgang Haase, 864–944. Berlin: Walter de Gruyter, 1984.

PHILO JUDAEUS ET ALEXANDRINUS:
The State of the Problem

EARLE HILGERT

Samuel Sandmel, at the beginning of his book on *Philo's Place in Judaism*,[1] quotes Louis Ginzberg:[2]

> There are few Jewish authors about whom so much has been written as about Philo. And yet the most important problem connected with Philo is not yet solved. Was he a Jewish thinker with a Greek education, or a Greek philosopher with Jewish learning?

These words set the focus of this study.

Philo Judaeus of Alexandria—the name itself epitomizes the problem: a Jew who is best known by the name of the Hellenistic city in which he spent his life. A contemporary of Hillel, Shammai, Seneca, Jesus and Paul, his life spanned at least the reigns of Herod the Great, Augustus, Tiberius and Caligula. He enjoyed wealth and prestige and leisure. A brother of Alexander Lysimmachus the "alabarch," who was rich enough to make a substantial loan to Agrippa I, and uncle of Tiberius Alexander, later Roman prefect of Egypt, Philo himself, when the Alexandrian Jews fell on evil days during the reign of Caligula, was chosen by them as one of a deputation of five envoys sent to Rome to intercede with the emperor. Philo's wealth and status provided the setting for the learning and the leisure required to produce the voluminous writings we have from his pen. The bulk of his *oeuvre* is devoted to exposition of and commentary on the Torah—and it is all written in Greek.

It is just at this point that our problem arises, for Philo interpreted the Torah as a treasure house of Greek philosophical insight. Using primarily the allegorical method, he drew seemingly at random on Platonic, Stoic and Pythagorean thought for the meanings he found in Scripture. At the same time, to quote Sandmel, "no Jew in history ever surpassed Philo in loyalty to Judaism."[3] Against more liberal souls, Philo insisted on the strict observance of the very rituals he allegorized into philosophical

---

[1] Samuel Sandmel, *Philo's Place in Judaism* (Cincinnati: Hebrew Union College Press, 1956) 1.

[2] Louis Ginzberg, *Legends of the Jews*, 7 vols. (Philadelphia: Jewish Publication Society, 1909–39).

[3] Samuel Sandmel, *Philo of Alexandria: An Introduction* (New York: Oxford, 1979) 134.

principles, and he risked his life in going to plead with Caligula that
Jewish synagogues not be desecrated and that the Jews' long-standing
civil rights not be curtailed.

The kaleidoscopic nature of Philo's writings has given rise to the most
varied evaluations of him. Writing in 1938, Walter Völker traced the way
in which each succeeding generation since the late eighteenth century
had thought to see its own characteristic understandings mirrored in
Philo. He was held to be a proponent of the Enlightenment (C.F. Bahrdt)
who was concerned to promote the principle of rationalistic super-
naturalism.[4] By the middle of the nineteenth century Philo was presented
as a Hegelian (Dorner, M. Wolff), while in the liberalism at the end of the
century he was once more seen as a rationalist. In the present century
Philo has successively been understood as a psychologist of religion (H.
Windisch[5]), a neo-Kantian (Falter: God is a "heuristic principle"), and an
existentialist (G. Kuhlmann). Völker's catalogue can be extended on
though the last half century since he made his survey. In our time Philo
has been hailed, in the main features of his thought, "as the most dominant force in the history of philosophy down to the seventeenth century"
(Wolfson[6]). He has been identified as the founder of a Jewish mystery
cult (Goodenough[7]), as a Heideggerian philosopher of language (Otte[8]),
and as an amazingly ingenious structuralist (J. Cazeaux[9]). At the same
time he is written off as an author without original thought whose only
value is in the traditions which he transmits: thus Peter Katz has likened
him to a beast of burden who is important only for the baggage he
carries.[10]

I

In light of such a spectrum of evaluations of Philo, it is no surprise that
attempts to locate him between the poles of traditional Judaism and

---

[4] Walter Völker, *Fortschritt und Vollendung bei Philo von Alexandrien* (Leipzig: Hinrichs,
1938) 42, quoting J. Chr. Schreiter, *Philos Ideen über Unsterblichkeit, Aufferstehung und
Vergeltung* (Leipzig, 1813) 1.126: "Philo, der sich bemüht, das Prinzip des rationalisti-
schen Supranaturalismus zu empfehlen."

[5] H. Windisch, *Die Frömmigkeit Philos* (Leipzig: Hinrichs, 1909) cited by Völker, 43.

[6] H.A. Wolfson, *Philo*, 2 vols. (Cambridge, MA: Harvard, 1948) 1.vii.

[7] Erwin R. Goodenough, *By Light, Light* (London: Oxford, 1935); see also the discussion and evaluation by Sandmel, *Philo* (n. 3) 140–47.

[8] K. Otte, *Das Sprachverständnis bei Philo von Alexandrien*, BGBE 7 (Tübingen: Mohr
[Siebeck], 1968).

[9] Jacques Cazeaux, *La trame et la chaine: structures littéraires et exégèse dans cinq traités de
Philon d'Alexandrie*, ALGHJ 15 (Leiden: Brill, 1983).

[10] P. Katz in *TLZ* 1956, 680 cited by V. Nikiprowetzky, *Le commentaire de l'écriture chez
Philon d'Alexandrie*, ALGHJ 11 (Leiden: Brill, 1977) 2.

Hellenism have been numerous and varied. From a very early date he was seen as standing in the wake of Greek philosophy. Thus Numenius (late second century) is said to have declared: "either Plato philonizes, or Philo platonizes."[11] This sense of a predominant Hellenism in his writings doubtless is also one reason for the fact that, as far as we know, he was totally ignored by Jewish thinkers and writers throughout antiquity and in the Middle Ages. His appeal seems to have been exclusively to Christians[12] (Jerome includes him in his *De Viris Illustribus*, a catalogue of Christian notables, and his influence on Origen, Gregory of Nyssa, and Ambrose was profound). The tendency, in fact, was to downplay Philo's Judaism for the sake of showing him, particularly through his logos-doctrine, to have been really a witness to Christ. In the Middle Ages he was, in fact, at times catalogued as a Christian saint, and after the Reformation his teaching regarding the divine potencies was called upon as a witness for the doctrine of the Trinity, in opposition to the Socinians.

This sense of Philo as a Hellenist, if not as a Christian, remained strong in the nineteenth century, and continues in some quarters today. We can mention only a few representative scholars who have focused their work on Philo's Hellenism. In 1875 Carl Siegfried, in the course of a study of Philo as an expositor of the Old Testament,[13] saw him as having taken a step beyond previous classical allegorists in that he systematized the allegorical process. Siegfried declared:[14]

> Wie wir gesehen haben, war Philo ebenso sehr begeisterter Verehrer griechi-scher Bildung und Wissenschaft als in seinem Herzen gläubiger Jude. Dieser Widerspruch fand zunächst in seinem Innern darin eine Ausgleichung, dass er die griechische Wissenschaft als einen Ausfluss der alttestamentlichen Offen-barung ansah .... Philo fand ... die Allegoristik bereits vor, er suchte aber dieselbe zu einer durchgebildeten Technik, die nach bestimmten Regeln verfuhr, zu erhoben.

---

[11] Quoted by Jerome, *De Viris Illustribus* 11.

[12] The only possible exception I know to this is Eusebius' report that within his own lifetime, during the reign of Caligula, "Philo became generally known as a man of the greatest distinction, not only among our own people, but also among those of heathen education" (*Ecclesiastical History* 2.4.2), and that during the reign of Claudius he read before the Roman Senate his "description of the impiety of Caius [i.e., Caligula]" and that his "words were so much admired as to be granted a place in libraries" (*Ibid.*, 2.18.8, Loeb). Eusebius' reference to Philo's fame at such an early time "among our own people" doubtless grows out of his notion that Therapeutae about whom Philo writes were really Christian monks, and further that Philo had been in touch with Peter while in Rome. There is, of course, no basis for either of these ideas, nor is there in pagan literature any indication of Philo's supposed influence.

[13] Carl Siegfried, *Philo von Alexandria als Ausleger des Alten Testaments* (Jena: Hermann Dufft, 1875).

[14] *Ibid.* 160–61.

Siegfried proceeded then to work out what he perceived these implicit rules to have been.

An enduring classic in Philo studies is the work of Emile Bréhier, *Les idées philosophiques et religieuses de Philon d'Alexandrie*,[15] first published in 1908. Bréhier worked systematically, topic by topic, through the thought of Philo and brought to it a host of analogies from Greek and Roman philosophy and political theory. In 1909 Hans Windisch published *Die Frömmigkeit Philos und ihre Bedeutung für das Christentum*, in which he saw the main stream of Philo's piety to derive from Platonic dualism.[16]

Closely related to the work of those scholars who have emphasized Philo's Hellenism is that of those who have seen the mystical element in his writings as dominant. This has been a particular interest of scholars working under the influence of the history of religions school. Two in particular may be mentioned. Wilhelm Bousset, in his *Jüdisch-christlicher Schulbetrieb in Alexandria und Rom*, saw Philo as[17]

> der Anfänger und erste Zeuge einer mystischen Gesammtanschauung ..., die sich weder aus dem Alten Testament noch aus der genuinen griechischen Philosophie ableiten und begreifen lässt und die dann in der grossen Bewegung der hellenistischen und der christlichen Gnosis ihre Fortsetzung findet.

Here Bousset stands in the tradition of Neander and Moses Mendelsohn at the beginning of the nineteenth century.[18]

Perhaps the most extreme portrait of Philo as a Hellenized Jew is that offered by the extensive works of Erwin R. Goodenough. He was convinced that Philo represented a unique, marginal strain in Judaism which took to its heart "the pagan idea of salvation; that is, that the spirit be released from the flesh in order to return to its spiritual source in God."[19] Philo's Judaism thus became, in Goodenough's view, a Greek mystery religion. The Jewish observances remained important, but that importance lay in their symbolizing the soul's departure from the defilement and confusion of this world by partaking of the logos and ascending mystically to stand, as Moses did, beside God. Thus, to quote Goodenough, Philo "claimed for Judaism all that was most inspiring in pagan religious, philosophic, and to some extent, ritualistic thought."[20]

---

[15] Emile Bréhier, *Les Idées philosophiques et religieuses de Philon d'Alexandrie* (Paris: Vrin, 1950³).

[16] Windisch, *op. cit.*.

[17] Wilhelm Bousset, *Jüdisch-christlicher Schulbetrieb in Alexandria und Rom* (Göttingen: Vandenhoeck & Ruprecht, 1915) III.

[18] I owe this insight to a remark of Arnaldo Momigliano.

[19] Erwin R. Goodenough, *An Introduction to Philo Judaeus*, 2nd ed. (Oxford: Blackwell, 1962) 14.

[20] *Ibid.* 158.

In 1955 Samuel Sandmel, a student of Goodenough, undertook to assess the issue of Philo's relation to the rabbis, with particular reference to the portrayal of the figure of Abraham.[21] Sandmel posed his question in this way:[22]

> To my mind, it is appropriate to alter the question from either 'Is Philo hellenized?' or 'How much is Philo hellenized?' to this, 'Granting some hellenization, how *measurably* much is Philo hellenized?' One needs always to recall that the little or greatly hellenized Philo is in his own light a loyal Jew, and that the philosophy, or anything else which he used in his writings, seemed to him either congruent with his Judaism or even derived from it.

After an extensive comparative study of conceptions of Abraham in Philo and in early rabbinic traditions, Sandmel concluded:[23]

> Insofar as the limited study of Abraham is decisive for the entire Philonic corpus, these conclusions seem to be in order. First, Philo either has little knowledge of or else rejects the characteristic content of rabbinic exegesis. Second, Philo's view of Judaism differs from that of the rabbis as philosophical mysticism based on the Bible differs from halakic legalism. Three, Philonic Judaism is the result of a hellenization which transcends mere language; it is as complete a hellenization as was possible for a group which retained throughout its loyalty to the Torah, and the separateness of that group. Fourth, as contrastable with normative, rabbinic Judaism, Philo and his associates reflect a marginal, aberrative version of Judaism which existed at a time when there were many versions of Judaism, of which ultimately only Rabbinism and Christianity survived to our day.

In 1968 Ursula Früchtel published a study in which she addressed the question of Philo's relation to Gnosticism, a connection proposed by Bousset and subsequently championed by others (Früchtel cites J. Jervell, F.-W. Eltester and W. Schmithals[24]). Focusing on Philo's cosmological conceptions as a test area, Früchtel concluded:[25]

> Philo hat diese Einzelüberlieferungen, deren Nahtstellen noch deutlich sichtbar sind, einer einheintlichen Denkstruktur untergeordnet und einem Ziel, der Erkenntnisfrage, dienstbar gemacht. Es wurde von Fall zu Fall gezeigt, dass weder die verschiedenen Traditionen noch der Gesamtaufriss also gnostisch im herkömmlichen Sinn bezeichnet werden können.

---

[21] Samuel Sandmel, "Philo's Place in Judaism: A Study of Conceptions of Abraham in Jewish Literature," *Hebrew Union College Annual* 25 (1954) 209–37; 26 (1955) 151–332; revised and enlarged as *Philo's Place in Judaism* (Cincinnati: Hebrew Union College Press, 1956).

[22] Sandmel, *op. cit.* (1956), 5.

[23] *Ibid.* 211.

[24] Ursula Früchtel, *Die Kosmologischen Vorstellungen bei Philo von Alexandrien*, ALGHT 2 (Leiden: Brill, 1968) 3, n. 9.

[25] *Ibid.* 184.

Rather, Früchtel found the rootage of these cosmological traditions to be in Middle Platonism. At the same time, however, she recognized that Philo's chief concern was not with philosophy as such, but with the exposition of scripture, to which he brought the rules of interpretation learned from Hellenistic scholarship. But scripture always remains at the center of his attention; she says: "Es ist nur dem Gegenstand her verständlich, mit dem er sich beschäftigt, dass er trotz aller Abhängigkeit wie ein erratischer Block wirkt."[26]

In the last decade, four works dealing with Philo's philosophical relationships may be mentioned: Georgios Farandos, *Kosmos und Logos nach Philo von Alexandrien*,[27] who sees Philo as the culmination of ancient metaphysical speculation on cosmos and logos and declares him to be "ein stoizierender Platoniker sui generis, Vertreter des kaiserzeitlichen Platonismus, ein Erneuerer des Platonismus und ein Kritiker der altgriechschen Philosophie und der jüdischen Religion."[28] More broadly focussed than Farandos' work is John Dillon's study, *The Middle Platonists*,[29] in which he treats Philo as a major representative of Middle Platonism and studies his thought in the context of such philosophers as Antiochus of Ascalon, who sought a synthesis between Platonism and Stoicism. Particularly valuable, and indeed a model of comparative scholarship is David T. Runia's two-volume study of *Philo of Alexandria and the* Timaeus *of Plato*.[30] Runia finds that Philo was deeply influenced by the Timaeus throughout his writings (he speaks of its impact as "impressively great" and "decisive"[31]). This influence covers a spectrum of issues: the doctrine of God, or the cosmos, and of the soul. Philo also becomes a witness to one form of Middle Platonism. Still another recent work of much merit is Thomas H. Tobin's *The Creation of Man*,[32] in which he demonstrates how widespread in classical thought were the roots of Philo's doctrine of creation.

---

[26] Früchtel, *op. cit.* 186.
[27] Georgios Farandos, *Kosmos und Logos nach Philo von Alexandrien* (Diss. Würzburg; Amsterdam: Rodopi, 1976).
[28] *Ibid.* II.
[29] John Dillon, *The Middle Platonists* (Ithaca, NY: Cornell, 1977).
[30] David (Douwe) T. Runia, *Philo of Alexandria and the* Timaeus *of Plato*, 2 vol. (Amsterdam: VU Boekhandel, 1983), Philosophia Antiqua 44 (Leiden: Brill, 1986).
[31] *Ibid.* 1.389.
[32] Thomas H. Tobin, S.J., *The Creation of Man*, CBQMS 14 (Washington D.C.: Catholic Biblical Association, 1983).

II

While much work was thus being done on Philo's relations to Hellenism, from the early nineteenth century onward a growing number of scholars focused on his connections with rabbinic, or at least "main line" Judaism. Thus in 1820 Jacques Matter could declare Philo "un croyant du judaïsme, il n'est jamais philosophe."[33] Similarly, Heinrich Ewald in 1859 offered the judgment that Philo's Greek language and education were worn only as "einen gefügigen Mantel um sich."[34] It remained, however, for Bernhard Ritter[35] to undertake a systematic investigation of Philo's relation to the halakah. Ritter worked through the rabbinic legal system topic by topic comparing Philo with it and with evidences from Josephus. He concluded that Philo's work contains "eine Anzahl palästinischer Halacha's" and also that "Philo's Schriftbehandlung, wo er eben als nüchterner Gesetzausleger auftritt, nicht so weit von der Weise der Halacha entfernt ist."[36] Ritter thought that Philo reflects the usages of the Jewish courts in Egypt (here he anticipates a thesis of Goodenough) and declared: "Eine Kenntnis der Halacha in grösserem Umfange gewahren wir erst bei Philo."[37] While Ritter worked with little sense of the chronological problems inherent in a comparative use of rabbinical literature, his book remains of interest for the evidence it provides of early themes in Mishna, Talmud, and Tosephta. It is, however, incomplete and fragmentary.

The first writer in English of whom I am aware who championed Philo as thoroughly Jewish and who sought to demonstrate this was Norman Bentwich, in 1910.[38] He declared: "I hold that Philo is essentially and splendidly a Jew, and that his thought is through and through Jewish."[39] Two decades later Edmund (Menachem) Stein published two essays[40] in which he undertook to determine the sources of Philo's allegory. Stein concluded that although Philo did not know Hebrew, nevertheless "die hebräische Etymologie alle Teile der philonischen

[33] Jacques Matter, *Histoire de l'école d'Alexandrie*, 2nd ed. (Paris, 1848) 3.184 cited by Völker *op. cit.* 30, n. 1; see also Matter, *Essai historique sur l'école d'Alexandrie*, 2 vols. Paris, 1820).

[34] Heinrich Ewald, *Geschichte des Volkes Israel bis Christus*, 3 vols. (Göttingen: Dieterich, 1843).

[35] Bernhard Ritter, *Philo und die Halacha: eine vergleichende Studie* (Leipzig: Hinrichs, 1879).

[36] *Ibid.* VII.

[37] Ritter, *op. cit.* 9.

[38] Norman Bentwich, *Philo Judaeus of Alexandria* (Philadelphia: Jewish Publication Society, 1910; 1940[2]).

[39] *Ibid.* 8.

[40] Edmund Stein, *Die allegorische Exegese des Philo von Alexandreia*, BZAW 51 (Giessen: Töpelmann, 1929); *Philo und der Midrasch*, BZAW 57 (Giessen: Töpelmann, 1931).

Philosophie beherrscht."[41] Therefore his allegorical system cannot have originated with him: "sein Verdienst besteht lediglich in der Erhaltung der überlieferung."[42] In seeking to determine the source of this tradition, Stein distinguished between "historical haggada," which simply elaborates the biblical narrative and which he identified as of largely Palestinian origin, and "allegorical haggada," of which Philo is the chief representative. On the basis of a systematic comparison of the treatment of names in Genesis by Philo and in the "historical haggada," Stein laid out his program as follows"[43]

> Es wird gezeight, dass die allegorische Agada eine Fortbildung der historischen ist. Ohne die historische Agada hätte die Allegoristik nicht entstehen können .... zur Darstellung der Philonischen Allegoristik diejenigen agadischen Momente des palästinensischen Midrasch [werden] herangezogen, die die Entstehung der allegorischen Deutung verständlich machen. Hat sich so die historische, grösstenteils palästinensische Agada als die Vorstufe zur Allegoristik herausgestellt, dann ist für die Entscheidung der Abhängigkeitsfrage ein neues Kriterium gewonnen.

At the end of his study, Stein then concluded:[44]

> Da der agadische Hintergrund, auf dem die Allegorisierung der biblischen Gestalten enstanden ist auf hellenistischem Boden nicht zu finden ist, wird man die palästinensische ausmalende Agada als Vorstufe der Allegoristik, d.h. weiter die Abhängigkeit der allegorischen Deutung von dem palästinensischen Midrasch anzunehmen haben.

Perhaps the most important work yet to address the issue of whether Philo was a traditional Jew or a Hellenist was Isaak Heinemann's *Philons griechische und jüdische Bildung*.[45] Like Ritter, but much more extensively and less tendentiously, Heinemann worked through the topics of Jewish law searching for backgrounds in both Greek and Jewish thought. He concluded that Philo knew only the LXX, and was ignorant of the oral law, though he did have access to certain traditions, particularly in regard to the Temple. On the Greek side, Heinemann showed the influence of Hellenistic legal systems, and that Philo's thought is related to a broad spectrum: Plato, the Peripatetics, the Cynics, the Middle Stoa, the Pythagoreans. Heinemann concluded:[46]

---

[41] Stein, *op cit.* 1929, 60.
[42] *Ibid.* 61; cf. 25–26.
[43] Stein, *op. cit.* 1931, IV.
[44] Stein, *ibid.* 51.
[45] Isaak Heinemann, *Philons griechische und jüdische Bildung* (Breslau: Marcus, 1932; Hildesheim: Olms, 1973).
[46] Heinemann, *op. cit.* 1973, 574.

Griechisches und Jüdisches wirken auswählend, umbildend, bisweilen verstär-
kend aufeinander ... Die Herstellung einer Synthese zwischen griechischer
Kultur und Jüdischer Frömmigkeit ist Philons geschichtliche Aufgabe.

The last sentence of Heinemann's book reads:[47]

Wohl aber ergibt sich, weshalb sich der hellenistische Jude mit voller Ehrlich-
keit als Bürger beider Kulturwelten fühlen durfte und welche Gefahren der
Hellenismus, auch in seiner philosophischen Form, für die Aufrechterhaltung des
Judentums in sich schloss.

This from a Jewish scholar in the Germany of 1932! The abiding value of
Heinemann's work, when compared with that of many of his contem-
poraries, lies not only in the depth and breadth of his investigation, but
also, and perhaps especially, in the balance of his judgments.

The most profound attempt to place Philo in a traditional Jewish setting
has been that of Harry Austryn Wolfson, whose two large volumes were
published in 1947.[48] Wolfson saw the relation between Philo and the
rabbis to have been extensive and fourfold, including: (1) those elements
from a common Palestinian source, which Alexandrian Jews had
brought to Egypt with them; (2) those that developed in parallel in
Palestine and in Egypt thanks to common methods of interpretation; (3)
those that filtered into Egypt from Palestine through normal channels of
communication; and (4) Philo's probable influence on later Palestinian
rabbis. All this makes good sense with the exception of the fourth item,
which also would be reasonable if we had any clear indication that the
rabbis read Philo. The real issue is *how much* relationship existed between
Philo and the rabbis, and indeed how much of our rabbinical material
existed in the early years of the first century. Wolfson thought this to be
considerable. He said: "Parallels to *many* of these unwritten traditions
reflected in the writings of Philo are to be found in the collections of
Palestinian traditions known as the Mishna, the Midrash, and the
Talmud."[49]

Another thoroughgoing, if not to say extreme, attempt to place Philo in
the company of the rabbis was undertaken by Samuel Belkin in a series of
books and articles in English and Hebrew. Initially writing under the
wing of Wolfson,[50] and in almost diametrical opposition to Heinemann,
Belkin argued that :[51]

---

[47] *Ibid.* 574.
[48] Wolfson, *op. cit.*
[49] *Ibid.* 1.90–91.
[50] Samuel Belkin, *Philo and the Oral Law* (Cambridge, MA: Harvard, 1940).
[51] *Ibid.* x.

the Oral Law which originated in Palestine was not limited to the borders of Palestine, but was also known and practiced among the Jews who lived outside of Palestine, and that Philo's Halakah is based upon the Palestinian Oral Law as it was known in Alexandria.

Belkin saw Philo to have "combined Pharisaic Halakism, practical allegorism, and mysticism."[52]

In evaluating the issue of relationships between Philo and rabbinic tradition there is no question of a certain amount of overlap. But, as Sandmel has pointed out,[53] this fact says little in regard to genetics. Many of the parallels are between Philo and rabbis who lived much later than he. While I would not suggest, as did Wolfson, that this points to their having read Philo, Sandmel was correct in arguing that parallels may be nothing more than parallel developments, and not necessarily concurrent ones, but developments growing out of similar circumstances and common presuppositions. Thus Philo's undeniably traditionalist traits prove little as far as his personal relation to the Palestinian rabbinism of his time is concerned.

III

Thus far we have focused almost entirely on questions regarding the sources of Philo's thought. In evaluating his orientation, it is important to consider also his method and his personal life situation.

The question of whether or not Philo knew Hebrew has been much mooted. On first thought it would seem that the answer would bear strongly on our classification of him as traditionalist or Hellenist, and it is indeed a fact that in general those who have identified him closely with Palestinian Judaism have held that he knew Hebrew, while those who have emphasized his Hellenistic connections have claimed that he did not. On second thought, however, the fact that we do not know whether he knew Hebrew and really cannot know, because a clear knowledge of Hebrew plays so little part in his writings, means that the question is really not a major issue. Philo builds much on the etymology of Hebrew names: some of his etymologies are linguistically sound, many are bad. There is nothing he could not have got from a previously existing *notarikon,* a list of names with their meanings, combined with perhaps a smattering of Hebrew vocabulary and an agile imagination. The question of Philo's knowledge of Hebrew is, I think, almost a non-issue for an understanding of his cultural location.

---

[52] Belkin, *op. cit.* 23.
[53] Sandmel, *op. cit.* 1979, 133–34.

Of greater importance is the question of Philo's exegetical method and its presuppositions, which has attracted the attention of a number of scholars in recent years. Yehoshua Amir (formerly Hermann Neumark), a pupil of Heinemann, in a series of articles published over several decades,[54] has continued investigation of the Hellenistic affinities of Philo's thought. He has traced specific motifs,[55] especially by analyzing Philo's concept of inspiration and its consequences for his exposition of the Torah,[56] as compared with that of the rabbis. In doing so he has placed himself in sharp contrast to Wolfson and become one of his most telling critics. Thus, after comparing the differences between rabbinic midrash and Philonic allegory in their understanding of the nature of the biblical text, Amir concludes:[57]

> Das Verhältnis zwischen dem Wortsinn und der eigentlichen allegorischen Intention ist ganz anders als das zwischen Wortsinn und Midrasch. Im Wortsinn breitet sich die Welt der sinnlichen Erfahrung aus, während die Träger des allegorischen Sinnes Abstrakta sind. Der Midrasch kann einen in der Bibel erzählten Vorgang in eine andere Zeit versetzen—die Allegorie hebt ihn aus der Kategorie der Zeit überhaupt heraus ... Alle diese Einzeldifferenzen aber weisen auf eine gemeinsame religionssoziologische Wurzel hin: Die Allegorie ist für die wenigen bestimmt [Abr 147] und soll vor der Masse geheimgehalten werden; der Midrasch hat seinen natürlichen Ort in der Volkspredigt in der Synogoge .... Die Allegorie stammt aus einer intellektuellen Entfremdung von der unmittelbar gegebenen Wirklichkeit des Gotteswortes; der Midrasch lebt und schafft aus eben dieser Wirklichkeit heraus.

In 1969 Irmgard Christenson published *Die Technik der allegorischen Auslegungswissenschaft bei Philon von Alexandrien*.[58] Here she demonstrated at

---

[54] Now collected in his *Die hellenistische Gestalt des Judentums bei Philon von Alexandrien*, Forschungen zum jüdisch-christlichen Dialog 5 (Neukirchen-Vluyn: Neukirchner Verlag, 1983).

[55] See, for instance, his article, "The Transference of Greek Allegories to Biblical Motifs in Philo," in *Nourished with Peace: Studies in Hellenistic Judaism in Memory of Samuel Sandmel*, ed. Frederick E. Greenspahn, et al. (Chico: Scholars Press, 1984) 15–25; republished as "Die übertragung griechischer Allegorien auf biblische Motive bei Philon," in Amir, *op. cit.* 1983, 119–28.

[56] See the following articles by Amir: "Philo and the Bible," *Studia Philonica* 2 (1973) 1–8; republished as "Philon und die Bibel" in Amir, *op. cit.* 1983, 67–76; and the following articles also in the same collection: "Mose als Verfasser der Tora bei Philon," 77–106; "Rabbinischer Midrasch und philonische Allegorie," 107–118; and "Philons Erörterungen über Gottesfurcht und Gottesliebe in ihrem Verhältnis zum palästinischen Midrasch," 164–85.

[57] "Rabbinischer Midrasch und philonische Allegorie" in Amir, *op. cit.* 1983 , 118; see also "Mose als Verfasser, *ibid.* 79–80.

[58] Irmgard Christenson, *Die Technik der allegorischen Auslegungswissenschaft bei Philon von Alexandrien*, Beiträge zur Geschichte der biblischen Hermeneutik 7 (Tübingen: Mohr [Siebeck], 1969).

length the frequency with which Philo employs the Hellenistic rhetorical technique of the dieresis in constructing his allegories. While she
may go too far in claiming for the dieresis that it "bildet die technische
Grundlage der allegorischen Auslegungswissenschaft,"[59] she has thrown
the spotlight on an important aspect of Philo that has roots in Hellenistic
philosophy. More recently and building partially on Christenson's work,
Robert G. Hamerton-Kelly has shown how Philo combines Hellenistic
dieresis with *gezerah shawa*, the second of Hillel's *middot*, or norms for the
exegesis of Scripture.[60] While the dieresis is a technique in which general
ideas are broken down into their component parts by a series of
contrasting sub-ideas, *gezerah shawa* argues on the basis of analogies both
in content and in identity of words. This presupposes, of course, that
Scripture is a unified whole, so that one text can be taken to elucidate
another. Hamerton-Kelly shows that Philo combines these methods in his
exegesis by setting up dieretic contrasts and then expounding on them by
the use of *gezerah shawa*. He concludes: "[This] also testifies to an author
equally at home in the Hellenistic and the Jewish conventions of
exposition."[61]

Moving in the same direction, Richard D. Hecht has recently investi-
gated the theological implications of Philo's use of Hellenistic rhetorical
techniques.[62] He focuses particularly on dieresis and anastrophe. In
regard to dieresis he points out that it is not confined in Philo to his
allegorical works, but that it is found widely across his corpus. At the
same time, dieresis is more than simply a "technique of composition": it
constitutes for Philo the structural relationship between the Decalogue, as
the overarching generality, and the rest of the laws, as the sub-ideas. This
is the relationship of genus and species, and thus ties the Law to the very
nature of cosmos.

Philo also uses anastrophe, in which it is possible to understand a text
backward or forward, or to rearrange its parts so as to nuance, and thereby
clarify its meaning. To be able to do this presupposes a particular theory of
Scripture, which assumes a certain degree of inspiration not only for

---

[59] *Ibid.* 29.
[60] Robert G. Hamerton-Kelly, "Some Techniques of Composition in Philo's Allegorical Commentary with Special Reference to *De Agricultura*" in *Jews, Greeks and Christians:
Essays in Honor of William David Davies*, ed. R.G. Hamerton-Kelly and Robin Scroggs
(Leiden: Brill, 1976) 45–56. There is, however, some evidence that the *middot* may
have been drawn from Hellenistic sources, in which case Philo's use of *gezerah shawa*
could have come directly from them.
[61] *Ibid.* 56.
[62] Richard D. Hecht, "Patterns of Exegesis in Philo's Interpretation of Leviticus,"
Studia Philonica 6 (1979–80) 77–115.

Scripture but also for the commentary on it. At this point Hecht quotes Yehoshua Amir with approval:[63]

> [Philo] takes for granted the Greek theory of revelation which is different from the theory of Jewish tradition. For the educated Greek, the Godhead does not speak *to* man but *within* man. Man at his highest is man working under inspiration.

Philo's interpretations thus come to be a "rewritten Bible," on the basis of a Greek point of view brought to bear on the Jewish sacred text.

One of the wisest and most balanced studies of Philo's method is that published by Valentin Nikiprowetzky in 1977, *Le commentaire de l'écriture chez Philon d'Alexandrie.*[64] He offers the following sober judgment on our problem:[65]

> L'on s'efforcera donc de ne jamais perdre de vue ... les deux poles de la personalité littéraire de Philon ... Il est rare qu'un enseignement qui, chez Philon, paraît provenir directement de la sphère grecque, ne soit autorisé ou suscité sinon par la littérature rabbinique, du moins par un passage scripturaire qui lui sert de garant. Ce n'est que lorsque l'on prend la peine de la situer avec précision deux pôles que la pensée de Philon apparaît sous son jour véritable et avec son véritable intérêt.

To say, as does Nikiprowetzky, that Philo's thought exists in a tension between two poles is not to conclude, however, that he sought to create a synthesis between Judaism and Hellenism. The possibility of such genuine bipolarity has been made more understandable by the growing recognition that, while Palestinian and Hellenistic Judaism exhibited marked differences, the chasm between the two was by no means as wide as has traditionally been thought. Not only was there constant intercourse between Palestine and the Diaspora, but within Palestine itself the impact of Hellenistic thought was marked; the Hellenistic motifs in the Qumrân literature are but one example of this.[66]

IV

Thus far, scholarship has paid relatively little attention to Philo's personal *Sitz im Leben* in Roman Alexandria as significant for understanding

---

[63] Amir, "Philo and the Bible" *op. cit.* 4; see also "Rabbinischer Midrasch" *op. cit.* 110–11.

[64] Nikiprowetzky, *op. cit.*

[65] *Ibid.* 8.

[66] This point has been emphasized by Peder Borgen, "Philo of Alexandria. A Critical and Synthetical Survey of Research Since World War II," in *ANRW,* ed. Wolfgang Haase (Berlin: De Gruyter, 1984) II.2.21.1.151–53, and by David T. Runia, "Philo, Alexandrijn en Jood," 13–14, an article forthcoming in *Lampas,* which the author has kindly shared with me. [The article has since appeared in *Lampas* 22 (1989) 205–218. EDITOR]

his cultural and religious orientation.[67] Philo's world was characterized by two areas of tension, one internal to the Jewish community and one external to it. Yet, the two inevitably were interactive. Both involved the polarity between rabbinic Judaism and Hellenism in different ways. Internally there was the ever present threat of assimilation by the ambient culture. Thus, Bentwich describes the situation, somewhat rhetorically:[68]

> Men started by thinking out a philosophical Judaism for themselves; they ended by ceasing to be Jews and philosophers. Philo foresaw this danger, and he tried to combat it by presenting his people with a commentary of the Bible which would satisfy their intellectual and speculative bent, but at the same time preserve their loyalty to the Bible and the Law.

Whether the locale in which Philo's treatises took shape be identified as the law court, the school or the exposition of the Torah reading in a synagogue service, all these were central functions of the Jewish community, and for the most part, at least, his writings were almost certainly intended first of all for his co-religionists. Borgen has described well Philo's response to the challenge of assimilation by Greek culture:[69]

> When Philo draws on Greek philosophy and various notions from pagan religions, etc., his intention is not to compromise Jewish convictions and aims. He is not interested in making a synthesis between Judaism and Hellenism as such, nor does he intend to transform Judaism on the basis of Hellenistic philosophy and religion. Philo's intention is to conquer the surrounding culture ideologically by claiming that whatever good there is has its source in Scripture and thus belonged to the Jewish nation and its heritage.

But cutting across the internal tension caused by the threat of assimilation was the mounting threat from outside, from the Gentile population of Alexandria. While the great pogrom of 38 C.E. came doubtless near the end of Philo's life, when probably all but his two historical works chronicling those troubles had been written, the violent events of that year were but the culmination of long-standing hostilities and pressures. We can be sure that Philo's treatises were written in a situation of conflict—internal conflict which was centrifugal in that it threatened to diffuse the Jewish community, and external conflict, which could only have been centripetal in its effect. Here the modern analyses of conflict propounded by the German sociologist Georg Simmel and the American Lewis Coser

---

[67] Two recent works which touch on this approach are Peder Borgen *op. cit.*, and Alan Mendelson, *Philo's Jewish Identity*, BJS 161 (Atlanta: Scholars Press, 1988), which contains many valuable insights regarding the tensions inherent in Philo's situation.

[68] Bentwich, *op. cit.* 96.

[69] Borgen, *op. cit.* 151.

are helpful.[70] They point out that conflict with out-groups tends to increase internal cohesion and to cause the group to define its boundaries. Self-identification of the community becomes a priority. Under such pressures the community must know and articulate who it is.

If we consider Philo from this angle of vision, we can understand that on the one hand, the threat of assimilation led him to try to speak intelligibly to the Jews of his world, to elaborate a "Wissenschaft des Judentums" for his day. At the same time, the mounting pressures from outside made it even more crucial that Jews should understand who they were. This is dramatically illustrated when, in introducing the story of his embassy to Caligula on behalf of Jewish rights and privileges, he reminds his readers that they are of that "race which the Father and King of the Universe and the source of all things has taken for his portion."[71] Philo was a Hellenist, but first and always a Jew.

V

To conclude, however, as we have, that Philo was at the same time a loyal Jew and a Hellenist, offers only a *description* of the Janus image that he presents. Two questions that deserve further investigation are these: (1) What sociological and political forces were at work in first-century Egypt to have called forth such composite culture as we find in Philo? As we have suggested above, modern insights from social psychology, if judiciously used, can be helpful in leading us behind the surface of Philo's image as Hellenistic Jew *par excellence* to a deeper understanding of why and how factors of such disparate origin interacted as they did in his mind. (2) To what degree is it then possible to extrapolate the results of such an analysis for a fuller understanding of the factors and the process by which the broader phenomenon of Hellenistic Judaism came into being? To answer this question it will be necessary to evaluate not merely Philo's loyalty to Judaism, but his location within it, a task to which Alan Mendelson has recently made an important contribution.[72]

---

[70] Georg Simmel, *Conflict*, tr. K.W. Wolff (Glencoe, IL: Free Press, 1955); Lewis A. Coser, *The Functions of Social Conflict* (New York: Free Press, 1956).

[71] *Legat.* 3.

[72] Mendelson, *op. cit.*

MOSES ON THE MOUNTAIN TOP:
A PHILONIC VIEW

Burton L. Mack

Prolog

Horst Moehring read Philo with the erudition of a scholar comfortably trained in the classics. His readings of Philo were invariably enlightening, for in text after text he was able to show Philo's indebtedness to Greek philosophical traditions. Horst knew, of course, that Philo preferred his readers to view his writings in quite a different light. As Philo would have it, the logos to be espied was derived from the books of Moses—a vision of the divine plan for the universe granted by special revelation. By tracing Philo's conception of the world to the philosophic systems of the Hellenistic age, Moehring was able to show that the vision of the logos attributed to Moses was really Philo's own. Horst's purpose in doing that was to set the stage for an honest discussion of Philo's exegetical strategies.

This essay in honor of Horst Moehring's work takes up his challenge. If Philo's view of the world was his own, why did he not say so? Why did he not write it up under his own signature? Why the effort to find it hidden in the depths of the books of Moses? Why the ruse of the allegorical enterprise, if the cogency of the system could be argued on philosophical grounds?

I. *Moses on the Mountain*

There is a wondrous image of Moses on the mountain in the *QE* 2, 27–49. As Philo portrays it, all Israel was gathered at the mountain. The people had to remain at the foot of the mountain, for it would be dangerous and foolhardy for them to approach the brilliance of the glory of God. Aaron, Nadab, Abihu, and the seventy elders were worthy to go up with Moses and witness the outward manifestations of the glorious appearance. But only Moses was worthy to enter into the presence of God:

> O most excellent and God-worthy ordinance, that the prophetic mind alone should approach God and that those in second place should go up, making a path to heaven, while those in third place and the turbulent characters of the people should neither go up above nor go up with them but those worthy of beholding should be beholders of the blessed path above. (*QE* 2, 29)

This picture hardly stays in focus throughout the extended interpretation of Exodus 24 of which it is a part, for, as is frequently the case in the *Quaestiones*, shifts in imageries and allegorical identifications occur rapidly in densely packed units. The pattern of three stations on the way was, however, a favorite with Philo. It was used, for instance, to interpret the exodus story as the story of the soul (with Egypt as the body and passions; the wilderness way as a time of testing and instruction; and the land as the goal of perfection). There is also a similar interpretation of the temple (using the symbolism of the forecourt, sanctuary, and holy of holies), of the three patriarchs, the so-called educational trinity (with Jacob as the symbol of learning by practice; Abraham of learning by instruction; and Isaac as naturally endowed), and of a variety of other scriptural phenomena that lend themselves to Philo's overarching allegory of the soul. So the picture of the path up the mountain with three stations fits a standard three-fold pattern.

The picture is nevertheless striking, for elsewhere Philo seems to shy away from the story of Moses on the mountain. This seems strange. One might expect, for instance, that the major event of the Exodus story would be central in Philo's rehearsal of the life of Moses, especially so since in *Vita Mosis* 1, the style is narrative and descriptive. But such an expectation is not met. There is only one brief allusion to this major event and it is curiously out of sequence when compared with the scriptural account, and thoroughly allegorical when compared with the rest of the account Philo gives. In this allusion, moreover, the focus is upon the singular authority Moses attained by means of entrance into the presence of God, not upon the giving of the law, and not upon Moses' ascent up the mountain according to the tripartite scheme of the soul's path to heaven (*Mos.* 1, 158). It is almost as if, in the case of Sinai, the scheme of the educational trinity would be in danger of loosing its allegorical and psychological moorings in the presence of the story's obvious point. That point, of course, was the giving of the law. One wonders how the path to heaven would look if Philo had said (as he almost did here and there throughout the section in *QE* 2, 27–49) that, then, Moses received the law, gave it to the elders, and they in turn instructed the people. Not only would the scheme of the soul's path to heaven lose its power; the reflection of Philo's actual program of instruction in the Alexandrian synagogue would be too obvious for comfort. It is at least most interesting that Philo did not tell the story of Moses on the mountain as the story of Moses' reception of the law. Neither did Philo, as far as I can see, try to account for the written text of the laws in the five books of Moses in relation to the story of Moses on the mountain. So we have a curious aporia on our hands.

This does not mean that the story of Moses' ascent up the mountain was

not important for Philo's program. It was, on the contrary, most important
as a narrative that could easily be interpreted as an ascent-vision. Note that
the allegorical allusion to this event in Vita Mosis I treats the moment not
only as an ascent-vision, but as a transformation into the divine:

> For since God judged him worthy to appear as a partner of His own possessions, He
> gave into his hands the whole world as a portion well fitted for His heir .... For
> he was named god and king of the whole nation, and entered, we are told, into
> the darkness where God was .... (*Mos* .1, 155–158)

The same is true of the description in *Quaestiones in Exodum* where, after
the passage cited above, it says:

> But that '[Moses] alone shall go up' is said most naturally. For when the prophetic
> mind becomes ... like the monad ... it is changed into the divine. (*QE* 2, 29)

This is a standard component of the ascent vision in Philo, an image of
coming to enlightenment and transformation that occurs again and
again, not only in application to Moses, but to other figures as well,
especially the patriarchs.

A close reading of *Quaestiones in Exodum* 27–49 shows that the imagery
of transformation abounds and that its appropriate pattern of two stages
regularly erases the underlying three-tiered elevation of Israel gathered at
the mountain. The imageries of transformation are the usual: translation,
relocation, purification, regeneration, sexual union, ecstasy, gaining
speed, monadic consolidation, empowerment, vision, and presence. Although these metaphors occur with frequency throughout the allegorical
commentaries, sometimes in connection with fantastic cosmic abstrac-
tions and mythologies, but often as well to explicate otherwise mundane
psychological, pedagogical and moral moments, they do appear to be
especially appropriate for Philo's descriptions of Moses. These descriptions
occur throughout the commentaries almost as clichés to enhance Moses'
authority as the sage par excellence, the *spoudaios* of incomparable virtue,
the kind of singular sovereignty, the prophetic mind who uniquely sees
God, the priest who performs the spiritualized high-priestly offices
appropriate within the world as cosmic temple, and even as the logos of
God, a "second god" whose powers include the governance and susten-
tion of the world. Through clichés, and thus without need of repeated
narrative description or exegetical grounding, these references to Moses
set him apart even when compared with the patriarchs and appear to
derive ultimately from Philo's imagination of Moses on the mountain.

It is clear that, for Philo, the importance of this Mosaic configuration is
primarily mimetic. In the text cited the mimetic relation is described in

terms of those at lesser stations "beholding" those in higher stations above them. In the text referred to from the Life of Moses the language of vision gives way to the language of impression:

> Thus he [Moses] beheld what is hidden from the sight of mortal nature, and, in himself and his life displayed for all to see, he has set before us, like some well-wrought picture, a piece of work beautiful and godlike, a model for those who are willing to copy it. Happy are they who imprint, or strive to imprint, that image in their souls. For it were best that the mind should carry the form of virtue in perfection, but, failing this, let it at least have the unflinching desire to possess that form. (*Mos.* 1, 158–59)

In these cases the metaphors of path and imprinting follow easily as mimetic explications of the vision model. There are, however, other instances where the language of vision gives way to metaphors of another kind in order to explicate the staged relationship to archetypal models. A familiar passage in *De Confusione Linguarum* explicates the mimetic model in terms both of sonship and instruction. It is therefore very suggestive for the purposes of this essay. Philo had taken note of some passages in Deuteronomy where Moses has referred to the Israelites as "sons of God." These are those, according to Philo, who "hold moral beauty to be the only good." He then explains to his readers/listeners:

> But if there be any as yet unfit to be called a son of God, let him press to take his place under God's first-born, the logos, who holds eldership among the angels, their ruler as it were.

He then gives the many names of the logos, the last of which is "he that sees," which Philo explains as referring to Israel. Returning to the theme of becoming a son of God, Philo now shifts to the first person and continues:

> For if we have not yet become fit to be thought sons of God yet we may be sons of his invisible images, the most holy logos. For the logos is the eldest-born image of God. And often indeed in the law-book we find another phrase, 'sons of Israel,' hearers, that is, sons of him that sees, since hearing stands second in estimation and below sight, and the recipient of teaching is always second to him with whom realities present their forms clear to his vision and not through the medium of instruction. (*Conf.* 146–48)

Moses is not in sight here, but his book of legislation certainly is, as well as express acknowledgement of a process of instruction concerned with a proper interpretation of that book. In this context, moreover, the metaphor of instruction pops up in the place of second level relationships normally described on the mimetic model. The educational trinity, mentioned above, hovers in the background, and one suspects that the meaning of the logos, the references to the textbook of Moses, and the metaphor of instruction all cohere in some theory that underlay the actual practice of instruction in which Philo was involved.

II. *In the School of Moses*

Taking the above considerations as clues, we can now shift to ways in which Philo attributed authority to Moses other than by depicting his ascent and transformation. We might keep in mind that the first book of the Life of Moses emphasized Moses' leadership as royal, and that the description of his ascent vision cited above ended with the notice, "So, having received the authority which they willingly gave him, with the sanction and assent of God, he proposed to lead them ..." (*Mos.* 1, 163). Then, in the second book of the Life of Moses, Philo organized his encomium around the offices of kind, (high)priest, and prophet. By collapsing the offices essential to a social definition of Israel, whether imagined as a structural or an historical entity, and attributing the complex configuration of roles to the singular figure of Moses, Philo automatically claimed for him an astounding authority. Of importance to the present investigation is the observation that these functions, though frequently said to have been granted to Moses as a result of (or on the occasion of) his ascent vision, are also regularly mentioned as roles that explain the peculiar nature and challenge of the five books he wrote. This means that, even though the moment of Moses' authorship was not mythologized as was his moment of vision, Philo clearly associated Moses' authority with his authorship. The question, then, is whether the authority of Moses for Philo was not actually derived from the authority of his writings.

At several points, Philo describes and evaluates the plan for the five books of Moses as a whole. (See, especially, *Abr.* 1–6; *Mos.* 2, 45–51; *Praem.* 1–3.) It consists, Philo explains, of (1) an account of creation, (2) a history of the patriarchs, and (3) the legislation of the laws. The sequence is significant, for the laws are thereby shown to reflect the structure of creation, and the history of the patriarchs describes lives lived in keeping with the principles by which both creation and the laws are ordered. Moses is to be credited with the design, according to Philo, an intentional invitation to discern the system by which philosophy, ethics, and Jewish practice are unified. And Moses' greatness is regularly praised in relation to the grandeur of this design. His sovereignty is manifest as divine because the design of the five books as legislation cannot be imagined except as the product of divine enlightenment. He is properly viewed as a prophet by virtue of the astounding vision granted to him of the hidden logos that holds all three parts of the legislation together. And one suspects that Philo thought of Moses as a priest primarily by virtue of the clues he left in the writing by which he, as mystagogue, guides the serious student to the vision of the whole that he intended.

So the story of Moses on the mountain was used to imagine the moment of his vision and locate his appointments as prophet, priest, and king. And, because the appointments were imagined on the model of an ascent vision, these roles of authority could be elaborated mythologically to create a divine and heavenly figure of cosmic proportions. But the authority of Moses expressed in these ways cannot be accounted for simply as the result of a mythic imagination taking its own fantastic lead. Moses was mythologized because the texts "he left behind," as Philo was wont to put it, had become authoritative in the Alexandrian synagogues and schools. The figure of Moses was enhanced in relation to the importance his books had assumed for Jewish life, thought, and orientation in the Alexandrian diaspora.

The historical process by which the books and figure of Moses came to be invested with such authority should not be too difficult to understand. The books of Moses had served as epic charter for all forms of Jewish social experimentation for at least four hundred years. In Judaea, the epic was read as charter for the temple state. The decisive moments for the constitution were lodged in the stories of archaic covenants, priestly genealogies, levitical codes, or the golden age of David and Solomon. The figure of Moses does not appear to have loomed that large, judging from the literature with orientation to the temple state in Jerusalem. But in the dispersion, with Jewish life and thought orientation to the synagogue, the books of Moses had to be read as charter for an institution hardly reflected in the epic history. It was here that Moses was mythologized as author and his books allegorized as constitution for Jewish practice in the Hellenistic city.[1]

The challenge to justify a diaspora institution as the heir of the grand epic traditions of Israel should not be underestimated. One problem was that the natural thrust of the epic clearly pointed to the formation and maintenance of a temple state in the land of Israel. That problem may have been solved in principle by focusing solely upon the five books of Moses as foundational charter for authentic Jewish identity located at a distance from Judaea. One of the curiosities about Philo's program, at any rate, has always been this delimitation of the scriptures held in highest

---

[1] On Moses as author and authority in Second Temple times see Burton L. Mack, *Wisdom and the Hebrew Epic,* Index (Chicago: University of Chicago Press, 1985); and "Under the Shadow of Moses: Authorship and Authority in Hellenistic Judaism," *SBLSP* 1982 (Chico, CA: Scholars Press, 1982) 299–318.

regard. Though he was not ignorant of the history of the kings, the prophetic corpus, the psalms and other writings, Philo treated them all as if they were "in the school of Moses," on a par, that is, with the exegetical traditions of the Alexandrian school in which he also labored. By eschewing the narrative histories that led from Moses to the temple state, the Alexandrian savants were able to trace their link with the archaic charter by taking another route.

A second problem was that the ancient Near Eastern temple state was really the only model in place for imagining Israel as a social and political entity. It was this conception of a social order that had guided the construction and history of the Second Temple state. It seems also to have governed reflection about Jewish presence in the world even in the diaspora. Philo accepted the model as given, thought of the temple at Jerusalem as the literal manifestation of Israel's proper destiny, and found it difficult to imagine the structure of the world apart from the temple pattern. But to think of the cosmos in terms of the temple already shifted the focus of orientation away from Judaea and onto the larger world within which Jews performed religious service wherever they lived. And to concentrate the offices integral to the model of the temple state in the singular figure of Moses effectively erased the historical significance of subsequent kings and high priestly commanders. If royalty, priesthood, and prophecy were now defined by the figure of Moses, and if Moses' legacy was available in the books he left behind, and if the books he left behind were in the hands of teachers in the Alexandrian synagogues, the proper shape of Israel as a social presence in the world was surely at the point of reconception.

A third problem can now be surmised. To understand it may throw some light upon the curious attribution of royal and sacerdotal authority to Moses. The problem also bears directly upon the questions we have raised with regard to Philo's hermeneutical strategy. The problem has to do with the role of the scribe as author and the place of the scribe subordinate in the ancient Near Eastern model of the state. As Jonathan Z. Smith has shown,[2] the temple state was structured on two systems of classification, with kings and priests presiding over hierarchical gradations of power and purity. Scribal activity is everywhere in evidence, and the function of the scribe is clear as the author of texts that provided for charter and mediated between the two systems of difference. Yet the scribe is seldom in the picture when the grandeur of the temple state is depicted, and as for

---

[2] On the social model of the ancient Near Eastern temple state, see Jonathan Z. Smith, *To Take Place: Toward Theory in Ritual* (Chicago: University of Chicago Press, 1987).

the scribe as an author and authority, acknowledgement seems to have been all but non-existent.

During the Hellenistic period, the Greek notions of authorship as an accomplishment and of a text as a memorial to its author became common coin. It was just during this period that Moses came to be imagined as a figure of imposing authority and that his books came to be regarded as texts that established epic precedence. So the Greek notions of authorship and authority must have been at work. But the authority of an author, even the author of an epic literature, could hardly become the central figure around which a substitute model for the people of Israel could easily be constructed. The profile of the scribe was simply not sufficient to incorporate the powers, privileges, and executive functions of the offices that organized the archaic model. Changes in social configuration always call for a reimagination of a people's epic or mythology. But reimagination must begin with the archaic model and recast it by means of rearrangements and displacements of elements essential to its structure. Thus the temple state model had to be reconfigured and its offices recast; it could not simply be set aside in favor of a novel institution based on textual authorization alone. So Moses was invested with the offices traditional to the temple state model, and viewed as a prophet in keeping with the importance of prophets for the traditional reading of Israel's history. But it is clear that, even for Philo, Moses was not an ordinary prophet, priest, or king. According to the myth, he was appointed as such by means of a vision. But according to function, Moses' authority was grounded in his authorship of the books he left behind. The story of Moses on the mountain, then, is a myth of origin for a novel social formation oriented to the five books he authored. Philo knew to call this social formation a synagogue. He also called it the "school of Moses."

III. *In the School of Philo*

Philo took his place in the school of Moses as a teacher. Instruction took the form of commentary upon the five books of Moses, commentary that purported to be exegetical with regard to the logos of Moses' vision, a logos held to be implicit in a text that, at the surface level, could easily be (mis)read merely as history or literal description. In order to buttress his project with methodological clarity, Philo proposed a rare and sophisticated rationalization.

The books of Moses were "well-written," according to Philo. By this he meant more than a reference to stylistic refinement. He meant that Moses composed his text according to the rules of rhetoric. The overall plan, mentioned above, was deliberative—designed to demonstrate that the law of Moses was superior to all other legislation by virtue of its correspondence with the orders of creation and the capacity of human beings to recognize its reason, live accordingly, and thus achieve their true end, moral excellence.

The smaller units were also composed in keeping with the art of persuasion. Narratives presented cases and examples; descriptions defined issues; speeches elaborated theses; dialogues revealed rhetorical questions and positions taken in debate; and as for the so-called "non-invented" arguments, Philo had no trouble identifying oaths, oracles, contracts, laws, precedent judgments, and the "witnesses" of innumerable illustrious figures from the grand age of the epic history, including sages, patriarchs, heroes, prophets, and angels. Naturally, since the sage par excellence was none other than Moses himself, Philo paid close attention to the speeches Moses delivered, especially to Deuteronomy, a veritable fund of maxims that could be used to clinch an exegetical argument with little need for further elaboration.

The goal, of course, was to persuade the reader of the all-encompassing logos Moses saw on the mountain. Such a persuasion could only be achieved ultimately by seeing the same vision. For that, words were inadequate. Even Moses' words, though born of that vision and designed to lead to that vision, were no substitute for the vision itself. Knowing this, however, Moses crafted the text with care, leaving clues that pointed to the vision of the logos behind and beyond the text. Philo was able to find these clues in the peculiarities of words, etymologies, numerical codes, phraseology, grammar and syntax. Questions about the meaning of the text were obvious invitations to explore the "deeper meaning," as Philo frequently called it. Moses had encoded the text intentionally, as Philo understood it, creating a composition that had two levels of meaning. The surface level was far from nonsensical, reporting as it did on the history that began at creation and led to Moses and the legislation of the law. But even that history was imagined in a kind of once-upon-a-time and, in reference to the vision of the divine plan for humankind implicit in the inaugural events, the surface level was like a riddle waiting to be solved. Philo's favorite term for the text, when viewed from this perspective, was oracle.

Philo's task was therefore exegetical with respect to both levels of the text. He had to pore over the surface level, say what it meant, and identify the codes that served as clues to the deeper meaning. Finding a clue, he had to explain how it worked to signal insight into the grand design Moses had envisioned. Just to be sure, supporting arguments had to be marshaled—examples, analogies, maxims, laws, considerations of logic, correlations with philosophical principles and truisms, and citations of other scriptural loci. Philo called his project allegory. But he also knew that, once he had made his move from a text to a statement of its deeper meaning, his assertion was a thesis that required argumentation. Philo was more than up to the challenge. In section after section of his commentaries, Philo composed complete argumentations on the model of what rhetors would have called an elaboration. So Moses' text was not the only text in Philo's hands that was well-written from a rhetorical point of view![3]

The tenor of the commentaries is consistently deferential with respect to the five books of Moses. As Philo sets his own work forth, he is merely at the task of disclosing the deeper meaning of Moses' text. His arguments are designed to demonstrate Moses' intentions, to lead his own readers to see the logos that Moses saw. But interwoven into the exegesis, and often explicitly at the end of an argumentation, Philo shifts to exhortation. The student must pay attention. The student must look for the logos. The student must grasp the consequences of failing to see the logos. The student must strive to pattern his life on the model of those whose goal was the vision of God. For the aim of the grand design of creation, the history, the laws, the five books of Moses, the exegetical labor, the allegory, and the instruction was moral inculcation of an ethical code. Seeing the logos, imitating the exemplars of vision, and receiving Philo's instructions on the meaning of the text were all ways of taking one's place among the sons of Israel, the nation that sees God.

So the student in Philo's school was confronted with two authoritative texts, not one. At first the rhetoric of commentary may have prevailed. Moses' text was the one that mattered, and Philo's text was merely the guide to the deeper meaning that Moses' text contained. But neither text made sense without the other. And taken together, what was one to do? Moses' text was mystified in the hermeneutical process. And Philo's text was partial by its exegetical arrangement. The logos to be espied was actually not all that difficult to comprehend and, one suspects, could have been spelled out much more efficiently in a series of treatises on the philosophical and theological grounds for a contemporary Jewish ethic. But, given the commentary format, the manner of its explication was fragmentary and disjointed. And so, after hearing (reading) an explication limited to a small selection of Moses' text, one waited for another round, a round that promised further enlightenment by means of yet another tryst with other oracles. There would be a new set of riddles, another chance for surprises, and of course there was always the expected

---

[3] On Philo's use of rhetoric, see Burton L. Mack, "Decoding the Scriptures: Philo and the Rules of Rhetoric," in *Nourished with Peace: Studies in Hellenistic Judaism in Memory of Samuel Sandmel*, edited by Frederick E. Greenspahn, Earle Hilgert, and Burton L. Mack (Chico, CA: Scholars Press, 1985) 81–115.

application to the story of the soul and a renewed exhortation on the importance of coming to the proper vision of God. Unfinished business, really. For working one's way through to the end hardly added new information. It merely established the rules of the game. In Derrida's terms, one might call Philo's program of pedagogy a game of deference. The object of the play was clearly set before as the logos that Moses saw and hid at the center of the text. But the game of getting to that goal was just as clearly not set up to come to an end.

In the meantime, one would have read (or listened to) a great deal of Philo. Two texts, two authors. According to the rhetoric, Philo's instruction was fully derived from Moses' text. But according to the program, the meaning of Moses' text was fully dependent upon Philo's exegesis. For Philo's students, then, the intention of the textbook and the teaching of the teacher in the synagogue school were interlocking. Ultimate authority was lodged expressly in the five books of Moses, with the teacher's authority granted as merely derivative and exegetical. But of course, within the social structure of the school it was the teacher's authority that prevailed and it was the logos espied by the teacher that the students actually were asked to see.

In the scheme of Moses on the mountain with its three levels of visionary perspective, Philo pretends to take his place with the elders who are privileged to occupy that middle position between Moses and the people. But because the logos that Philo saw in Moses' text, the logos that mattered, was actually his own, a more accurate application of the myth of origin would put Philo in Moses' place. Philo's reticence to elaborate that scheme more fully may have been due to the question of authority that would naturally have been raised. The myth of mimesis at the origin of the Jewish vision of the world works, after all, only by shifting attention away from questions of authorship and authority and onto a logos beyond the text held to be the goal of all authorial and exegetical activity.

Philo's myth of Moses was not a result of speculative imagination taking its own lead. It was worked out as a myth of origin for a social institution within which the five books of Moses had been settled upon as a sufficient corpus of epic and constitutional literature. To position the synagogue correctly required linkage with Jewish tradition as well as orientation to the Hellenistic culture of context. Intellectual labor was called for in order to rethink the shape of Jewish society, retain the codes and sensibilities of Jewish identity, and relate the synagogue to Jewish heritage and authority without drawing directly upon Second Temple history. Philo's program is evidence of the vigor with which that challenge was pursued in Alexandria. Jewish intellectuals in Alexandria apparently thought that the synagogue was worth the investment.

The myth of Moses and his five books that arose in Alexandria may be compared with the myth of Moses as the source for both the written and the oral Torah that emerged later in Rabbinic Judaism. Both can be seen as strategies by which the end of the Second Temple could be survived. Both have the diaspora synagogue in view as a fully appropriate social formation for the inculcation and celebration of Jewish life and thought. Both viewed the Torah of Moses as epic legislation. And both settled upon the role of the teachers, instead of the offices of king and (high) priest as the locus for the authority that would sustain and interpret Jewish ethos and identity. But there are also significant differences between the two mythologies and mentalities.

Rabbinic Judaism avoided the riddle of locating unique authority in the written text, and thus also the ruse of denying the authority that the teacher actually assumed as exegete in the Alexandrian solution. In the Alexandrian solution, the danger lay in the lack of control over questions of authority where differences of opinion and interpretation mattered. That is because the text of Moses had been mystified, the logos reified, and the authority of the exegete as thinker left unexamined. The Rabbinic solution positioned the oral tradition of the teachers parallel to the written tradition of Moses' text. By so doing, the logos that counted was repositioned away from the text of Moses as sole repository, and located in the tradition of exegetical activity. Recourse could then be made to precedent opinion and not directly to the text. And the chain or oral tradition was imagined to have unfolded through a series of pairs of teachers in debate. Debate, moreover, focused on issues of halakha, not upon a psychology of internalized piety on the model of Greek notions of virtue. And so the Rabbinic sages created a myth of Moses that supported the wisdom inherent in a dialogical process and avoided the logocentric desire implicit in the Alexandrian experiment.

Epilog

Philo's vision of the world was indebted to contemporary systems of philosophical thought, as Horst Moehring knew. He also knew that Philo was engaged in a serious exegetical enterprise designed to anchor that view of the world in the books of Moses as manifest authority for Jewish tradition. Horst granted to Philo his grand design and took his place among the modern students of Philo as a player intrigued by the riddle Philo posed. The questions a modern scholar can ask are seemingly without end, for Philo's text is strong and his readings of the text of Moses are fascinating. Horst played the game of reading Philo reading Moses, but not on Philo's terms. He played to find the points of departure where

Philo thought to join two texts and thus two ways of being in the world. He found the seams and figured out the codes that Philo used to make the connections. If we now expand upon Horst's work to suggest the social concerns and cultural motivations for Philo's global enterprise, Horst would surely understand. He was fully aware, as well, that Philo's program prepared the way for Christian exegetes, not the Rabbis. It was in the Christian tradition that the logos hidden beneath Moses' text was turned to advantage, and that the commentary as a form of scriptural explication found a home.

PHILO'S DOCTRINE OF REPENTANCE

DAVID WINSTON

Metanoia *in Greek Thought*

Greek philosophy had little interest in the feelings of regret or remorse that may at times lead an individual to a complete reassessment of his former life path and his conversion to a fresh course of existence. The single favorable statement on *metameleia* remorse, in classical Greek literature is that by Democritus (DK 68.B.43): "Remorse for shameful deeds is salvation in life." This is offset, however, by fragment 66: "It is better to deliberate before action than to repent (*metanoein*) afterwards."[1] Aristotle does indeed note that there is no cure for one who does not regret his error (*ametameletos: EN* 7.1150a23), but not only does he nowhere say that repentance is a virtue, but further asserts that for the good man "the same thing is at all times painful and the same thing is at all times pleasant, and not different at different times. He is, one might say, a person who knows no regrets (1166a29).[2] "Bad people," on the other hand, are full of regrets." Following in the footsteps of Aristotle, the Stoics declare: "The philosopher surmises nothing, repents of nothing, is never wrong, never changes his opinion (Cicero *Pro Murena* 61)."[3]

From the polemic of the Stoics against *metanoia*, however, Werner

---

[1] Cf. Epicharmus, DK 23.B.41: "The wise man should think before hand (*pronoein*), not afterwards (*ou metanoein*)." Eduard Norden, *Agnostos Theo* (Leipzig, 1913) 136 commented on fr. 43 of Democritus as follows: "Either this saying, which is not in Stobaeus, is not by Democritus, or, if it is genuine, it must have anticipated future development of the concept by centuries." Norden also speaks of the oriental character of *metanoia*. See O. Michel, *Theological Dictionary of the New Testament*, ed. G. Kittel, trans, and ed. G.W. Bromiley (Grand Rapids, 1967) 4.626. (All translations from Philo are taken from the Colson and Whittaker edition of Philo in the Loeb Classical Library. *FE* refers to the French edition of Philo by Arnaldez, Pouilloux, and Mondésert. The following abbreviations are used for rabbinic sources: *PRK, Pesikta de Rav Kahana; Pesik. R., Pesikta Rabbati; ARNA, Abot de Rabbi Nathan*, version A; b, *Babylonian Talmud*; y, *Jerusalem Talmud*; m, *Mishnah*; t, *Tosefta*; Midr., *Midrash*.

[2] Cf. Plato *Resp.* 9.577E; Aristotle *EN* 1150b29–35; 1152a27–33; *EE* 7.1240b14: "But a good man does not rebuke himself either at the time, like the uncontrolled, nor yet his former self later, like the penitent (*ho metameletikos*) nor his latter self his former." According to Aristotle, a man who regrets what he has done in ignorance is considered an involuntary agent (*EN* 3.1110b18).

[3] Cf. Cicero *Tusc.* 5.81; *SVF* 3.548: "Nor do they suppose that the sensible man repents, for repentance (*metanoia*) is classified in Ps-Andronicus' list of *pathe* as a species of *lupe*"; 3.563; Seneca *Ben.* 4.34.3–4; Epictetus, fr. 25; M. Aurelius 8.53.

Jaeger had already surmised "the widespread existence of a type of ethics in which it had high value."[4] A faint echo of such a religious tradition has been detected by Rudolf Pfeiffer. The statue of the Delian Apollo held the graces in his right hand and bow and arrow in his left. This gave rise to an allegorical-ethical interpretation, namely, that the god holds the bow in his left hand "because he is slower to chastise if man repents" (Callimachus *Aitia*, fr. 114.8–17, Pfeiffer).[5] Pfeiffer has pointed out that[6]

> there were commands believed to be given by Apollo carved on the front hall of the Delphic temple; to the original few inscriptions, of which the most famous was *gnōthi seauton*, more sentences were added in the course of time. A sort of copy of an inscription from the Delphic temple was found at the beginning of this century in Miletopolis in Asia Minor; in this new inscription (SIG³1268.II.8), not to be dated much later that 300 BC, we read amongst the other precepts: 'repent when you did wrong,' *metanoei harmartōn*. This sentence itself is not new to us; it had been registered in literary collections of Delphic exhortations of late imperial or Byzantine times, but had been neglected as some quite arbitrary very late addition. Now, the inscription of Miletopolis proves its relatively early existence at least in the third or perhaps fourth century BC ... Any doubt about the pre-Christian existence of the idea of the god's demand of and even his waiting for man's repentance is now, I think, removed ... How very different appears this Apollo from the terrible god who at the opening of our Iliad shoots his deadly arrows immediately after his wronged priest's prayer for revenge, from the god who is the merciless slaughtering avenger of the Niobides, leaving no time for repentance to the insolent Niobe.

---

[4] Werner Jaeger, *Göttingische gelehrte Anzeigen* 175 (1913) 590.

[5] Cf. Pausanias 9.35.3, who records that "Angelion and Tektios, in making the Apollo for the Delians, placed three Graces on his hand;" Ps-Plutarch *De Musica* 16, where it may be his own mistake or a slip in the archetype of our manuscripts, that the Graces are said to be attached to Apollo's left hand and the bow to his right hand; Apollodorus, *Peri Theōn, FGrHist* 95 in Macrobius 1.17.15: "Apollo's images are holding the Graces in the right hand, the bow and arrows in the left, because he is slower to do harm, and the prompter hand provides well-being;" Philo *Legat,* 95: "Then when it pleased him he [Gaius] would strip them off and change his figure and dress into Apollo's, his head encircled with garlands of the sun-rays, wielding a bow and arrows in his left hand and holding out Graces in his right to signify that it was fitting for him to extend good things readily and that these should hold the superior position on the right, while punishment should be kept in the background and allotted the inferior place on the left." See Rudolf Pfeiffer, *Ausgewählte Schriften* (München, 1960) 55–71.

[6] Pfeiffer, *Schriften* 69–70. Jaeger, *Anzeigen*, n. 4, refers to the use of *metanoia, metameleia,* and *ametamelētos* in the *Tablet of Cebes* 10.4; 11.1; 35.4; 32.2. Cf. also *Corp. Herm.* 1.28. See also E. Bréhier, *Les idées philosophiques et religieuses de Philon d'Alexandrie* (Paris, 1950) 41–42.

Philo on Repentance

Although Philo clearly knew this interesting Apolline tradition (*Legat..* 95; cf. *Leg* 3.105–06), and we can find a close parallel to it in rabbinic sources,[7] he was certainly aware that it could not easily be harmonized with Greek philosophical thought. It had arisen out of the context of a religious concern with god's forgiving or punishing relationship to man, and was rooted in the profound human need for divine grace amid deep and ubiquitous feelings of sinfulness. Yet the centrality of the doctrine of repentance[8] in Jewish prophetic literature[9] and in the Palestinian (and probably also Alexandrian) traditions of Philo's own day was such that he not only could not ignore it but felt impelled to give it a prominent place in his writings, devoting a separate segment of his treatise *On Virtues* to it. He thus reads it into the Scriptural text even when it is not there, after the manner of a similar Palestinian tradition. Commenting on Gen. 6:3, he notes that "perhaps one hundred and twenty years are not the universal limit of human life, but only of the men living at that time, who were later to perish in the flood after so great a number of years, which a bene-volent benefactor prolonged, allowing repentance for sins" (*QG* 1.91).[10] Similarly, in response to the question "why, after their entering the ark, did seven days pass, after which came the Flood," Philo answers that it

---

[7] See *Sifre Numbers, Pinḥas* 134. God's right hand, representing the attribute of mercy which is extended to all, is also called "the mighty hand," inasmuch as it has to represent the attribute of strict justice.

[8] The term Philo generally employs for repentance is *metanoia*, although he also describes it as a 'turning' (*tropē*) toward the better, thus approaching the biblical term *śub* (*Abr.* 17; *Mig.* 148; *Spec.* 1.227, 238). The terms *epistrephō* and *apostrephē* that are used in the LXX and the Apocrypha and Pseudepigrapha to render the Hebrew *śub* are, except for *Jos.* 87, not found in Philo.

[9] In the early biblical narratives, repentance plays virtually no role. The generations of the Flood and the Tower of Babel, the men of Sodom, and the Canaanites are not called upon to repent. Nor does Moses avert God's wrath from Israel by rousing them to repentance (Yehezkel Kaufmann, *Toledot ha-Emunah ha-Yisraelit* (Tel Aviv, 1947) 2:1, pp. 285–86. "Repentance is found in P and D (Lev. 26:40–42; Deut. 4:29–31; 30:1–10), but there, contrary to the prophets, it can only terminate the punishment but cannot prevent its onset. Moreover, the term *śub*, meaning 'repent' never appears in P. Neither does it appear in the Tetrateuch and early narratives. Though the power of repentance in P is such that it can reduce a deliberate sin to an unintentional one, P insists that for the complete annulment of sin sacrificial expiation is mandatory. It also does not know the prophetic teaching that repentance suffices in itself to nullify sin." (J. Milgrom, *The Interpreter's Dictionary of the Bible*, ed. Keith Crim [Nashville, 1976] Supplementary Volume, s.v. Repentance). As Kaufmann has noted, the Israelite concept of repentance receives its full expression in the book of Jonah. For repentance in Qumran, see 1 QS 5:1, 8; 10.20; 1 QH 2.9; CD 19.16.

[10] For a similar Palestinian interpretation, see Ps-Jonath, on Gen. 6:3; Rashi. *ad loc.*: *Midrash ha-Gadol* on Gen. 6:3; *Seder Olam R.* 28.

was to grant them repentance of sins (*QG* 2.13).[11] Moreover, in contrast to the Stoics, who denied that the wise man would ever repent, Philo asserts that "to do no sin is peculiar to God; to repent, to the wise man" (*Fug.*157; cf. *Leg.* 2.60; *Virt.* 177),[12] and like the Greek version of Sir.44.16, he finds in Enoch a paradigm of the penitent (*Abr.* 17; *Praem.* 15; *QG* 1.82–86).[13]

Man's privilege to repent for his sins and be forgiven is rooted in God's Gracious Power which makes allowance for human proneness to sin (*Fug.* 99, 105).[14] Like parents who, especially concerned with their wastrel

---

[11] Cf. *Mek, Shirta* 5; *ARN* 32; *Tanḥ, Buber, Bereshit* 37. Similarly, notwithstanding their rebellion God stretched out his hand to the builders of the Tower of Babel and bade them repent (*Tanḥ.* Buber. *Noah* 28). So also from Gen. 18–21 it is inferred that God opened to the people of Sodom and Gomorrah a door of repentance (*Gen. R.* 49.6, Theodor-Albeck: 504; *Mek. Shirta* 5), and when God communicated to Abraham his purpose to destroy the cities of the plain, Abraham began at once to make a plea for them, thinking that perhaps they might repent (*Tanḥ,* Buber, *Wayyera* 9; cf. Philo *QG* 4.16). The same is true with regard to the Egyptians: "Ten plagues Thou didst bring upon the Egyptians in Egypt, and Thou didst not condemn them to destruction until after they had perpetrated the full measure of their wickedness (*Mek. Shirta* 5)." Cf. also Wis. 11:23 and 12:9–10 (God gave the Canaanites space for penance). Of the woman undergoing the ordeal of the bitter waters, R. Eliezer says, "It was done to tire her, in order that she should repent (*Sifre. Num.* 11)."

[12] At *Virt* 177 Philo writes that "sinlessness belongs to God alone, or possibly to a divine man." In Jewish tradition, too, there were some exceptional men who were described as pure, or free from sin. In Ps. Sol. 17:41, the Messianic king is stated to be pure from sin, and Josephus relates that, when Agrippa I offered the high priesthood to Jonathan, son of Ananus, he declined the honor and recommended instead his brother Matthias, whom he declared to be "pure of all sin against God" (*Ant.* 9.315). R. Eliezer asserted that in the patriarchs there was neither iniquity nor sin (*Mek,* on Exod. 16:10), and Elijah was believed never to have sinned (*Lev. R,* 27; *PRK,* Mandelbaum: 152). An anonymous *Baraitha* states that four men died only in consequence of the advice given by the serpent to Eve, Benjamin, Amram, Jesse, and Kileab, i.e., there was no sin in them to account for their death (*bShab.* 55b; *bBB,* 17a). According to one view, Moses and Aaron died only because death had been decreed upon all men without exception (*bShab,* 55b). An anonymous *Baraitha,* in referring Deut. 32.25 as a prophecy to the generation of the destruction of the first Temple, says, "They were all pure from sin, like the virgin who tasted not sin (*Sifre Deut.* 321)." See A. Büchler, *Studies in Sin and Atonement* (Ktav repr., N.Y., 1967) 331–32.

[13] Cf. *Gen. R.* 25.1, Theodor-Albeck: 238; *Qohel. R.* 7.32.

[14] Cf. *Mut.* 181–85; *Sac,* 42; *Som,* 2.292; *Mos,* 2.147; *Spec.* 1.242; 2.196; *Praem,* 163; *Deus* 74–81; *QG* 1.84. K.J. Dover writes: "The gods as portrayed in Greek legend and poetry were not conspicuously compassionate ... The scheme of Euripides' *Hippolytus* presupposes a divine willingness to treat human beings as pawns played in a fierce game between deities; Aphrodite does not care how Phaidra suffers, so long as punishment can be contrived for Hippolytus, and Artemis proposes to hurt Aphrodite in return by killing some mortal of whom she is fond ... When a god does take pity on a human being, he does so because that human is a friend, ally or loyal subject who has established by piety and sacrifices a claim on pity and help. Aristophanes satirizes this aspect of the relation between god and man in *Peace* 363–425, where Hermes, at first implacable towards Trygaios and the chorus, is softened by extravagant promises

children, lavish on them more care and attention than on the well behaved, God the father takes thought also "for those who live a misspent life, thereby giving them time for reformation." (*Prov.* 2.15 [635]; *QG* 4.198).[15] There is, nevertheless, for Philo, as well as for the rabbis, a point of no return:[16]

> The soul that is widowed but not yet cast out of the good and beautiful, may still by steadfast persistence find a means of reconciliation and agreement with right reason, her lawful husband. But the soul that has once been dismissed from hearth and home as irreconcilable, has been expelled for all eternity, and can never return to her ancient abode. [*Det.*. 149; cf. *Cher.* 2; *Leg.* 3.213]

The rabbis similarly say: "No pardon is granted to five persons, to him who repents too much, sins too much, sins in a sinless generation, sins with the idea to repent, and to him who profanes the name of God (*ARNA* 19, 58b)."[17]

---

and finally won over by a gift of gold vessels ("Ah! How compassionate I always feel—to gold plate!"). Nevertheless, characters in plays sometimes ask gods for forgiveness and offer excuses which are apparently accepted (Aristophanes *Clouds* 1476–85; *Peace* 668 ff.; Euripides *Electra* 1327–30; Menander *Epitr*, 855.874 ff.)." (*Greek Popular Morality in the Time of Plato and Aristotle* [Oxford, 1974] 78).

[15] The rabbis place a similar emphasis on God's mercy: "R. Johanan said: Were it not written in the text, it would be impossible for us to say such a thing; this verse (Exod. 34:6) teaches us that the Holy One, blessed be He, drew his robe round Him like the reader of a congregation and showed Moses the order of prayer. He said to him: Whenever Israel sin, let them carry out this service before Me, and I will forgive them ... R. Judah said: A covenant has been made with the thirteen attributes that they will not be turned away empty-handed, as it says, 'Behold I made a covenant' (Exod. 34:10) (*bR.H.* 17b). We read further in *bBer.* 7a: [What does God pray?] "May it be My will that My mercy may suppress My anger, and that My mercy may prevail over My other attributes, so that I may deal with My children in the attribute of mercy and, on their behalf, stop short of the limit of strict justice." The parade example of God's unrestricted responsiveness to human repentance is the case of king Manasseh: "The divine justice would have hindered the reception of King Manasseh's supplication, but God made a kind of loophole in the firmament in order to receive him in repentance (*bSanh.* 103a; *ySanh.* 10.2, 28c; *PRK*, Mandelbaum: 364–66; 369; cf. *bPesaḥ.* 119a; *Exod. R.* 31.1; 45 *fin.*). In a famous parable, God is likened to a king who addresses his son, who is reluctant to return to him after having strayed into evil ways, as follows: "My son, are you indeed ashamed to return? Is it not to your father that you return?" (*Deut. R.* 2.24). Philo similarly speaks of the penitent Israelites' finding favor with God, "as sons may with their father" (*Praem*, 167–68).

[16] Cf. Seneca *Ep.* 94–31: "But when [his natural disposition which has been over-shadowed and kept down] wins support and receives the aid of precepts, it grows stronger, provided only that the chronic trouble has not corrupted or annihilated the natural man. For in such a case, not even the training that comes from philosophy, striving with all its might, will make restoration;" Cicero *Fin.* 4.56: "Some fools are so foolish as to be utterly incapable of attaining wisdom."

[17] Cf. *ARNA* 40, 60b; *tYoma* 5.13; *Fug.* 84; *Mark* 3:29; yḤag, 2.1, 77b: "*Return ye wayward children, save Elisha b. Abuyah, who knew my power and rebelled against it;*" bḤag. 15a; *Qohel.*

The effects of repentance are such that sin is expunged, "the old reprehensible life is blotted out and disappears and is no more found, as though it had never been at all (*Abr.* 19; cf. *Spec.* 1.187–88; *QG* 1.84; *Mut.* 124). This was also the prophetic view and it was emphatically repeated by the rabbis.

> Concerning the meaning of *këbaśim*, he-lambs (Num. 28:3), the disciples of Shammai and the disciples of Hillel differ. The disciples of Shammai read *këbaśim*, as though written *kabbaśim*, 'they that put out of sight.' That is, the daily offering of the lambs brings it about that God puts Israel's iniquities out of sight, as the verse tells us, 'He will turn again and have compassion upon us; He will put our iniquities out of sight (*yikboš*)' (Mic. 7:19). But the disciples of Hillel said: The phrase *këbaśim, bëne šanah*, he-lambs of the first year (Num. 18:3), is to be understood as though written *kabbasim bëne šanah*, they that cleanse the things which are of many a year. That is, the daily offerings cleanse the sins of Israel, as is said 'Though your sins be as of many a year, they shall be as white as snow' (Isa. 1:18). And Ben Azzai said: The phrase *këbaśim bëne šanah* means that they cleanse the sins of the people of Israel and make them as innocent as an infant in its first year. [*PRK*, Braude-Kapstein: 135][18]

The efficacy of repentance, however, clearly depends on its sincerity: "The man who lying against the truth, maintains while still doing wrong that he has repented, is a madman. It is just as if the sick man were to act the part of the healthy man: he will certainly get worse through declining to have recourse to any means conducive to health (*Fug.* 160)."[19] A sure sign of sincere repentance is that it is marked by bitterness, weeping, sighing, and groaning:[20]

R. 7.8; *mAbot* 5.18: "One that leads the many to sin, to him shall not be given the means to repentance;" *Midr. Psalms* 1.22: "He who is confirmed in transgressions cannot repent, and there is never forgiveness for him;" *Exod. R.* 11.1; *bErub*, 19a; *Tanḥ* Buber, *Naso* 18; *Num. R.* 11.5.

[18] Cf. *Pesik. R.*, Braude: 781: "They said to Him: Master of the universe, upon our return what wilt Thou do with all our iniquities? He replied: Resolve upon a return, and they will be swallowed up from the sight of the world, as is said 'The iniquity of Israel shall be sought for, and there shall be none, and the sins of Judah and they shall not be found' (Jer. 50:20);" *yR.H.* 4.8, 59c: "When you are gathered to judgment before me on New Years Day and go forth in peace, I impute to you as if you were created a new creation (or creature);" *PRK*, Mandelbaum: 346; *Lev. R.* 229 end; *Tanḥ* Buber, *Wayyera* 16; *Wayyeṣe.* 22; *ySanh.* 10.1, 27c; 2 Cor. 5:17; *bYeb.* 48b (a proselyte is like a newborn child). Both Philo and the rabbis also assert that repentance brings about redemption (*bYoma* 86b; *Praem.* 163–64).

[19] Cf. *Tanḥ.* Buber, *Bereshit* 25 (Cain's repentance was insincere); *PRK*, Mandelbaum: 358–62 (the repentance of Cain, Ahab, and the people of Nineveh was insincere. See E. Urbach, "The Repentance of the Ninevites and the Jewish-Christian Debate," *Tarbiz* 20 (1949) 118–22). Philo even suggests that if one returns to God out of duress, He does not in all cases follow His law of mercy (*Sac.* 71).

[20] Cf. *LA* 3.211–13; *Det.* 95; Joel 2:12–13; Wis. 5:3–14; *Exod. R.* 38.4; Aristotle *EN* 3.1110b: "[Acts] are involuntary only when they bring sorrow and regret in their

For those who naturally and genuinely repent become bitter toward their former way of life and are vexed with their wretched life, weeping, sighing and groaning because they have given over the most necessary part of time to that seductive and deceitful mistress, Desire, and have spent the prime of their youth in being deceived by her when they ought to have renewed themselves and advanced in the contemplation of wisdom toward the goal of a happy, fortunate and immortal life. And so, we who desire repentance eat the unleavened bread with bitter herbs, that is, we first eat bitterness over our old and unendurable life, and then we eat the opposite of overboastful arrogance through meditation on humility, which is called reverence. [*QE* 1.15]

Quoting Hos. 14:3 ("Take words with you, And return to the Lord"), the *Pesikta* similarly remarks:

The Holy One blessed be He, said to Israel: My children, I will not accept burnt offerings, or sin offerings, or guilt offerings, or meal offerings from you. Propitiate Me only with prayer, with supplication, and with right direction of the heart. If you suppose, however, that you can propitiate Me with idle words, heed what Scripture says: "Thou art not a God propitiated by [one retaining] wickedness; evil sojourneth not with Thee' (Ps. 5:5)–propitiation requires confession, supplication, and tears. [*Pesik. R.*, Braude: 847]

Like the rabbis, however, Philo is concerned that the penitent's sins not be unduly publicized. In his interpretation of Lev. 5:20–26, which coincides with that of the Tannaitic tradition (*mShevuot* 8.3; *B.Q.* 9.7–8; *B.M.* 4.8), he insists that the biblical text is dealing with one who, convicted by his own conscience (*hupo tou suneidotos*), has voluntarily confessed his wrong (apparently to the victim)[21] and verifies his repentance by restoring the deposit or property which he has seized or usurped from his neighbor, adding a fifth as a solatium for the offense. This must be followed up by his proceeding to the temple to ask remission for his sins and offer a sacrifice.

The prohibition against carrying the flesh of the sacrifice outside the temple is due to Scripture's wish that any sin which the penitent has previously committed should not be made notorious through the ill-judged judgments and unbridled tongues of malicious and acrimonious persons, and blazed abroad as a subject for contumelious and censorious talk, but be confined within the sacred precincts which have also been the scene of the purification. [*Spec.* 1.235–41]

The rabbis similarly explain that the Torah deliberately stated that the sin offering and the whole-burnt offering are to be slaughtered in the same place, in order not to embarrass the sinner, since no one would be able to

---

train."
21 See S. Daniel, *FE* 24.152, n. 4; and the detailed discussion in Jacob Milgrom, *Cult and Conscience* (Leiden, 1976) 84–114.

tell whether the sacrifice was being brought as a burnt offering or as a sin offering (*yYeb.* 8.3, 9c).[22]

Up to this point, we have found nothing in Philo's account of repentance that differs from Jewish tradition. In analyzing the process of repentance, however, Philo appears to introduce a philosophical mode of description. In an allegorical interpretation of Exod. 12:9a, he tells us that "those who change by the principle of knowledge and are hardened as though by the force of fire have acquired a stable and unmoving usefulness" (*QE* 1.16). Similarly, in *Mig.*148, he speaks of "those who are irresolute, swaying up and down as though as on a pair of scales," as "not being praiseworthy even in their taking a turn to the better course, since it is the result not of judgment but of drift (*phorai gar, all' ou gnōmei gignetai*) (cf. *QG* 4.45). More revealing is his description of repentance at *Fug.* 159 as "a restricted and slow and tarrying thing" (*estalmenon kai bradu kai mellon hē metanoia*). This is spelled out further in his allegorical interpretation of Gen. 8:11:

> What is the meaning of the words, 'The dove returned again to him at evening, holding an olive-leaf, a dry branch in its mouth'? All these are chosen symbols and tests–'the returning again,' the 'at evening,' the 'holding an olive leaf,' the 'dry branch,' the 'oil' and the 'in its mouth.' But the several symbols must be studied in detail. Now the return is distinguished from the earlier flight. For the latter brought the report of a nature altogether corrupt and rebellious, and one destroyed by the flood, (that is) by great ignorance and lack of education. But the other repents of its beginning. And to find repentance is not easy but is a very difficult and laborious task. For these reasons it comes at evening, having passed the whole day from early morning until evening in inspection, in word by passing over various places but in deed by looking over and inspecting the parts of its nature and in seeing them clearly from beginning to end, for the evening is a symbol of the end. And the third symbol is the 'bearing a leaf.' The leaf is a small part of the plant. And similar to this is the beginning to repent. For the beginning of improvement gives a slight indication, as if it were a leaf, that it is to be guarded and also can be shaken off. But there is a great hope withal that it will attain correction of its ways.... [*QG* 2.42]

The rabbis, in contrast, emphasize the instantaneousness of the process of repentance. We read in *Pesik. R.* 44, Braude 779:

---

[22] Similarly, the silent recitation of the Amidah is explained by the rabbis as intended to avoid embarrassing those who committed transgressions (*bSotah* 32b). Cf. *bYoma* 86b, where the apparent contradiction between Ps. 32:1 and Prov. 28:13 is resolved in two different ways. According to one answer, if a man's sin is known then it is his duty to confess publicly, but if it is unknown, then he may confess without acknowledging his sin publicly. According to the second answer, sins committed against God require no public confession, but those committed against one's fellowman require a public confession. See Samuel Belkin, *Philo and the Oral Law* (Cambridge, 1940) 59.

'Return, O Israel, unto the Lord thy God.' Our holy rabbi [Judah] expounded the verse as follows: So great is the power of a return in repentance that the repentance soars straight up to God. Indeed, as soon as a man resolves in his heart upon the act of repentance, his repentance soars up not to height of ten miles, nor of twenty, nor of one hundred, but to a height that would require a journey of five hundred years to accomplish.

A similar sentiment is expressed in *PRK* 24.12, Braude-Kapstein 738:[23]

R. Tanḥuma citing R. Ḥnina, and R. Aibu citing Resh Lakish, said: Vow repentance for as little time as it takes to wink an eye, 'and you will be aware that I am the Lord [of mercy] (Ps. 46:11). For as R. Levi said: Were Israel to vow repentance for but one day, they would be redeemed forthwith. And the proof? 'We would be the people of his pasture, and the flock of His hand, if only for but one day you would hearken to His voice' (Ps. 95:7).

On the other hand, at *Praem.* 15, Philo describes repentance as being "suddenly possessed with an ardent yearning for betterment," and at *Virt.* 182, he speaks of the proselytes as acquiring all the virtues at once. Moreover, at *QG* 2.13, he speaks of the "extraordinary abundance of the seemly kindness of the Savior and Benefactor in loosing man's evil of many years, extending almost from birth to old age, in those who repent for a few days." We may perhaps reconcile these apparently conflicting passages by distinguishing between the psychological events that ultimately lead up to a complete change in the individual's psyche, and which may constitute a slow, lengthy process, and the moment of conversion (*metabolē*) itself to wisdom.[24] The Stoics, for example, believed that the transition of the man who is making moral progress (*prokoptōn*) to the state of perfected wisdom is instantaneous, and supervenes suddenly upon a long course of self-mastery, without the individual being conscious of it (*SVF* 3.539–42, 510, 637–70. For Philo's knowledge of this Stoic teaching, see *Agr.* 161; *Som.* 2.270).

---

[23] Cf. *bQidd.* 49b: [If a man betroths a woman] on condition that I am righteous, even if he is absolutely wicked, she is betrothed, for he may have meditated repentance in his thought. In *Midr. Psalms* on Ps. 45:4 we are told that the sons of *Qoraḥ* could not confess with their lips, but when their heart was moved in repentance, the Lord received them.

[24] Cf. *Mut.* 124: "But in Caleb we have a total change of the man himself. For we read 'there was another spirit in him' (Num. 14:24), as though the ruling mind in him was changed to supreme perfection. For Caleb is by interpretation 'all heart,' and this is a figurative way of showing that his was no partial change of a soul wavering and oscillating (cf. *Mig.* 148), but a change to proved excellence of the whole and entire soul which dislodged anything that was not entirely laudable by thoughts of repentance; for when it thus washed away its defilements, and made use of the illustrations and purifications of wisdom, it could not but be clean and fair." For a similar contradiction in Epictetus, see Adolf Bonhöffer, *Epictet und die Stoa* (Stuttgart, 1890) 303.

Finally, in assessing the relative rank of the penitent and the man who is perfect, Philo gives the palm to the latter. "Repentance," he says, "holds the second place to perfection, just as a change from sickness to health is second to a body free from disease (*Abr.* 26)." The unbroken perfection of virtues stands nearest to the divine power, and[25]

> the perfect man [i.e., Noah] is complete from the first. The transferred [i.e., Enoch] stands half-way(*hēmiergos*), since he devoted the earlier part of this life to vice but the latter to virtue; the hoper [i.e., Enosh], is defective inasmuch as though he always desired the excellent he has not yet been able to attain it, but resembles sailors eager to put into port, who yet remain at sea unable to reach their haven. [*Abr.* 47]

Furthermore, in *Aet.* 40, Philo reports the view that repentance is a "*pathos* or distemper of the soul (*nosēma psuchēs*)," with apparent approval,[26] and in *Spec.* 1.103 (in spite of his brave words at *Abr.* 19 cited above), he points out that "in the souls of the repentant there remain, in spite of all, the scars and prints of their old misdeeds (*oulai kai tupoi tōn archaiōn adikēmatōn*).[27]

The rabbis, too, however debated the question of the relative merit of the penitent and the man of perfection:

> R. Ḥiyya b. Abba said in the name of R. Yoḥanan: All the prophets prophesied only on behalf of penitents; but as for the wholly righteous, 'Eye has not seen, O God, beside Thee.' He differs in this from R. Abbahu. For R. Abbahu said: In the place where penitents stand even the wholly righteous cannot stand, as it says: Peace, peace to him that was far and to him that is near' (Isa. 57:19)—to him that was far first, and then to him that is near. [*bBer.* 34b][28]

Moreover, Philo's assertion that the scars of old misdeeds cannot be effaced also appears to be paralleled in the Talmud:

---

[25] Cf. *Praem.* 15; *Virt.* 176; *Som.* 2.91.

[26] It is generally accepted that *Aet.* 39–43 is a fragment of Aristotle's lost *De Philosophia* (fr. 19c, Ross).

[27] Cf. Plato *Gorg.* 524D: "Nay, often when Rhadamanthus [the judge of the dead] has laid hold of the Great King or some other prince or potentate, he perceives the utter unhealthiness of his soul, striped all over with the scourge, and a mass of scar, the work of perjuries and injustice (*oulōn mestēn hupo epiorkiōn kai adikias*) where every act has left its smirch upon his soul." The Stoics admitted that "even the wise man's mind will keep its scar (*cicatrix manet*) long after the wound has healed." (Seneca *De Ira* 1.16.7, trans. Colson, LCL 7.620. Cf. Epict. 2.18.11). In *Spec.* 1.187, however, Philo says that God has given to repentance the same honor as to innocence from sin, and in *Som.* 1.91 he describes repentance as "younger brother of complete guiltlessness." See E.K. Dietrich, *Die Umkehr im A.T. und im Judentum* (Stuttgart, 1936) 287–305, especially 297–98, 304–05.

[28] Cf. Luke 15:7: "There will be more joy in heaven over one sinner who repents than over ninety-nine righteous persons who need no repentance."

R. Ḥama b. Ḥaina pointed out a contradiction: It is written: 'Return ye backsliding children' (Jer. 3:22), i.e., you who were formerly backsliding; it is written: 'I will heal your backsliding.'[29] This is no difficulty: in the one case the reference is where they return out of love, in the other out of fear [bYoma 86a].

On the other hand, Philo's assertion that repentance is an irrational emotion (*pathos*) naturally finds no echo in rabbinic literature, but it must be noted that that assertion is found in one of his purely philosophical treatises and in another context.

In sum, although Philo has not succeeded completely in assimilating the concept of repentance to his philosophical thought, he does nevertheless emphasize its secondary rank in the hierarchy of virtue, explicitly refers to the scars of old misdeeds, and clearly indicates the lengthy intellectual process that precedes conversion to a better life.[30] Revealing, too, is his casual reference to repentance as an irrational emotion, a view that derives inevitably from the fundamental philosophical principles of his ethical theory. It should further be noted that Philo was undoubtedly aware of a Neo-Pythagorean preoccupation with self-examination that was later taken up by the Roman Stoa, and this may have made it easier for him to incorporate the Jewish emphasis on repentance into his own writings in the manner that he did.[31] Philo's treatment of the doctrine of

---

[29] According to Rashi, the first part of the verse implies that having repented they are perfect as children, whereas the second part, which speaks of 'healing,' implies that they still retain a taint of their former backsliding.

[30] Cf. *Jos.* 86, where the repentance of his fellow prisoners is partially induced by Joseph's doctrines of philosophy.

[31] Self-examination is recommended in the Ps-Pythagorean *Golden Verses*:

Also allow not sleep to draw nigh to your languorous eyelids,
Ere you have reckoned up each several deed of the daytime:
'Where went I wrong? Did what? And what to be done was left undone'? [40–44]

This advice was quoted with approval by Epictetus (3.10.2), trans. Oldfather, LCL) and practiced by Seneca (*De Ira* 3.36.1–4; *Ep.* 28.9–10: "'The knowledge of sin is the beginning of salvation.' This saying of Epicurus seems to me a noble one. For he who does not know that he has sinned does not desire correction ... Therefore, as far as possible, prove yourself guilty, hunt up charges against yourself; play the part, first of accuser, then of judge, last of intercessor. At times be harsh with yourself." (Cf. *Ep.* 6.1; 53.8; Epictetus 2.11.1; M. Aurelius 1.7). M. Aurelius similarly writes: "I do penance, I am cross with myself, I am sad and discontented, I feel starved." (Fronto *Epist.*, vol. 1, LCL, p. 216). See E.R. Dodds, *Pagan and Christian in an Age of Anxiety* (Cambridge, 1965) 28. It should also be noted that Plutarch, in an effort to explain why God is slow to punish, says that he does so in order "to make room for repentance" (*pros metanoian; Ser. Num.* 551D; cf. *Gen. Soc.* 592B). In *On Tranquility of Mind* (476F) he says that conscience, "like an ulcer in the flesh, leaves behind it in the soul regret (*metameleian*) which ever continues to wound and prick it. For the other pangs (*lupas*) reason does away with, but regret is caused by reason itself, since the soul, together with its feeling of shame, is stung and chastised by itself (*tēn de metanoian*

repentance thus exemplifies the pervasive tensions that characterize much of his writing and the resulting ambivalence which follows in the wake of a head-on clash between his philosophical impulse and religious conceptions that are native to his ancestral tradition and are irreconcilable. with it. His writing under these conditions reveals a studied ambiguity of expression that seeks to camouflage his true philosophical position.

---

autos ergazetai daknomenēs sun aischunēitēs psuchēs kai kolazomenēs huph' autēs. Plutarch's use of the term *daknomeñes* here suggests that Philo's high evaluation of *metanoia* could have been further softened for him by the fact that he may have conceived of it not as a pathos, as the Stoics did, but either as a *propatheia*, just as he had done with Abraham's tears at the death of his wife Sarah (*QG* 4.73; Greek frag., LCL, supp. 2, Marcus, p. 220), or even as an *eupatheia*. Although the Stoics did not consider *dēgmos* (biting, sting) to be a *pathos*, neither did they consider it an *eupatheia*, but placed it instead in the category of an automatic bodily reaction such as pallor, shuddering, or contraction of the brow. The Stoics were frequently attacked on this account for fudging and resorting to linguistic quibbles in order to escape from reality (Plutarch *Virt. Mor.* 449A). But Philo classified *dēgmos* as an *eupatheia* (*QG* 2.57). He was either following some minor Stoic disciple sensitized by the criticism, or more likely he did this on his own. (See my forthcoming article, "Philo's Conception of the Divine Nature," note 50).

"NUL N'EST PROPHÈTE EN SON PAYS
Contribution à l'Étude de Joseph d'après Philon

Jacques Cazeaux

Introduction : Les Trois Héros de la Politique

Dans les *Lois*, Platon commence par une feinte curiosité à l'endroit des Institutions de Sparte et de la Crète, comme si une comparaison pouvait conseiller à l'Athénien une réforme rationnelle et idéale. La Loi reste à venir, et l'ordre politique reste une construction réfléchie, rapportée à la raison universelle. Mais Philon le Juif possède une seule référence, la Bible, qu'il ne s'agit pas de peser et d'estimer comme une esquisse entre d'autres esquisses, mais d'adopter d'emblée comme l'unique modèle. Et ce modèle est déjà existant. La Loi d'Israël est un donné. Philon ignorant tout messianisme politique, le Logos au-dehors et l'achèvement personnel au-dedans tiennent lieu de Fin; et il suffit à l'homme de bonne volonté de lire et de faire.

Dans la Bible elle-même, il existe une réflexion politique, dissimulée dans la composition des récits historiques, des *Nombres* aux *Rois*. Mais Philon ne descend pratiquement jamais si bas dans l'Histoire d'Israël. Il ne prend jamais appui sur les expériences effectives du pouvoir et de la vie politique en Israël. Il ne se présente pas davantage en penseur politique. Il n'a même pas écrit, semble-t-il, un de ces nombreux traités *Peri Basileias* qui fleurirent durant la période hellénistique. Et, s'il fut ambassadeur auprès de Caligula puis de Claude, rien ne prouve que ce soit au titre d'une carrière politique. Depuis longtemps, on utilisait comme porte-parole des Cités les notables, voire les médecins réputés, les philosophes, des personnages dont les cours hellénistiques aimaient à orner leur réputation de culture et de libéralisme.[1]

Pourtant, sans traiter *ex professo* de l'ordre "politique", Philon en est comme assiégé. Tantôt, sa réflexion première, de l' "âme", emprunte les images du monde social et politique, la Cité devenant l'image de l'homme individuel, étant donné que celui-ci n'est pas un être simple; tantôt, la réalité sociale et politique d'Israël (Moïse n'est-il pas d'abord le Législateur, et la Bible n'est-elle pas d'abord la Loi ?) a besoin d'être interprétée à l'image de cette république en miniature que représente l'homme. À mi-

---

[1] Les thèses d'E.R. Goodenough sur Philon politique ont été saluées comme un pur roman. Voir, à propos de son *The Politics of Philo Judaeus* (Olms: Hildesheim, 1967), Ray Barraclough, *Philo's Politics*, dans ANRW, II, 21, 1, pages 417–453.

chemin entre ce microcosme et le macrocosme de l'Univers, conçu immédiatement par les Anciens comme tout à la fois physique et moral, l'ordre politique est, pour Philon comme pour tous les penseurs, la réalité première, le premier donné empirique : à partir de la Cité,[2] libre à la réflexion de descendre en soi, comme si l'homme était un groupe humain à "gouverner", ou de monter jusqu'à l'Éther, comme si le monde des Dieux était une Monarchie, par exemple. Le Moderne se représente lui-même comme au centre de trois cercles concentriques, le Moi, la Cité, l'Univers. L'Ancien est chose de la Cité, et il rayonne à partir de là, vers soi-même ou vers Dieu. Philon ne fait pas exception. Fanatique de l'"âme", du "moi", son plan de référence reste la Cité. Mais cela ne suffit pas plus à en faire un Politicien que la référence immédiate du Moderne à son "moi" n'en fait un psychologue. Nombre de passages "politiques" dans l'oeuvre de Philon ne dépassent pas ce réflexe de la référence naturelle ou "du premier degré". D'autres, bien entendu, passent au "second degré", et Philon y parle vraiment de Politique. Héritier du Stoïcisme et des Cyniques, on verra ce Juif, parfaitement Juif et comme tel conscient d'une singularité raciale, mentale et religieuse surtout, annexer les concepts universalistes de l'École, l'*"homme-roi"*, le *"citoyen du monde"*, le *"peuple-philosophe"*—à la fois, disions-nous, comme des images du Moi décrit à ses yeux par la Bible, et comme concepts approchant la réflexion réellement politique.[3]

Les trois politiques

Les traités allégoriques de Philon se limitent par définition à la Torah ou, pour parler son grec, au Pentateuque, et, de fait, à la *Genèse*, voire à ses ch. 1–17, pour ce qui nous reste de son Commentaire suivi (avec de grands vides: absence des ch. 5; 7–8, c'est à dire de tout le récit du Déluge; 10; 13–14). Cependant, l'histoire de Joseph fait l'objet de deux synthèses, dans le *De Josepho*, qu'on veut rattacher au genre hellénistique de l'"encomion", et le troisième traité *De Somniis* (actuellement, *De somniis* II, par la perte du premier traité); et le personnage de Moïse, héros de l'*Exode*, se profile tout au long des allégories consacrées à la *Genèse*. Que ce soit un hasard dû à la rédaction de Philon lui-même ou à l'oubli de telle et telle oeuvre, que ce

---

[2] La recherche rationnelle du meilleur ordre "politique", chez Platon, prend en fait pour balises l'équilibre psychique, d'un côté, et, de l'autre, une sorte de gravitation physico-morale de l'Univers (voir en particulier, le *Gorgias*, par exemple, 507–508).

[3] Avertissons le lecteur d'une ambiguïté entretenue par le vocabulaire propre de Philon : chez lui, le terme *politikos* est plus étroit que notre "politique", puis-que, pour Philon, *politikos* designe le mauvais politique, armé de sophismes et condamné à la variation indéfinie (*poikilos*).

soit l'effet d'une volonté, nous restons en présence de trois grandes figures du Politique : Abraham, Joseph, Moïse. Hasard ou volonté, ces trois figures se trouvent agencées de façon dialectique, autour d'un axe (moral, et non directement géographique) formé par deux régions "infernales", la Mésopotamie et l'Égypte. Abraham et Moïse s'arrachent violemment et arrachent leur famille ou le Peuple entier du pays maudit; mais, entre les deux héros, Joseph descend en Égypte, y vit, s'y installe et y prend même une grande part du gouvernement. Abraham et Moïse, de plus, incarnent tout deux la Loi d'Israël en même temps que la loi naturelle: Abraham est "*loi vivante, non écrite*", et Moïse donne à Israël la plénitude de la "*Loi écrite*"; l'un résume Israël en sa naissance, et le second, dans sa résurrection; l'un exerce le gouvernement sur une simple maison, et l'autre prend la tête d'un Peuple entier;[4] tous deux s'élèvent à des expériences hors du commun, et Abraham est introduit à la première initiation, tandis que Moïse jouit des mystères accomplis (on ne verra dans ce vocabulaire des Mystères qu'une image, bien entendu). Entre les deux, Joseph incarne la tentation du Politique, et c'est d'ailleurs à lui seul que Philon accorde le nom même de *politikos*, comme un blason péjoratif. Il est engagé dans l'épaisseur et le "nombre" qui définissent le corps, puisque l'Égypte symbolise précisément le corps, avec ses passions matérielles, le souci du boire et du manger ... Il n'est pas l'homme du "oui ? oui ! Non ? non !", mais il compose, pactise avec le mal; il met sa sagesse au service d'un panetier, d'un échanson, du Pharaon inquiet pour le ravitaillement de son pays en vivres (on se souviendra que Platon fait déjà coïncider les désirs populaires et les plaisirs de la cuisine—*Gorgias* 462, etc.). Bref, d'Abraham à Moïse, et de tous deux à Joseph, il existe dans la Bible allégorisée suffisamment d'homothéties et d'antithèses pour alimenter la rhétorique savante d'un Philon.

D'Abraham je ne dirai pas ici grand-chose, sinon ceci : le traitement que lui impose Philon fait que l'image d'un Abraham-roi nous oriente très vite vers l'*apolitisme* plutôt que vers une *Politique*. À force de sublimation et d'utopie morale, Philon nous éloigne du champ clos où la Politique, bonne ou malsaine, doit précisément s'exercer. L'intransigeance et la sublimité de Moïse, à l'autre bout de l'Histoire patriarcale, aboutiront au même paradoxe; et le seul personnage à tenter les nécessaires conciliations et les contingences, à savoir Joseph, sera d'emblée réputé sophiste et traître à Israël.

---

[4] Selon Platon et d'autres philosophes, mais non pas selon Aristote, le gouvernement d'une maison présage utilement de celui d'une cité; et Philon opère souvent le va-et-vient de l'une à l'autre forme d'autorité. Voir aussi la parabole évangélique des "talents" (*Matthieu*, ch. 25, v. 21 et 23).

Abraham, roi sans royaume

Abraham domine la guerre et la paix; Abraham gouverne sa maisonnée. Il est royal. Sa conversion à l'Unique lui fait rejoindre d'emblée l'origine de toutes choses et l'équilibre universel. Et cela lui confère aussitôt le titre et le rôle de *Nomos empsuchos*. Il faut voir que par sa conversion à l'Unique, Abraham est associé à la Création première dans son *fieri* : il est initié à la *Division* par laquelle toutes choses ont vu le jour et l'équilibre, tant dans le Cosmos que dans la Constitution d'Israël. C'est le sens du long "chapitre" du *Quis heres.* § 125–236. L'art suprême et proprement divin de la "séparation adéquate",[5] en deux parties égales, de toutes choses y est découvert à Abraham quand il partage lui-même les victimes de son sacrifice (*Genèse*, ch. 15). Les exemples pris par Philon associent Cosmos et Loi, de telle sorte que les deux mots français "justesse" du partage métaphysique et "Justice" morale et quasi politique deviennent superposables. C'est donc par les sommets qu'Abraham se trouve doté de la Loi, à la fois naturelle et politique et morale. Il devient le *kosmopolitēs* accompli. Il est encore seul, et ce n'est qu'en promesse de Dieu qu'il se sait père d'Israël. Mais, dans le monde païen qui l'entoure, il est reconnu comme roi; dans la famille restreinte qui est la sienne, il exerce un gouvernement harmonieux (voir ici le *De migratione Abrahami* § 118–126, et le *De Abrahamo* § 116, etc.). On devine déjà le caractère déductif et comme *a priori* du "pouvoir" d'Abraham; et le peu de rapport qui subsiste (pour ce que nous appelons "politique") avec l'expérience, voire l'empirisme, qui ne peut manquer d'entre dans sa définition réelle.

Aussi bien est-ce à partir de l'Expérience mystique d'Abraham que Philon peut classer les divers régimes politiques concrets—en cela, il transpose et aggrave l'idéalisme d'un Platon. Pour Philon, l'étude des régimes politiques peut être menée à partir de l'étude des états de l'âme, comme, à son tour, celle-ci doit être menée en fonction de la plus ou moins grande participation à l'Unité, idéal divin. La *monarchie* imite au mieux le gouvernement de Dieu et l'harmonie cosmique : elle reflète en réalité l'unité du Moi. La *démocratie*, reposant sur l'égalité, accomplit en un sens la monarchie : la Loi, imposée par la monarchie, devient en un sens l'instinct de chacun. Malheureusement, si la démocratie devient le champ clos des opinions diverses et du désordre, elle tourne à l'*ochlocratie*, le pire des fléaux pour les nations comme pour les âmes. La démocratie consacre l'harmonie de toutes le parties du Moi, solidement intégrées, et l'ochlocratie représente l'anarchie d'une âme livrée aux passions. Reste la

---

[5] Pour les Anciens, la division juste, le partage des "insécables", évoque la perfection divine. Ici, Abraham est rendu contemporain de la Création (en amont) et de l'Histoire et Loi d'Israël (en aval).

tyrannie : elle caricature la monarchie, comme l'ochlocratie caricature la démocratie.[6] La tyrannie renvoie à l'impiété fondamentale, celle qui fait croire à l'esprit qu'il est Dieu. Vertu unifiée (monarchie), engendrant l'harmonie (démocratie théorique), les deux premières formes sont positives; passions en désordre (ochlocratie) et méritant le fouet (tyrannie), les deux derniers régimes sont négatifs : les quatre hypothèses, deux à deux, composent une histoire de l'âme. Mystique et psychologie expliquent d'ailleurs pourquoi Philon n'a pas exploité pour ses références "politiques" la succession des régimes dont Israël a fait bel et bien l'expérience au long de son histoire. Il s'en tient aux images domestiques de la *Genèse*; il sait encore utiliser celles de la horde tirée d'Égypte par Moïse selon l'*Exode*, ou de l'armée disciplinée qu'on voit s'ordonner au début des *Nombres*. Mais il ne tire aucun enseignement des règnes de Saül, de David , de Salomon, le roi des rois, non plus que de la vague amphictyonie qui réunit les Tribus d'Israël, au temps des Juges et de Samuel commençant.

Le commentaire de Philon constitue lui-même une sorte de république morale, où tous les héros du bien entretiennent des relations d'homothétie et de transparence tout en gardant leur personnalité propre, leur degré de vérité. Ainsi, Abraham a beau symboliser le premier degré de la sagesse, puisqu'il incarne le *désir de savoir*, l'étude en son commencement, il y a dans son histoire biblique suffisamment d'événements et de traits capables de nous faire pressentir en Abraham les étapes suivantes, la lutte même de Jacob et même la perfection immobile d'un Isaac. De la sorte, il est difficile d'isoler ce qui revient à l'exemple d'Abraham ou à l'exemple propre de Moïse, dans la théorie politique de Philon. Les héros positifs se *communiquent leurs idiomes*.[7] Nous pourrions ici passer directement au troisième modèle de Philon, à savoir Moïse, sans quitter réellement Abraham.

Si nous parlons de la "politique" et de la royauté d'Abraham, il est un aspect très précis des spéculations sur le Pouvoir que Philon rejoint à l'occasion d'Abraham : c'est l'extension de la Providence (du pouvoir royal ...) jusque dans les cantons les plus obscurs. Le Roi devant assurer justice et prospérité, c'est dans sa capacité à les assurer là où elles sont le plus nécessaires, dans les zones reculées, loin de la Cour, loin du cercle des gens de mérite et de valeur, loin des villes prospères, à la frontière de la nuit politique et morale. Dieu[8] comme Roi provident, le Dieu de la Bible

---

[6] Philon n'invite pas à la revolte les sujets du tyran : la tyrannie est le châtiment des folies, et le tyran, un fléau de Dieu.

[7] La théologie chrétienne de la Trinité désigne ainsi la communauté des trois Personnes en ce qui touche à la Création ou à l'activité divine *ad extra*.

[8] Voir déjà Platon, *Lois*, 10, 900c–903a.

surtout, bon pour les pauvres et les petits, étend précisément sa puissance pour sauver ce qu'il y a de plus infime dans l'Univers et dans l'humanité. Abraham, pour Philon, est justement associé à cette vertu divine. Il étend son regard jusqu'aux êtres les plus éloignés de la Source divine et qui semblaient voués à une obscurité de plus en plus impénétrable. Dieu confie à ses Ministres, les Puissances, ce que Philon appelle les *affaires secondaires*, mais Il se réserve les *affaires capitales*. Que sont-elles? Les malheurs des êtres les plus faibles, l'étranger, la veuve, l'orphelin (selon la terminologie des Lois d'Israël, en particulier dans le *Deutéronome*). Les êtres qui ont seulement pour soutien de leur existence la Justice du Prince symbolisent d'autant mieux l'efficacité de la Cause suprême, qui vient jusque là conférer l'unité et la forme, aux confins de la *materia prima* politique et ontologique.[9]

Mais, pour Philon, en cette providence même, Abraham n'a rien d'un Hammurabi. Il n'édicte pas de sages lois qui seraient destinées à régler concrètement le sort des déshérités. C'est par en-haut et de façon aussi invisible que celle[10] de la Justice divine que tout est réglé. Nous verrons en conclusion comment Philon répugne à faire entrer les lois même de Moïse, et donc le gouvernement, et donc la Politique, dans l'ordre du concret. Abraham est un Chef idéal, pour lui, parce qu'il exhorte, preche d'exemple, encourage, et ne s'abaisse pas à la coercition pas plus qu'à ces ruses proprement symboliques du Pouvoir concret que sont les jugements psychologiques de Salomon ou les expédients divins qui, depuis les derniers chapitres des *Juges* jusqu'aux livres des *Rois*, permettent d'apaiser les conflits, en admettant une réduction de la Justice à l'équité, à l'équilibre, aux compromis inévitables de la Politique et du Pouvoir. Nous verrons aussi que les Lois de Moïse, pour Philon, sont plutôt des modèles, des exhortations, que des instruments contraignants.

L'*a-politisme* d'un pareil système va éclater lorsque, des grands Politiques, Abraham et Moïse, Philon passe à Joseph, qu'il leur oppose comme le "*politique*", au point de lui réserver le qualificatif. C'est avec l'étude de son Joseph, pourtant, que le lecteur de Philon peut espérer aborder une conception concrète de la politique. Mais, en un premier temps, cet espoir sera déçu. Entre la *Loi non écrite incarnée par Abraham, Jacob et Isaac*, d'une part, et, d'autre part, la *Loi écrite* grâce à *Moïse*, Joseph n'a plus aucune chance de

---

[9] Ainsi, dans le beau texte du *De migratione*, § 118b–126; voir *De spec. leg.*, I, § 308ss; II, § 108, 218; IV, 176, etc., pour le gouvernement divin.

[10] Caractéristique à cet égard la conclusion du *De migratione* et d'autres traités ou "chapitres" philoniens, sur le thème des *fautes involontaires*. Dieu rétablit mystérieusement et au-delà de toute vérification empirique, au-delà de toute intervention d'une instance humaine de justice ou de pouvoir, et par Sa Justice, des situations perdues. La transcendance dispense les rois et les juges d'intervenir …

dépasser le domaine misérable de l'instinct. Il ne nous apprendra pas grand-chose sur la direction rationnelle des affaires de la Cité idéale.

Nous devrons cependant y regarder de plus près. Nous devrons en particulier éviter de projeter sur les deux grandes réalisations exégétiques du *De Josepho* et du *De somniis II* les traits un peu raides qui servent à opposer rapidement Joseph aux nobles figures de la vérité et du Bien public: Joseph est compromis dans les sophismes et l'animalité, quand Abraham et Moïse s'en éloignent au plus vite—trop vite, précisément, pour rester des "politiques", au sens pratique du mot. Je soulignerai tout de suite un phénomène étrange, en guise de préalable. Le terme couramment appliqué à Joseph dans les traités qui ne lui sont pas directement consacrés, ce fameux adjectif de *politikos*, ne se trouve pas une seule fois tout au long du *De somniis II*; et une exégèse férue de statistiques pourrait en conclure que le ce livre n'est pas l'oeuvre de Philon. Au contraire, le *De Josepho* semble contenir tout ce qu'il faut à la définition péjorative de Joseph comme "*politique*". Nous allons entrer dans la comparaison de ces deux ouvrages majeurs.

Le "De Josepho" : Joseph, Prophète de l'Égypte

Le Joseph de la Bible

Le Joseph de Philon a contre lui son nom et sa naissance. Né de Rachel, la "*sensation*", et nommé Joseph, l'"*excédent*", il est voué au matérialisme égyptien et à l'enflure mondaine.[11] Il est lié à Pharaon. Et là nous touchons à la "politique" philonienne: Pharaon est bien *roi*, mais au lieu de dominer le monde divers et animal, il n'a d'autre souci que les valeurs du corps; et il est donc une caricature de royauté—l'esprit devrait être le maître du corps, et non le servir. Joseph va participer, en second seulement, il est vrai,[12] à cette perversion. Tel est le départ de l'allégorie de Joseph.

Au premier abord, le *De Josepho* renonce à l'allégorie pour se rapprocher du genre synthétique de l'*encomion* hellénistique. Philon y raconte la vie de Joseph en suivant l'ordre anecdotique des épisodes de la *Genèse*. Il s'agit même de louer Joseph : la récapitulation finale compose même une image naïve (§ 268–270). L'histoire biblique de Joseph suit elle-même une progression ascendante, et Philon n'a pas à recomposer un éloge suivant une logique oratoire qui bouleverserait plus ou moins l'ordre des événements, comme c'est le cas dans le *De Abrahamo*. Or, pour comprendre la

---

[11] Selon sa méthode d'interprétation synthétique, globale, totalisante, Philon montre que tous les éléments du dossier "Joseph" conspirent entre eux, depuis le nom jusqu'à tous les événements de sa vie, ses comparses et ses adversaires.
[12] Voir la réhabilitation de Joseph, dans le *De migratione*, § 161, en écho des § 16-24.

portée exacte de l'éloge contenu dans le *De Josepho*, il est bon de garder en mémoire l'ironie et la déception organisées déjà par la *Genèse*.

Les ch. 37 à 50 de la *Genèse* déroulent avec complaisance une sorte de roman de cour. Joseph réunit progressivement en lui prédestination, sagesse variée, allant de la soumission à la chasteté, à la divination, à la faculté de gouverner, au pardon enfin. Mais la conclusion de son histoire déçoit l'espérance secrète du lecteur. En effet, Jacob accorde la grande Bénédiction, non pas à Joseph, mais à Juda, son *"quatrième"* fils (plusieurs fois, le *De Josepho* souligne ce chiffre— § 15, 189 et 222). Cette issue surprenante a été dûment préparée : Ruben, Siméon et Lévi, les trois aînés, ont péché (*Genèse*, ch. 34, v. 25s; ch. 35, v. 22), tandis que Juda reçoit une consécration étrange dans l'affaire de sa bru Tamar (ch. 38) et qu'il joue un rôle efficace dans le salut de Joseph ou les négociations ultérieures (ch. 43, v. 3, 8; ch. 44, v. 14, 18; ch. 46, v. 28). Ainsi, le personnage de Joseph a grandi à nos yeux, mais inutilement, en vain, pour ainsi dire, comme un nuage glorieux : Philon le dira à sa manière, *tuphos, kenē doxa*. La *Genèse* livre à Philon un Joseph déjà complexe, déjà dialectique, puisqu'à la fois exalté[13] et écarté, déjà presqu'allégorique. Philon a tenu compte de l'ambiguïté conférée par la *Genèse* à Joseph, mais il l'a transposée d'une façon curieuse et habile. Il a admis dans le déroulement de l'histoire de Joseph des passages allégoriques, nettement repérables. Ce sont la place, la proportion (et l'absence même de ces plages d'allégorie durant la seconde partie du *De Josepho*) qui nous guideront durant notre lecture. Pour garder notre premier repère, ajoutons ici que le terme exprès de *politikos*, avec son parent, *politeia*, sont utilisés seulement au cours des allégories et dans les paragraphes de transition entre "récit" linéaire et allégorie (§ 1, 31, 34, 54, 58, 61, 64, 75, 76, 79, 125, 143, 148, 149; et § 38, 39). Voici le plan sommaire de l'ouvrage.

1.– L'ENFANCE : PRÉDESTINATION–ÉPREUVE FONDAMENTALE DE L'ENLÈVEMENT

§ 1–15   a) RÉCIT : Joseph, marqué par les rêves de gloire, est haï de ses frères. Sauvé de justesse grâce au *"quatrième"* des frères, il est vendu et entraîné en Égypte par des marchands en transit d'Arabie.

§ 16–21   b) DISCOURS : La fin du "récit" est consacrée à deux discours, – celui de l'aîné, qui flétrit le crime de ses frères;

---

[13] Les péripéties de l'Histoire de Joseph permettent au *De Josepho* de cumuler les caractéristiques de l'*encomion* et celles d'un petit roman hellénistique : enlèvement, périls extrêmes, retrouvailles, merveilleux.

§ 22–27   – celui du père, qui exprime sa douleur et plaint un enfant mort sans sépulture.

§ 28–36   c) ALLÉGORIE : Assimilable au "*politique*", le personnage de Joseph doit être interprété de façon symbolique :

a.– son nom, "*addition au Seigneur*" signifie qu'il incarne "*une politique ajoutée à la Loi de Nature*" (§ 28–31);

b.– son vêtement "*bigarré*" – *poikilos* – symbolise les variations inhérentes à la politique (§ 32–34);

c.– enfin, la triple circonstance de son enlèvement convient au "politique" : il est un "*vendu*" (§35); il est censément "*livré aux fauves*" § 36a), et il est *vendu à nouveau* (§36b – on note le chiasme formé par le retour de la notion de "vendu").

2.– L'ÉPREUVE SECONDAIRE : LA FEMME DE L'EUNUQUE

§ 37–53   a) RÉCIT : Joseph devient intendant d'un eunuque (lequel est ainsi préparé par la nature à son rôle de politicien – § 37–39). La femme de son maître le provoque (§ 40–41), mais Joseph résiste ...

b) DISCOURS : la résistance de Joseph est exprimée par une plaidoirie, logique, appuyée (§ 42–48).

c) RÉCIT 2 : accusé par la femme, Joseph est jeté en prison, au mépris de la justice et de l'intelligence (§ 49–53).

§ 54–79   d) ALLÉGORIE : •Joseph a donc la maîtrise de soi, utile au roi;

•l'*eunuque* symbolise le Peuple (§ 58–60),

•lequel Peuple est un *maître-cuisinier* (§ 61–63) et parle comme la femme-sensation (§ 64–66);

e) DISCOURS : •Mais le véritable "*politique*" résiste et affiche un programme de justice et de vérité (§ 67–78).

3.– LA RESTAURATION

§ 80–124   a) RÉCIT : Joseph, en prison, interprète les songes prémonitoires des ministres de Pharaon (§ 80–99), puis les songes de Pharaon lui-même; Joseph est alors élevé au rang de vice-roi (§100–

122), ce qui est un effet de la justice immanente (§ 123–124).

§ 125-156   c) ALLÉGORIE :   •le Politique est un *interprète de rêves* – de ce grand rêve qui marque l'homme au milieu des variations universelles, dont seuls les astres sont exempts ... (§ 125–147);

•le Politique monte *le second char*, il reçoit l'*anneau* et le *collier* – ce sont trois signes de son ambiguïté... (§ 148–150);

•certains interprètes ajoutent l'allégorie des serviteurs de Pharaon, cuisinier, échanson, panetier, en suivant l'ordre de nécessité des biens corporels que ces métiers symbolisent (§ 151–156).

4.– LE GRAND ŒUVRE DE SAGESSE

§ 157–270   a) RÉCIT :   Philon raconte les missions successives des fils de Jacob en Egypte;

les épreuves auxquelles Joseph les soumet[14] (§ 157–231);

b) EXPLICATION SAPIENTIELLE[15] : en tout cela, Joseph a voulu vérifier l'amour fraternel de ses frères les uns pour les autres (§ 232–236) – explication elle-même généreuse et optimiste.

c) RÉCIT 2 : Scène de reconnaissance de Joseph et de ses frères; discours de Joseph (§ 237–245);

réconciliation,

sécurité des frères,

amitié de Pharaon,

joie et arrivée du père, Jacob,

heureuse gestion de Joseph,

caractère définitif de son pardon

(discours de Joseph),

RÉSUMÉ triomphant (§ 267b–270).

---

[14] Philon note soigneusement les âges respectifs des fils de Jacob (§ 173, 175, 187, 188, 189, 193, 207, 210, 222).

[15] Ce n'est plus une allégorisation des événements qui vient doubler le récit, mais une interprétation psychologique et morale de la conduite suivie par Joseph à l'égard de ses frères. Au § 250, Philon prend soin d'en effacer les traces objectives : tout le monde croit que la famille de Joseph vient en Égypte pour la première fois. L'´Egypte ignorera toujours que la famille de Jacob a pu se trouver divisée par un complot criminel ...

Ce résumé appelle quelques commentaires. Le dernier des quatre "chapitres"que j'ai distingués dans le *De Josepho* équivaut aux 3/4 des trois premiers réunis. Et, comme l'allégorie s'arrête justement au § 157, on pourrait diviser letout en deux parties : du § 1 au § 156, première partie, avec alternance de récit et d'allégorie; du § 157 à la fin, seconde partie, avec récit seulement, marqué par le style de l'éloge ou du roman.

Mais cette division simple demande à être précisée.

Tout d'abord, on notera la maîtrise rhétorique de Philon. Le récit est conduit de façon suggestive et cependant discrète.[16] La première partie (§ 1–156) est coupée de discours, selon les lieux-communs attendus; et ils sont placés avec art : dans le premier "chapitre", un discours (§ 16–27) sépare le récit de son allégorie; dans le second "chapitre", deux discours concluent, l'un, le récit, l'autre, son allégorie (§ 42–48; puis § 67–78). Durant le troisième "chapitre", les discours sont réduits à de courtes paraphrases des dialogues de la *Genèse*. La seconde partie (ou le "chapitre" quatrième) suit ce modèle plus lâche pendant longtemps, et nous retrouvons de plus longs discours à la fin (§ 222–231; § 238–245; § 262–266). Mais abordons la question plus importante, celle de l'allégorie. L'observation de sa répartition dans l'ouvrage et de son rôle nous permettra de mieux définir le *De Josepho*. Le contraste que nous verrons ensuite entre ce *De Josepho* et le *De somniis II* nous fera alors parvenir à une vision harmonieuse du "politique" Joseph.

Un point de départ : la place de l'allégorie dans le De Josepho

L'allégorie est donc présente dans les § 1–156 (une première partie, de trois "chapitres"); elle est absente des § 157–220 (une seconde partie, formée du quatrième "chapitre"). D'autre part, dans la première partie, il existe dans les sections-récit des *amorces d'allégorie*. Ainsi, le récit des § 49–53 prépare sa propre allégorisation : le § 53 excuse le maître-cuisinier dans des termes incompréhensibles à quiconque n'est pas initié aux codes philoniens : "*Le maître de Joseph est peut-être pardonnable pour son inculture : il passe sa vie dans une cuisine, remplie de sang, de fumée et de cendres, et le raisonnement, en lui, n'a pas le loisir de se recueillir et de s'apaiser en soi-même, car il est définitivement embrouillé, ni plus ni moins que son corps ...*". On dira que ce § 53 est contigu à l'allégorie explicite des § 54–79. Mettons. Mais, plus loin, par exemple, au § 106, et donc, là, sans contact avec l'allégorie explicite, Philon prête à Phaune comparaison entre Joseph et les interprètes Égyptiens : "*Mon âme augure[17] que l'ombre de l'indécision ne s'étendra pas définitivement sur mes rêves. Ce jeune homme est marqué du signe de la sagesse et il découvrira la vérité. Comme*

---

16 Sans aucun des débordements pathétiques ou moraux qu'on pourrait attendre.

17 Noter la subtile harmonie de redoublement : Pharaon *devine* qu'il y aura *divination*.

la lumière le fait des ténèbres, son savoir chassera l'ignorance de nos sophistes." Les derniers mots n'ont de sens que replacés dans l'allégorie globale de Philon, où les sages d'Égypte sont des sophistes. Philon n'insiste pas, et, seul, un lecteur familier du système allégorique peut prolonger en lui-même ces débuts de moralisation. Ajoutons que ces commencements d'allégorie ne se limitent pas à la première partie, ornée elle-même de franches allégories : les § 157–270 sont eux aussi parsemés d'expressions qui dépassent le niveau stylistique du récit. Voici une liste de ces passages *supérieurs au contexte* :

§ 7 :	les frères de Joseph, les fils d'Israël sont donnés comme des interprètes sagaces (résultat d'une traduction implicite, *Israël = Voyant ?*).
§ 15 :	le fils efficace est, Philon souligne, *quatrième par rang d'âge* (voir aussi § 189 et 222).
§ 26 :	Jacob est désigné comme *l'athlète* (voir aussi § 223 et 230).
§§ 26–36:	… ALLÉGORIES EXPLICITES, "politiques" (trois *item*).
§ 44 :	l'Égypte est synonyme de *vie licencieuse.*
§ 53 :	la cuisine, image de *fumée, obscurité, trouble* (depuis le *Gorgias…*).
§§ 54–79 :	… ALLÉGORIES EXPLICITES, "politiques" (trois *item*).
§ 84 :	le mal, unifié et pourtant *multiforme.*[18]
§ 86–87 :	par Joseph, la prison devient école de vertu.
§ 90 :	la révélation des sens cachés est donnée à qui la *désire* (aussi § 106).
* § 91–96 :	noter que, paradoxalement, Philon reste très sobre à propos des rêves eux-mêmes et de leur interprétation par Joseph. Nous n'avons *pas* de début d'allégorie là où nous l'attendons le plus …[19]
§ 93 :	on lit cependant, en incise, que la corbeille du panetier contient des *délicatesses bigarrées – poikilas periergias.*
* § 100 :	Philon anticipe sur l'explication que Joseph donnera lui-même (§ 107 et sv.); Philon en désamorce l'originalité (cette observation rejoint celle que nous venons de faire sur les § 91–96 : Philon curieusement *en-deçà* de l'allégorisation …)
§ 103 et 106 :	les *sophistes* Égyptiens.

---

[18]   Le mot *pamphurton* rappelle le *pephurthai* du § 53.

[19]   Cette observation sur un effet *a contrario* est un argument *a silentio*, difficile à utiliser. Je la fais cependant, la croyant plausible dans la masse des autres.

§§ 125–156 : Allégories explicites, "politiques" (deux *item*)

}(trois *item*)

Allégorie explicite, "psychique" (un titre)

§ 170 et 174 : personnification de la *Justice*, du *Logos*, de la *Loi divine*.[20]

§ 175–177 : (Siméon), le *deuxième fils* de Jacob, occupe une place symétrique de Joseph, qui est *avant-dernier* (voir § 187; et § 15, 189 et 222, à propos de Juda).

§ 179 : une expression curieuse, *à chaque voyage* : nous sommes au premier voyage, seulement. Y a-t-il anticipation ou inadvertance de Philon?

§ 189 : (Juda) désigné comme *quatrième par rang d'âge* (voir § 15 et 222).

§ 203–206 : dans cette belle page (qui fait penser au *De Abrahamo*, § 107s, avec le repas de Mambré), la délicatesse d'un repas joyeux évoque la vertu.[21]

§ 218 : annonce l'explication sapientielle des § 232–236.

§ 222 : Philon insiste sur le rang d'âge de (Juda), le *quatrième* (voir § 15 et 189; également les § 175–177).

§ 223 et 230 : (Jacob), désigné comme *athlète* menant les *combats de la vertu*. Ici, le profil allégorisé de Jacob est plus net qu'au § 26.

§ 232–236 : explication sapientielle[22] de ce qui précède. Deux remarques :

1) on notera la finesse psychologique de l'enquête;

2) le § 234 évoque la meilleure part donnée à Benjamin, mais dont le récit n'a pas parlé (au contraire, le § 203 pouvait suggérer que les aînés reçoivent plus d'honneur …).

§ 246–249 : par leur éloge, qui reste d'abord sur le plan de l'*encomion* et du roman, les frères de Joseph laissent entendre que la vérité de Joseph était *cachée*, mais que la force des choses, ou la *nature* l'a révélée; son intendance sert de témoin à la Bonté originelle, Dieu. On peut voir dans ces propositions comme une définition de l'allégorie elle-même, derrière le personnage de Joseph.

---

[20] La personnification relative de certaines entités morales n'a pas la même portée allégorisante, me semble-t-il, et reste sur le plan de la rhétorique simple : l'*Envie* (§ 5), la *Nature* (§ 38, désignant en fait Dieu), ou la *Pitié-Humanité* (§ 240). De même le *Pasteur*, le *Sage-maître de soi*, métaphores utiles pour parler de l'apprentissage du rôle politique (§ 2–3; § 38–39; § 54), mais qui ne reviendront pas lors du résumé final, des § 267b–270.

[21] Nous reviendrons sur ce point.

[22] "Sapientielle" et non plus "allégorique".

§ 250 :   la réconciliation des frères semble tenir lieu du blé dont on était privé par la famine. La *fraternité* tient lieu de la vie.

§ 254 :   l'inquiétude de Jacob suppose que le lecteur connaît le combat mené par la *vie corporelle*, symbolisée par l'Égypte, contre la vie véritable[23]

§ 258 :   Joseph préfère la *richesse authentique* à toute sa fortune, ce qui fait des biens matériels des réalités *bâtardes et aveugles*, formules proches de l'allégorie.

§ 265 :   de même, sans doute, est-ce déjà allégorisation que le passage du *père* au *Père*.

Tels sont les passages qui nous ont paru suggérer l'existence d'un plan nouveau, que le "récit" ne demandait pas. Il est vrai que leur interprétation relève d'une appréciation qui peut paraître subjective. Je la tente cependant, en fournissant les repères les plus objectifs possible.

Par exemple ceci : les trois plages directement *allégoriques* de la *première partie* (§ 26–36; 54–79; 125–156) ont pour répondant, dans la *seconde partie*, trois passages soutenus qui ne sont pas allégoriques, mais relèvent le récit proprement édifiant. Il s'agit de la considération prolongée sur le repas servi par Joseph à ses frères (§ 203–206); de l'explication sapientielle fournie à l'étrange comportement de Joseph éprouvant ses frères (§ 232–236); enfin, de l'éloge de Joseph tel qu'il est prononcé par ses frères, sur le *caché / visible* (§ 246–249). À la différence des trois longs passages allégoriques de la première partie, ces pages ne se réfèrent pas au thème unifié et clair de la "politique". Du coup, leur unité est moins évidente. Pourtant, c'est le thème de la *paix fraternelle* qui assure cette unité, au point que l'explication de type sapientiel des § 232–236 annule artificiellement tout ce qui a divisé la famille de Jacob : l'amour fraternel passe avant tout, et Joseph conclut lui-même à l'innocence de ses frères, instruments de la Providence divine. Mieux : par une harmonie calculée, on voit Joseph, au milieu (§ 232–236), et ses frères, de part et d'autre (§ 203–206; puis § 246–249), découvrir et célébrer la valeur divine de la fraternité.

Premiers résultats

Arrêtons-nous un instant. Parlons "politique" appliquée. Le *De Josepho* conduit le "politique" (première partie) à cette valeur essentielle de la "fraternité" (seconde partie). S'il en est bien ainsi, le *De Josepho* ne saurait être adressé à quelque Gouverneur d'Égypte, un étranger à qui Philon

---

[23] Voir le commentaire de Philon au cri de Jacob, "*Mon fils Joseph est en vie!*" (de *Genèse*, 45, 28), dans *De migratione*, § 21, *etc.*

suggérerait discrètement la voie de la modération. S'il fallait tirer une leçon globale, on serait mieux inspiré en cherchant du côté de la Communauté juive d'Alexandrie : Philon se servirait de l'histoire de Joseph dans l'esprit même où elle fut rédigée, à savoir en vue de la réconciliation des fils d'Israël, *à l'intérieur*, entre eux. Et, ajoutons, en vue d'une réconciliation qui ne serait pas due à la volonté ou à la décision d'un Prince, mais bien à tous les frères. Car le *De Josepho* commence par nier la valeur du "Politique" : l'allégorie de la première partie est pessimiste; elle déconsidère le Politique. Mais la seconde partie, usant de sapience plutôt que d'allégorie, est au contraire positive, optimiste. Et cette seconde partie est relevée par endroits, disions-nous : or, ces passages (les § 250, 254, 258 et 265) mettent en relief l'harmonie familiale. C'est la *famille rassemblée* qui vaut mieux que le pain (§ 250); c'est de la sauvegarde des traditions familiales en Joseph que Jacob se montre soucieux (§ 254); c'est sans doute de la *philanthropie* que se compose pour moitié la richesse authentique préférée par Joseph (§ 258); c'est enfin la référence du *père* au *Père* qui assure la fraternité (§ 265). De plus, par une discrète invitation à consulter l'allégorie, on peut penser que l'insistance de Philon à noter l'âge du meilleur fils de Jacob, ce fameux *quatrième*, évoque les mérites du nombre Quatre : c'est le chiffre de la solidité, de la *solidarité*, notion connexe de la *cohésion familiale* ou *fraternité*.[24]

En ce qui concerne la compréhension globale du *De Josepho*, nous pouvons avancer quelques résultats. Le Traité est équilibré : la répartition de l'allégorie (première partie) et de la sapience (seconde partie) pose même la question de leurs rapports, et le lecteur peut opter entre deux interprétations. En effet, le *De Josepho* commence par l'allégorie et finit en sagesse, et ce mouvement est aussi celui qui conduit de la critique du "politique" à la célébration de la fraternité—ce qui donne au *De Josepho* une portée à l'intérieur du Judaïsme. Mais faut-il privilégier l'Allégorie comme mode de réflexion (première partie) ? Dans ce cas, le *De Josepho* va en "descendant" relativement, du meilleur au bon. Ou bien faut-il voir dans l'Allégorie du début le ferment, l'outil, qui est destiné à servir la sagesse de la seconde partie ? Nous avons largement souligné le fait que l'Allégorie reste présente, d'une présence subtile et pour ainsi dire inchoative, dans la seconde partie : elle viendrait au titre de servante montrer que la simple fraternité est un trésor en réalité. Le lecteur n'est d'ailleurs pas obligé de choisir, et il peut féconder l'une par l'autre l'Allégorie et la Sapience, pourvu qu'il n'oublie pas le contenu : à savoir que le Prince est au service de la Paix fraternelle.

---

[24] Un Traité, ou du moins un excursus, était consacré par Philon à la Tétrade, semble-t-il (voir le *De opificio mundi*, § 52). Le 4 définit les "solides".

L'allégorie spécifique de la première partie.

Revenons à l'Allégorie. Durant toute *la première partie*, en dehors des trois pages d'allégorie (§ 28–36; § 54–79; § 125–156), les brefs "dépassements" que j'ai notés ci-dessus restent de l'ordre de la définition symbolique. Ainsi, au § 7, les fils d'Israël sont donnés comme *Voyants*; au § 26, Jacob est *l'Athlète*; au § 44, l'Égypte apparaît comme le pays *du corps*; au § 53, le vice prend l'image de la *cuisine*; le § 84 rappelle que le mal est du côté du *multiple*; le § 93 rapproche mal, nombre et politique, par le thème de la *variation-bigarrure*; les § 103 et 106 définissent les sages d'Égypte comme des *sophistes*; le § 124 donne l'équivalence rapide du Juste-solitaire et de la *braise*, suffisant à rallumer tous les feux du monde … Nous avons vu qu'au contraire la plupart des allusions de la *seconde partie* au plan de l'Allégorie ouvraient des développements plus que de simples définitions ponctuelles. On peut en conclure que la première partie concentre l'Allégorie dans ses trois passages plus étendus et que, par une sorte de croisement, ses brèves définitions ont pour rôle de préparer les insinuations de la seconde partie, à mi-chemin entre Sapience et Allégorie.

Durant la première partie, l'Allégorie est donc limitée à trois pages. Mais elle est également limitée du dedans. Non seulement les noms de Jacob, d'Israël, de Juda, de Siméon, de Ruben, de Benjamin, ne sont pas cités, ce qui souligne par contraste le fait que seul le nom de Joseph subisse l'alchimie de l'allégorisation,[25] mais les éléments du récit biblique qui se prêteraient le plus aisément à l'interprétation symbolique sont négligés par Philon. Il résume au plus juste les rêves de Joseph[26] (§ 6, 8). Il ne les paraphrase même pas. Il ne laisse filtrer, en guise d'interprétations, que les seules réponses qu'il trouve dans le récit de la *Genèse*, sur les lèvres de la famille du visionnaire (§ 7, 9). On peut même se demander si Philon considère les rêves de Joseph comme une faveur ou un mauvais signe. Jacob redoute surtout que ces avertissements ne provoquent la rupture de l'"*égalité*", cette valeur qui peut servir d'axe à tout le *De Josepho* (le Prince s'élève; les frères assurent unanimement la paix). On peut admettre, sous réserve d'analyse rigoureuse, que le *De somniis* prendra justement pour objet d'étude les rêves, négligés par le *De Josepho*. Les deux ouvrages sont complémentaires, en cela aussi.

Les trois allégories de la première partie traduisent le récit de la *Genèse* en symboles de l'ordre *politique*. Le lecteur peut même être surpris de cette uniformité, comme il l'est par l'insertion abrupte des trois transpositions allégoriques, et plus encore par le caractère négatif de l'interprétation. Ce lecteur partait sur le sentier de l'admiration qu'on allumait en lui pour

---

[25] On peut ajouter que Ruben, Siméon, Joseph et Benjamin sont désignés par leur rang d'âge, et que le *premier* et le *deuxième*, puis le *dernier* et l'*avant-dernier* forment harmoniquement une Tétrade, celle que Juda incarne à lui seul.

[26] Laconisme qui continuera dans la seconde partie.

Joseph. Or, il bute soudain sur trois réflexions qui, mises bout à bout,[27] forment une solide diatribe contre l'univers "politique". La première (§ 26–36) trace du personnage politique un portrait peu flatteur, s'achevant sur le spectacle de sa *vente* répétée. La deuxième (§ 54–79) retourne le problème : le Prince peut être moral autant qu'on voudra (Joseph est resté noble et chaste), mais le peuple, partenaire obligé et naturel du Prince, sa raison d'être, est un monstre—à la fois eunuque et vicieux. La dialectique du *Gorgias* est ici active et ... simplifiée à l'extrême. Peu importe : nous sommes avertis que tantôt le Prince, tantôt le Peuple, "matière" du Pouvoir, composent à eux deux un univers malsain, voué à la multiplicité, à l'équivoque, à la variation qui blasphème de toutes manières l'Unique Vérité.

Le troisième volet de l'Allégorie (§ 125–156) s'annonce par deux traductions : du nom nouveau donné à Joseph par Pharaon (§ 121a); des trois insignes du pouvoir, le "*second char*" – *l'anneau* – *le collier*" (§ 120). Les deux premières sections de l'Allégorie reprennent et développent ces thèmes, d'une façon surprenante en ce qui concerne le premier. La troisième (§ 151–156) quitte Joseph : il s'agit de ses comparses, les ministres Égyptiens, serviteurs des désirs matériels. Philon qui vient de transposer l'histoire de Joseph et ses titres en symboles politiques, extérieurs, dit maintenant ce que ce spectacle extérieur signifie pour chacun de nous, à l'intérieur de son âme. C'est donc cette toute dernière page de l'Allégorie qui se rapproche le plus de l'allégorisation ordinaire de Philon, psychique; et cela, au moment où l'Allégorie va s'effacer définitivement du *De Josepho* ...

La troisième allégorie

Revenons un peu sur les § 125–156, le troisième déploiement allégorique. Une diatribe (§ 127–147), essentiellement; une belle composition symbolique, dans sa brièveté (§ 148–150); et une "psychologie" morale sommaire (§ 151–156) : telle sont les subdivisions.

• La *diatribe* (§ 127–147) part du surnom donné à Joseph, "*Qui tranche dans les rêves*" (§ 121a). Disons tout de suite que "*trancher*" recevra commentaire à la fin, dans les § 143–147. C'est la réalité ou l'étendue du "*rêve*" et surtout l'incessant mouvement aléatoire ainsi désigné dans l'humanité qui font le sujet essentiel. Il ne s'agit pas ici de reprendre la question des sources de Philon en ce qui touche cette page "sceptique", mais de l'insérer dans l'ensemble des § 125–156. Cet ensemble pose bien des problèmes, et en particulier celui de son rapport avec la figure précise de Joseph, occasion de l'allégorie. Mais commençons par accepter la logique du passage. Regardons-le sans exigence quant au contexte, en un premier temps.

---

[27] Avec la précision que nous apporterons, au sujet des § 151–156.

Il faut évidemment en respecter le phrasé : le Politique "*tranche*", coupe, dans la fluidité irrationnelle du rêve. Les § 143–147 contrebalancent les § 127–146 : à l'incertitude le Politique impose un cran d'arrêt. Philon y joue sur le mot de départ, *oneirokritikos*: au lieu de "discernement", d' "exégèse", le Politique sage prononce un "*jugement qui tranche*". Et ce jugement opère selon la loi divine des Contraires. C'est la Loi de conscience, "*Ceci est bien – ceci est mal*", reflet de la loi cosmique des Contraires, qui remplace le "devin" ou l'interprète des songes. Pour Philon, ici, le surnom de Joseph lui fait dépasser l'efficacité empirique de ses oniromancies, telles que la Bible les décrit. Absolutment, la Loi fait cesser le Rêve. Mais cette Loi morale garde quelque chose de la loi quasi physique voulant précédemment que l'homme soit balloté du bonheur au malheur (§128–139) : seulement, elle fixe deux pôles bien définis et repérables, le Bien, le Mal. Dans ce "double" persistant, ele apprend à l'homme la stabilité : au sein du malheur, il prévoira le bonheur, et réciproquement, comme il usera de générosité dans l'abondance (§ 144). Et même, par une propédeutique qui fait songer au jeu du Même et de l'Autre dans le *Timée*, l'homme (ce Politique supérieur, avisé) apprend que la contrariété du Bien et du Mal entre dans un couple transcendant, celui du "contraire" et du "même" : un univers purement stable et lumineux englobe le tout (§ 145–147).[28]

Notons deux choses. Tout d'abord le caractère sublimé de ce "Politique". Ce que nous appelons "politique", ordinairement, c'est d'emblée le monde fluctuant, dans la mesure où une autorité commune le morigène en fonction d'une image supérieure, la Cité, par exemple, mais une Cité réele, où précisément aucune autorité ne peut "trancher", ni dans les conditions géographiques, ni dans la nature humaine.[29] Ici, la séparation entre la matière, le "rêve", et la forme, le Politique, brise la notion même de gouvernement, dans une sorte de platonisme naïf, extrême, mystique. Supprimons d'un coup de baguette magique les contingences, et tout ira bien—évidemment.

Mieux : on peut ensuite se demander si ce Politique idéal a quelque relation avec le personnage de Joseph, qui a servi de point de départ. Non seulement les "lois" des § 143–144 ne définissent pas une "politique"— c'est plutôt une morale—mais on devine que Philon répugne précisément

---

[28] C'est cette dialectique qui permet ailleurs à Philon de résorber finalement la Puissance de *Maîtrise – Kurios*, en l'unique et définitive Puissance de *Bonté-Création – Theos*. Voir J. Cazeaux, *La création chez Philon*, in La Création dans l'Orient ancien – coll. Lectio divina, no. 148, éd. du Cerf (Paris, 1985) pages 345–408, et, plus spécialement, les pages 380–403.

[29] Le phénomène de la "colonie" a eu pour cause ou pour effet l'utopie : où se porter pour fonder à partir de rien une Cité, idéale tant pour le climat que pour les hommes, et donc pour la Constitution?

à descendre jusqu'aux déterminations concrètes. Il en reste éternellement aux *"préambules"* que Platon préconise à plusieurs reprises dans les *Lois*, comme introduction à l'autorité. Or, Joseph incarne les déterminations concrètes. Ici, Philon semble lui substituer un Moïse, contemplateur de l'Ordre divin des Astres et proposant la Tora. Le stoïcisme des formules du § 144 s'accorde bien avec le Décalogue et les préceptes deutéronomiques. Plus rien de la vie de Joseph n'entre dans ce portrait du Philosophe-roi.[30] Le récit précédent (§ 110–115) donnait pourtant un début de "politique" réaliste : Joseph conseillait au Pharaon une série de mesures contre la famine, et ces mesures étaient de sagesse politique, faisant sa part à la ruse même, disons à la psychologie condescendante. La transposition héroïque dont l'Allégorie nous gratifie ensuite (§ 144) n'en tient plus compte.[31]

Ainsi, partis de Joseph, vite généralisé en Politique sage, nous quittons subrepticement la Politique : toute l'humanité dort, rêve et flotte dans l'instabilité, sauf un unique Sage, hors de la Caverne. Et, comme les deux premières allégories du *De Josepho* s'acharnaient sur Joseph et sur l'homme "politique", on peut dire que Philon, par le bas puis par le haut, élimine Joseph. S'il faut le regarder en face, il est illusion, tromperie et superflu; s'il faut le louer, il n'est plus là, tellement il est loin de ce qu'il fait et de ce qu'il a à faire …

• Cela est si vrai que, dès le retour à l'histoire concrète de Joseph (§ 148–150), nous retrouvons aussi la fatale ambiguïtè du réel. Une triple allégorie des honneurs proposés à Joseph, le *second char*, l'*anneau* et le *collier*, réunit les deux complices que la première allégorie (§ 28–36) puis la deuxième (§ 54–66) avaient stigmatisés séparément, à savoir le "politique" et le "peuple". C'est une dialectique simple et exemplaire qui nous est ici proposée. L'image du *char*[32] n'est considérée que sous l'angle du succès— même si l'hypothèse contraire est indirectement annoncée dans le *kai malisth' hotan*…; l'image du *collier* permet de poser clairement les deux issues de l'alternative, succès ou ruine, et son interprétation s'achève sur la ruine. Entre les deux, et comme leur axe, l'image de l'*anneau* reste neutre : elle permet seulement de marquer l'alliance pour le meilleur et pour le

---

[30] Sauf peut-être le cadre très général : l'Égypte doit connaître une période de surabondance puis une période de misère; le panetier et l'échanson héritent, l'un de la mort, l'autre de la vie.

[31] Les deux premières allégories du *De Josepho* restaient sur le plan politique. La troisième pouvait donc le faire, elle aussi : elle s'échappe vers le domaine "psychique", l'objet habituel de l'allégorie philonienne.

[32] Le § 148 est un modèle du style "adversatif" de Philon : Joseph est sur un char, et cette image sera prise pour elle-même au § 149. Mais ce char est le second : en jouant sur cette position, Philon apparie ce qui est au-dessus et ce qui est au-dessous de ce moyen-terme, de sorte que le "roi" de Joseph devient le Peuple.

pire qui lie le prince et le peuple. Le "meilleur" est supposé à partir du char; le pire sévit à partir du collier—donc, de part et d'autre de l'anneau, les deux branches de l'alternative déclarée universelle dans les § 127–142 se trouvent réparties. Je dis dialectique, et non pas seulement équilibre, parce que l'alliance du prince et du peuple, à l'occasion de l'anneau, élément médian, est la raison de l'alternative elle-même. Le peuple, par définition versatile et en tout cas matiére changeante du gouvernement,[33] domine le Prince, paradoxalement "*second*".

Bref, si le Joseph de la *Genèse* revient, il bascule du côté de la mauvaise politique. La dernière allégorisation (§ 151–156) renforce cette impression : les soucis du maître de l'Égypte sont tournés vers le corps, et l'on ne sait pas bien si de tels soucis vont au *plaisir* ou aux exigences de la *vie*[34] (témoin, l'ambiguïté du mot *anagkaion*, entre le § 154a et le § 155). Les § 151–156 achèvent le mouvement d'intériorisation de toutes les allégories du *De Josepho*. L'ordre "politique" est ramené à l'ordre "psychique". Le *De Josepho* cesse d'être le discours *ad usum Delphini*, et il s'adresse à toute "*âme*". Le rêve décrit dans la troisième allégorie n'est plus le beau rêve prémonitoire de Joseph adolescent, comme un signe distinguant le héros; il n'est pas davantage le rêve prémonitoire et occasionnel qui annonce au panetier sa condamnation et à l'échanson son élargissement, ou au Pharaon la succession de sept années et de sept autres années : le *rêve* s'élargit à totalité de l'humaine condition. Du fait même, c'est chacun qui est visé par la parabole "politique", puisque la Politique est devenue parabole de l'âme. De ce point de vue, les étranges § 151–156 sont bien à leur place, même si Philon ne les a pas entièrement fondus à l'ensemble.[35] Nous comprenons mieux maintenant pourquoi Philon a négligé les données du récit qui auraient permis à l'Allégorie de se déployer : les premiers rêves, ceux de Joseph. Philon se réservait une interprétation entièrement pessimiste du rêve, et il la réservait donc à l'Égypte, terre morale de toute dispersion, de toute sensualité.

---

[33] La souveraineté du peuple est impensable chez Philon. La position "seconde" du char oú monte Joseph fait encore de lui un *intermédiare*, d'un autre point de vue, dans le *De migratione*, § 160b–161.

[34] Les § 151–156, apparentés par le style au genre des *Quaestiones*, sont difficiles à intégrer. Je ne peux entrer ici dans le détail, comme je le fais ailleurs (dans une étude moins condensée du *De Josepho* et du *De somniis II*).

[35] Le rêve universel s'oppose à la loi naturelle, censément universelle, dont Philon parlait dans les § 28–31, sa première allégorie. Il disait que les politiques "*ajoutent*" le superflu de la volonté de puissance à cette unique loi de Nature. Le vrai Politique de la dernière allégorie revient à la Loi, universelle et naturelle – dont la philanthropie et l'*isotēs* familiale à l'oeuvre parmi les frères, fils d'Israël, de la seconde parti du *De Josepho* sont en réalité le premier et le dernier mot.

Situation des allégories dans le plan général

Je reviens sur la suppression du personnage propre de Joseph au cours des pages allégoriques—en opposition assez nette avec le tissu global du "récit", favorable à Joseph. Comme "politique", Joseph est *"vendu"*, conclut la première allégorie (§ 35–36); et il est vendu à un maître *"pervers"*, le peuple (§ 58–66), ajoute la deuxième. La troisième oublie Joseph, oublie la mauvaise politique, et elle s'élance dans l'idéal. Ainsi, condamné ou volatilisé, Joseph disparaît, durant l'Allégorie. Et l'Allégorie s'arrête au terme de ce double jeu, lorsque, Joseph étant ou trop ou trop peu lui-même, la *"décision"* qui est celle de la *Loi* nous est manifestée. À la fin, il faut dire, comme dans l'Évangile : Il y a ici *plus* que Joseph. Au début, il y avait *moins* que Joseph.

Et la question essentielle au sujet du Joseph de Philon se noue à cet endroit théorique, en même temps que celle de l'équilibre du *De Josepho*. Le nerf de la réponse me paraît être la relation de l'Allégorie avec une forme de *géographie*. L'Allégorie est circonstrite, matériellement, aux pages du *De Josepho* dans lesquelles Joseph traite avec l'Égypte. Philon, au début, n'a reien dit des rêves personnels de Joseph, et il n'y reviendra pas, alors que l'Allégorie pouvait s'y donner carrière.[36] Pourquoi ? Parce qu'alors Joseph était dans le cadre *familial d'Israël*. La seconde partie de l'ouvrage ne recourra pas davantage à l'Allégorie, mais à la Sapience, avons-nous répété, et c'est aussi parce que, là encore, Joseph n'a plus qu'à assurer l'*isotès famimiale*. C'est au moment précis où Joseph passe en Égypte que l'Allégorie commence. Nous lisons, à la fin du § 27, la phrase de *Genèse*, ch. 37, v. 36, ou ch. 39, v. 1 (selon les LXX) : *"Il fut vendu en Égypte à l'un des Eunuques du roi—c'était le cuisinier en chef."* Tous les mots portent, depuis le sinistre *"vendu"*[37] jusqu'au *"cuisinier"*, et ils entreront tous dans l'Allégorie. Ou plutôt tout se passe comme s'ils la déclenchaient. C'est donc sur le territoire de l'Égypte abordée que le nom de Joseph et son vêtement (§ 28–31, puis § 32–34) deviennent significatifs de la versatilité. C'est la *"revente"*, et donc le passage en Égypte de Joseph, qui polarise les trois allégories des § 28–36.

Pourquoi et comment l'Allégorie est-elle liée à l'Égypte ?

Et tout d'abord, quel rôle y joue le personnage de Joseph ? Il a lui-même des rêves, mais l'Allégorie ne s'en préoccupe pas. Il est seulement l'interprète des rêves *égyptiens* ou, ce qui revient au même, de la réalité *égyptienne*, toute faite de multiplicité, d'enlisement de l'esprit-roi dans la

---

[36] Voir le *De somniis II.*

[37] Ou plutôt *"revendu"*, puisque Joseph, d'abord vendu aux Madianites, fut par eux vendu aux Égyptiens. Cette multiplicité de transactions est en fait le véritable point de départ des trois allégories des § 28–36, qui tournent autour du multiple pervers et inquthentique.

masse corporelle, de fumée et de variation. Joseph sert d'abord de révélateur à l'Égypte. Se condamnant quand il s'y installe, il la condamne, en un premier temps (celui des deux premières allégorisations). Puis, cheval de Troie de la vérité d'Israël, voici qu'en un second temps (la troisième allégorisation, celle des § 125–156), il convertit l'Égypte, en un sens. C'est en effet le Pharaon qui lui reconnaît le rôle et le titre de "*tranchant dans les rêves*".

Ainsi, par le biais des trois Allégories, la première partie du *De Josepho* instaure une dialectique complexe d'Israël à l'Égypte : condamnation puis conversion. Le Pharaon en vient à confesser qu'il n'est dans le monde que rêve, mais qu'il existe un vrai Politique, capable de mettre un point d'arrêt au flux universel, par la Loi universelle " nous avons suggéré que les § 143–144 tenaient lieu d'un amalgame opéré entre un héraclito-stoïcisme cosmologique et moral, d'une part, et la Loi juive, d'autre part. Mais c'est dans la seconde partie du *De Josepho* que nous allons trouver la confirmation de cette situation de charnière attribuable à l'Allégorie et à Joseph dans la logique du Traité. Ce sera une preuve par la *réciproque*, puisque la seconde partie n'accorde à l'Allégorie qu'une ombre d'elle-même; que l'Égypte odieuse y est oubliée; que c'est la *famille de Jacob-Israël*, et non pas Joseph aux prises avec l'Égyptien, qui forme l'horizon du débat moral. Il ne faut pas s'étonner de cette dialectique d'Israël à l'Égypte : au début du *De Josepho*, la première allégorie posait innocemment la question de l'universalité morale et politique. Philon y déplorait la séparation des "*Barbares et des grecs*", selon le schéma stéréotypé de la philosophie classique, mais l'on peut et l'on doit y lire la séparation d'"*Israël et de l'Égypte*", sachant que les deux entités peuvent alternativement se considérer comme "Barbares" et "Grecs", c'est à dire "civilisés", policés, "naturels". Le *De Josepho* met en images une réflexion sur la *frontière*. Nous allons éclairer ce propos en ne retenant de la seconde partie rien d'autre sinon dux passages où précisément l'*Égypte* fait mine d'entrer en scène. Ce sont deux passages *sapientiaux*, comme prévu. Ce sont deux passages complémentaires, l'un accordant beaucoup à l'Égyptien, l'autre le rejetant apparement. Ce sont enfin deux passages sur l'*échange*, positif ou négatif, d'Israël à l'Égypte, et, par là, deux passages sur la *frontière*. Ils achèveront de montrer que, pour Philon, la Politique est sublimée en la morale et donc, à nos yeux, supprimée. L'unanimité familiale sera le type d'un monde unifié.

Politique et "frontière" dans la seconde partie

Les deux passages que nous allons regarder de plus près sont le repas servi par Joseph à ses frères (§ 201b–206) et l'hesitation de Jacob: Joseph est-il resté fidèle aux moeurs de sa race (§ 254–255) ? Dans les deux cas, il s'agit d'une appréciation portée sur Joseph et sur l'Égypte par ceux qui lui sont tout à fait étrangers, les frères de Joseph comme visiteurs et invités, le père de Joseph, invité à son tour. La question qu'ils se posent tous est celle du *passage*, les frères de Joseph essayant de mesurer le rôle civilisateur joué par Joseph, et Jacob inquiet du rôle de perversion jouable par l'Égypte. Commençons par le second aspect.

1) *La fidélité à la race* (§ 254–255) : Là, l'inquiétude de Jacob vient, tout près de la fin du *De Josepho*, en donner pour ainsi dire la clef. Tous les termes que nous avons proposés comme étant les paramètres réels du livre se trouvent alors rassemblés. À commencer par l'Allégorie, présente ou absente, ou voilée : ici, elle est voilée en Sapience. En effet, la *Genèse* ne dit rien de l'inquiétude de Jacob, mais seulement qu'il se réjouit de savoir Joseph *"vivant"* (ch. 45, v. 28);[38] Dieu le rassure tout de suite, mais c'est au sujet de l'avenir temporel de sa race (ch. 46, v.1–7). Philon allégorise discrètement, en traduisant *"vivant"* par *authentiquement doté de la Vie divine par la Loi*; et il détourne la parole de Dieu, en lui faisant dire que Joseph l'attend en Égypte. Mais ces inflexions ne sont pas soulignées, et elles coulent aisément à même ce que Philon donne comme une simple paraphrase de l'Écriture sous forme de récit édifiant. Sous cette banalité, Philon cache en réalité l'essentiel. Car cette fidélité à la Loi que Jacob souhaite à Joseph vient donner son sens aux réflexions antérieures, celles que le festin offert par Joseph à ses frères leur suggérait, comme nous le dirons. Elle donne également son dernier mot à la Législation idéale qui formait le coeur de la dernière allégorie, à la fin de la première partie. Le scrupule décisif de Jacob (§ 252–256) est placé entre deux éloges de Joseph comme Politique honnête et avisé (les § 246–249; puis les § 258–260). Et il devient clair que cette Politique reflète, d'une part, les *"moeurs ancestrales"* du § 254a et, d'autre part, la grande vision de la Loi universelle, professée dans les § 143–144—les deux ne faisant qu'un en réalité, comme la Loi naturelle et la Loi mosaïque.

Mais l'inquiétude de Jacob est seulement utile au lecteur qui n'aurait pas encore compris. Elle lui rappelle qu'on ne peut plus opposer sinon de façon oratoire l'Égypte et Israël. La scène du repas égyptien contenait, non plus la différence des deux Nations, mais au contraire leur réunion.

---

[38] Repris au ch. 46, v. 30. Le § 256 du *De Josepho* insiste sur la scène des retrouvailles de Jacob et de Joseph. Sans exagérer dans l'émotion, il obéit au genre littéraire, qui veut émotion et édification. Mais l'on notera qu'il parle de la *"frontière"* où les deux héros se rencontrent. Cette image me paraît symbolique, surtout si l'on prévoit que le *De somniis* II s'arrête (par hasard ?) sur un thème identique, le rôle de l'Euphrate, l'autre frontière du grand Israël.

2) *Le repas des Anges* ... (§ 201–206) : Là encore, Philon dépasse sensible-ment la narration biblique. Déjà, le tabou exigeant la séparation des nationalités à la table (*Genèse*, ch. 43, v. 32) avait subi une interprétation pudique dans les LXX : les Égyptiens refusant de manger en compagnie de bergers. Philon y voit un respect des coutumes de chacun (§ 202). Surtout, le repas de Philon s'élève à une transparence imprévue de la Bible. Dans la Bible, le repas n'est que la première partie d'une machi-nation de Joseph : il honore Benjamin, avant de le compromettre par le vol simulé de la coupe (ch. 43, v. 34, et ch. 44). Dans Philon, rien de tel. Le repas ressemble à celui de Mambré dans le *De Abrahamo*, § 107–118. Équilibre, bienséance, proportion, exactitude du détail, accord, telles sont les valeurs, qui, dans les deux repas, transfigurent ce qui pourrait rester trivial en exactitude de l'Univers et de Dieu. Le *De Abrahamo* est plus explicite. Le *De Josepho* est, comme prévu, voilé, inchoatif.[39]

Plus important, Philon prête aux frères de Joseph, qui ne l'ont pas identifié, une admiration sans bornes pour son oeuvre : il a donc civilisé l'Égypte (§ 203–204). Mieux : on pouvait accorder à l'Égypte un grand et beau respect des traditions ancestrales de chaque nation (§ 202), mais les frères vont plus loin : on dirait, pensent-ils, que les Égyptiens ont adopté la mentalité des "*Hébreux*" (§ 203). Il y a donc eu une sorte de croisement. En étant adopté par l'Égypte, Joseph courait le risque de perdre l'essentiel pour trouver le superflu, l'enflure, la "politique". En adoptant Joseph, l'Égypte a au contraire adopté les moeurs d'Israël. Qu'il s'agisse bien de cela, la répétition d'une formule semblable, *ta patria* et *palaious nomous* du § 202, ou *hē tōn patriōn ekdiaitēsis* du § 254, le démontre suffisamment. L'inquiétude ultime de Jacob rappelle les deux premières allégories de la première section du *De Josepho*; la réflexion admirative des frères de Joseph reprend l'admiration même du Pharaon : celui-ci avait reconnu en Joseph le grand Législateur du Monde, qui suspend et "*tranche le rêve*" universel—ce rêve, à son tour, n'étant qu'un autre nom de la folie des factions, des peuples, de l'humanité qui a refusé la Loi naturelle unique et universelle (théorème de base, formulé aux § 28–31). Cette Loi était la base de l'Harmonie, de l'*isotēs*, de la fraternité.

C'est ainsi que les deux passages de la seconde partie du *De Josepho* qui sortent le plus loin dans la direction de l'Allégorie, au mépris de la lettre du récit de la *Genèse*, s'adaptent parfaitement aux deux aspects successifs des allégories de la première partie.

---

[39] Ajoutons que, dans le *De Abrahamo*, le repas servi par Abraham est décrit pour faire pièce à l'inhospitalité et à la grossièreté égyptiennes. Les Égyptiens, barbares, inhumains, meurtriers de leur hôte, étaient "*en cet autre temps*" – c'est sans doute l'allusion de notre *De Josepho*, § 204a – des sauvages. Le retournement de situation est d'autant plus remarquable, de l'un à l'autre "Éloge".

C'est ainsi que l'idéal de l'*isotēs*, mis en exercice durant la seconde partie, apparaît comme la plus haute Politique, touchant immédiatement à la Loi de Nature, laquelle a trouvé son expression sur terre, parmi les Peuples, en Israël. Aussi le Pharaon pourra-t-il sans erreur désigner Joseph comme Politique suprême, puis Jacob, comme son *"père"* (§ 257): comme souvent, le détail qui entre de plain-pied dans les obligations lyriques ou émotionnelles du Roman et de l'Éloge sert en même temps la théorie— discrètement, de façon sapientielle et non plus violemment imposée par l'Allégorie, puisque nous sommes dans la seconde partie du *De Josepho*.

C'est ainsi que Joseph a conduit l'Égypte aux portes de la gouverne sublime de l'Univers. L'ordonnancement du banquet en est le symbole. On notera que le texte de la Bible, LXX y compris, termine ce banquet par l'*"ivresse"* générale. Le débordement "égyptien" est remplacé par la perfection de la mesure, en Égypte même. Le premier choc avec l'Égypte (premières allégories) a révélé la folie égyptienne de la "politique", menaçant aussi bien Israël, s'il s'y complaisait; la suite renverse la situation : un Joseph qui laisse déjà presentir Moïse[40] sert de prophète à l'Égypte. Ce ne sont d'ailleurs pas les mérites personnels de Joseph qui lui valent ce rôle prophétique. Personnellement, il est le possible *"superflu"*, par son nom, et, par son vêtement,[41] il est tout proche du *"rêve"* universel et "politique", indéfiniment *"bigarré"*. Ce qui le désigne comme prophète de l'Égypte, et, par elle, des Nations, c'est sa qualité d'*"Hébreu"*.[42] De ce point de vue concret, d'une lecture attentive aux inflexions de cet "Éloge", le *De Josepho* fait l'éloge, non pas de Joseph, mais d'Israël *dans* Joseph ou *malgré* Joseph.

C'est ainsi que, plus Joseph s'enfonce en Égypte, et plus il y révèle Israël. Ce point de vue de la *géographie* morale déplace le point de vue strictement politique de nos lectures philoniennes. En effet, que cette géographie commande les positions successives de Philon à l'égard de

---

[40] Comme si l'histoire de Joseph précontenait l'*Exode*. Philon y pense : il fait dire à Pharaon que l'interprète des rêves venu d'Israël surpasse les interprètes d'Egypte, purs *"sophistes"* (§ 90, 103 et 106, d'après *Genèse*, ch. 41, v. 8 et 15), et nous avons là une anticipation d'*Exode*, ch. 7, v. 8–12, *etc.* Nous avons répété que les § 125 et 143–144 subliment Joseph en Moïse; la Politique en Décalogue.

[41] Nom et vêtement, deux symboles décisifs de la personnalité.

[42] Le livre de *Jonas*, dans la Bible, joue le même jeu. Apparemment, il s'agit d'enseigner l'universalisme, Dieu ayant pitié de Ninive, l'abominable, et Jonas ne voulant pas de cette génrosité divine. Mais, plus finement, on peut voir que la parabole met en cause, *à l'intérieur et à l'usage d'Israël*, le désir d'avoir des "prophètes". Car Jonas convertit les marins et Ninive de telle sorte que l'action efficace soit celle de la Loi (citations de la *Genèse*, citation de l'*Exode*, au coeur des deux épisodes); mais, *personnellement*, comme prophète charismatique, Jonas est nul: " il fuit sa mission (premier volet), ou il l'exagère (second volet). La Loi, dite à *chacun* en Israël, vaut mieux que la "prophétie". Universalisme ? Oui, mais d'abord vérité de la Loi en Israël.

Joseph, nous en aurons la preuve, la contre-épreuve, par l'analyse du *De somniis II*, tout entier consacré à la même matière narrative de la *Genèse*. Philon s'y place, quant à notre géographie, sur le terrain opposé : Joseph y est aperçu depuis Israël, et non plus depuis l'Égypte. Ce sont ses rêves enterritoire familial d'Israël qui vont être critiqués, et sévèrement, et, ajoutons, critiqués parce qu'ils n'ont pas leur place en Israël. Plus précisément, ils introduisent en Israël la démesure égyptienne, tout comme, selon le *De Josepho*, Joseph introduit la mesure juive en Égypte.

Autour du personnage de Joseph, il se dessine une grande harmonie entre le *De Josepho* et le *De somniis II*. Le souci proprement "politique" de Philon a pour axe dans les deux ouvrages l'*isotēs* que toutes les politiques oublient. Au début du *De Josepho*, le premier scrupule de Jacob portait sur l'exaltation que les rêves de Joseph risquaient de lui promettre, en le distinguant. Nous retrouverons tout au long un tel reproche dans le *De somniis II*. De telle sorte qu'il serait loisible de se représenter le *De Josepho* et le *De somniis* comme deux branches issues de ce § 9 du *De Josepho*, où sont formulées les deux hypothèses : exaltation ou mesure de Joseph ? Le *De Josepho* opte pour l'hypothèse heureuse; l'*isotēs* y triomphe, sous la forme de la *fraternité* (seconde partie, en ce qui touche la famille d'Israël; première partie, en ce qui touche la réunion des Nations et d'Israël). Le *De somniis II* examine l'hypothèse malheureuse : aussi les rêves propres de Joseph seront-ils le point de départ de l'Allégorie, et, en dépit des apparences, resteront-ils son seul terrain; aussi retrouverons-nous le thème *géographique* de la frontière; aussi Philon usera-t-il d'une ruse symétrique de celle qu'il déploie dans le *De Josepho* : là, il sauve finalement l'Égypte, perdue en principe; ici, il va finalement réhabiliter Joseph au moment où tout le perd selon l'Allégorie—nous dirons comment. Disons pourquoi : parce que Joseph est substantiellement fils d'Israël.

Le "De Somniis II" : Joseph, Tentation D'Israël

Je me contenterai ici d'amorcer l'étude du *De somniis II*.[43] Ce beau livre est difficile. Il considère la troisième catégorie des songes, celle qui appelle l'exégèse[44] : en sont les sujets successifs *Joseph—Pharaon—ses officeirs* (l'ordre annoncé au § 5 ne sera pas celui de l'exposé; le rêve du Panetier

---

[43] Je rappelle qu'il s'agit en fait du troisième "chapitre" d'un Traité complet, le premier ayant disparu. J'aimerais mieux, également, analyser ce livre de façon désintéressée, pour lui-même et sans le rapporter immédiatement à la "Politique" de Philon : c'est ce que je fais ailleurs, mais, faute de place, je m'en tiendrai ici à ce qui entre directement dans le cadre politique (d'ailleurs essentiel).

[44] De ce point de vue, la nécessité d'un interprète, toute la Bible qui a besoin de l'Allégorie, fait figure de "rêve" …

sera brièvement traité, § 205–214; et nous n'avons pas le commentaire de la plupart des phrases bibliques citées en exergue aux § 216–218, puisque le § 302, lui-même suspendu en cours de phrase, nous laisse avec les premiers mots du lemme …). Voici, d'abord, le plan de l'ouvrage subsistant :

§ 1–4 :	LA TROISIÉME FORME DE RÊVE : OBSCURE, APPELANT UN EXÉGÈTE.
§ 5 :	SUJETS DE CETTE FORME : *JOSEPH – PHARAON – LES DEUX OFFICIERS:*
§ 6–7 :	1. LES RÊVES DE JOSEPH : terre et ciel (la lettre);
§ 8–16 :	a) synthèse allégorique de Joseph …
§ 17–109	b) *Premier rêve* (la terre) – les *gerbes* :
§ 21–77 :	1. – *"lier"* au lieu de *"moissonner"* (*début ou fin ?*);
§ 78–92 :	2. – *"se dresser"* en "tyran";
§ 93–109 :	3. – *"la* révolte *de ses frères"* : *conversion de Joseph.*
§ 110–154	c) *Second rêve* (ciel) – les *astres* :
§ 110–132 :	1. – l'exaltation *cosmique* •Xerxès,
	•un gouverneur d'Alexandrie;
§ 133–154 :	2. – *la réponse du père* sauve Joseph …
§ 155–214	2. LES RÊVES DES MINISTRES DE PHARAON :
§ 159–204 :	a) *Rêve de l'échanson* : la *"vigne"*
§ 159–163 :	*mauvaise ivresse;*
§ 164–168 :	*ambivalence de la vigne;*
§ 169–180 :	*bonne vigne, de la Joie;*
§ 181–189 :	*ambivalence de l'échanson;*
§ 190–204 :	*mauvaise vigne de Sodome.*
§ 205–214 :	b) *Rêve du panetier* : les *"trois corbeilles"* du Temps …
§ 215–302… "	3. LE RÊVE DE PHARAON :
§ 216–218 :	*ênoncé du rêve;*
§ 219–236 :	1. – *"se dresser debout"*, blasphème;
§ 237–260	2. – *"le fleuve"* = *la parole*
§ 239–254 :	il y a une *bonne parole*
§ 255–260 :	il y a la *mauvaise parole* – d'Égypte.
§ 261–302	3. – *"la lèvre"* du *fleuve* :
§ 262–268 :	il y a un *bon silence,*
§ 269–273 :	il y a une *bonne parole* – louange;
§ 274–299 :	il y a *l'abus du silence et de la parole – les Sophistes*
§ 300–302 :	seul, le *fleuve d'Égypte* a une *"lèvre"* … (*valeur de ces recherches subtiles*).

Je donne la plan du livre II en son entier. C'est qu'il s'agit de la même réalité de bout en bout, le cas des "*âmes du gynécée*" (§ 9); et l'on peut montrer que Philon considère les songes de Pharaon, sa démesure et son orgueil, comme les limites où tendaient de soi les rêves de Joseph.

On doit faire tout de suite quelques remarques :

– les rêves du *De somniis II* ont besoin du "prophète", de l'exégèse : or, jamais Philon ne commente le rôle de Joseph, qui fut précisément cet interprète ...

– le *De somniis II* complète exactement le *De Josepho* : là, Philon ne disait rien du contenu des rêves; ici, seul, le contenu entre dans le commentaire;

– enfin, l'absence de toute référence à Joseph comme *politikos* est d'autant plus remarquable que la fin du livre I du *De somniis* y insistait : le mot *politeia* y apparaissait même au moment décisif de la belle dialectique des § 200–227, laquelle établit une série de variations sur la "*variation*"— *poikilos*. On ne saurait donc dire sans nuance que le *De somniis II* traite de Joseph en tant que "Politique" ...

Reprenant le *De somniis II* dans son ensemble, nous allons simplement esquisser notre interprétation globale, à partir de la composition de l'ouvrage (bien qu'inachevé[45]), et, en second lieu, à partir du rôle de Joseph.

Les compagnons de l'apparence

Philon a pris soin d'emboîter les différents "chapitres" du *De somniis II*, de telle sorte qu'*une seule* histoire psychique s'y trouve déployée sur le thème du rêve. En faisant de Joseph, non directement un *politikos*, mais un ami du plaisir efféminé, parmi les "*âmes du gynécée*", il réunit étroitement ce Joseph, perdu dans la mollesse, les Ministres de Pharaon, soucieux de vin et de cuisine, et enfin le Pharaon lui-même : ses visions ont aussi pour objet la nourriture du corps, et Philon souligne l'intérêt qu'il portait à l'échanson (§ 182). Mieux, dès le début du livre, Philon réunit les tois parangons de la sensualité. Il établit Joseph dans la souci de la vaine *gloire*, qui est en fait l'apanage de Pharaon, et la *goinfrerie*, qui est en fait le péché des Ministres de Pharaon. D'autre part, si Philon déplace les éléments de

---

[45] Personne ne peut se hasarder à donner le contenu des pages qui prolongeaient le *De somniis II*. Je pense, simple hypothèse, qu'elle n'étaient pas très nombreuses, en dépit de tout le lemme des § 216–218 : il arrive que Philon accélère, en fin d'ouvrage, de telle sorte que beaucoup du Texte entre en peu d'espace (voir la fin du *De migratione*, celle du *Quis heres* ou du *De fuga*). Évidemment, la perte des derniers "chapitres" du *De somniis II* rend plus délicate l'application de ma méthode ordinaire d'analyse, fondée sur les ensembles ... On prendra donc avec précaution tout ce qui, dans mon interprétation, fait appel à la vision synthétique du livre.

son trio, s'il annonce "Joseph, Pharaon, les Ministres", mais suit dans son commentaire la ligne de la *Genèse*, "Joseph, les Ministres, Pharaon", c'est aussi qu'avec Pharaon, nous arrivons au somment de l'orgueil et de la folie sensuelle. Pharaon accomplit sans plus aucune réserve, explicitement, la démesure qui restait inchoative, implicite, dans les premiers rêves, ceux de Joseph au début. Pris comme un tout, le *De somniis II* prend la forme d'une composition régulière : une première *exaltation*, celle de Joseph, reste formelle, puisque la vanité se limite aux manifestations du luxe; vient ensuite le constat et la condamnation de l'*ivresse*; mais une seconde forme d'*exaltation*—bien plus profonde—entraîne Pharaon jusqu'au défi porté à Dieu. Nous verrons que, curieusement, Philon "sauve" deux fois son Joseph, au moment même où l'Allégorie l'accable, et Joseph, de toutes façons, disparaît (à partir du § 155) : Pharaon le remplace dans son rôle d'orgueil, et l'on peut dire que ce Pharaon est le bouc émissaire qui décharge Joseph de sa noirceur. L'Égyptien remplace le Palestinien, serons-nous amenés à reconnaître. Philon dessine une courbe descendant vers l'Enfer, où les personnages, Joseph, les Ministres de Pharaon et Pharaon lui-même, occupent des places en dégradé.

La géographie politico-morale

Pour que le lecteur aperçoive la continuité qui mène de Joseph à Pharaon, dans l'orgueil, et qu'il voie comment Joseph *pouvait* aboutir à l'athéisme noir de Pharaon, Philon a ménagé une sorte de substitution. Aux rêveries déplacées de Joseph on voit successivement ses frères (§ 93–109) et son père (§ 133–154) opposer une souble fin de non-recevoir, habilement contrastée de l'une à l'autre réponse. Les frères de Joseph brisent d'abord en lui l'ambition du rêveur : ce faisant, ils l'en purifient; puis son père Jacob le sauve tout à fait et de façon positive. Pourquoi ces deux opérations de sauvetage, sinon pour que le blasphème reste tout entier, par "transfert", au compte de Pharaon ? Israël est ainsi venu deux fois au secours d'Israël, et il reste l'Égyptien ...

Car c'est au milieu des siens, de sa *famille*, que Joseph rêve, et c'est là le drame. Joseph peut être "roi" en Égypte, à l'usage des Nations, mais il ne peut pas l'être à l'intérieur de la Nation idéalement *égalitaire*. Alors, les frères de Joseph, si jaloux, si lâches et si criminels du *De Josepho*, deviennent ici des modèles de la saine piété et justice. Dans le *De Josepho*, ils n'étaient pas nommés; quelques-uns avaient tout juste droit à leur numéro d'ordre symbolique, "*premier – quatrième ...*". Ici, Philon donne leur nom et l'explique par le symbolisme d'une vertu correspondante, de façon à composer un tableau harmonieux (§ 33–36). C'est au nom de l'*isotēs*, lentement conquise et démontrée au cours du *De Josepho* que d'emblée, les frères se font ici les champions de la lutte contre la *tyrannie* commençante en Joseph. Ils lui évitent d'ailleurs d'entrer dans l'ordre "politique": l'*isotēs* est moins un système politique qu'une valeur transcendante, voire cosmique.[46] Sans doute est ce l'une des raisons pour lesquelles Philon a évité complètement l'usage des mots exprès de *politikos—politeia* au long du *De somniis II*. Les frères de Joseph, en somme, gardent la frontière d'Israël contre le "mal égyptien", une frontière qui se trouve menacée *du dedans* par les rêveries de leur frère.[47]

Jacob à son tour morigène son fils Joseph (§ 133–154). Philon lui prête une visée complémentaire par rapport à celle des frères du rêveur. Ils luttaient contre la *tyrannie*, et, en cela, ils étaient bien dans leur position, celle du "nombre" idéal des fils d'Israël; Jacob, le père, le "Monarque", a le souci d'éviter à Joseph et à Israël l'égarement le plus odieux, celui de l'*anarchie*. On voit la correspondance des deux admonestations, anarchie et tyrannie formant les deux vices extrêmes de la "Politique" et surtout de la vie psychique. Elles sont criminelles et contre-nature à l'intérieur d'Israël.[48]

Que ce point de vue *géographique* soit décisif dans l'ensemble de nos deux traités, nous allons en avoir la preuve par la suite même du *De somniis II*. Notons auparavant le procédé majeur de Philon dans son premier "chapitre", explicitement voué à Joseph (§ 6–154). Au lieu d'accabler Joseph, sujet de ces rêves qui peuvent aboutir aux deux excès contraires, de la tyrannie et de l'anarchie, Philon le fait paradoxalement relever, ou mieux : sauver, par ses frères puis par son père. Or, ce procédé va pour-suivre ses effets de maniére encore plus voyante durant les "chapitres" suivants, qui n'ont plus trait à Joseph, mais aux Ministres de Pharaon, puis à Pharaon. Au lieu, encore, de condamner sans mesure la démesure des Égyptiens, pris au piège du "corps" et de ses flatteries, l'allégorisation conduit à deux hyperboles *exaltant Israël*. Et elles exaltent Israël dans des formules *géographiques*, de géographie morale, en relation surprenante avec les Prophéties d'Israël.

---

[46] Rappelons que l'*isotēs* est le terme qui, dans *Gorgias* 508a, résume et soutient l'harmonie des cinq autres termes de la "*chaîne adamantine*".

[47] Dans le *De Josepho*, Joseph était le "cheval de Troie" d'Israël en Égypte, et il l'illuminait. Ici, Joseph risque d'être le même piège, mais venu de l'impiété égyptienne en Israël : c'est ce que révèlera le "chapitre" consacré à Pharaon.

[48] On voit l'échange harmonieux : les fils de Jacob sont le "nombre", et leur tentation pourrait être l'*anarchie*, dérèglement du multiple; Jacob est seul, en tant que Père, et sa tentation pourrait être la *tyrannie*. Or, les fils de Jacob récusent la *tyrannie*, et le père, Jacob, refuse l'*anarchie*. Il y a donc un croisement.

Le "chapitre" essentiellement consacré à l'Échanson (§ 172–180) nous parle d'"*Israël*", donné comme la "*Vigne*" plantée de Dieu. La condamnation prévisible du "vin" tourne à l'exaltation de la "Vigne" d'Israël. Le "chapitre" ultime, occupé tout entier par Pharaon, son orgueil, son délire verbal, le défi qu'il porte à Dieu, se met à exalter le nom propre de "*Jérusalem*" (§ 246–254), au moment où l'on attend une malédiction sur l'Égypte orgueilleuse. Il faut se rappeler que le nom même de Jérusalem ou son équivalent ne se trouve pas ailleurs, dans les oeuvres de Philon qui nous restent,[49] en un sens autre que matériel.[50] Ajoutons que la dernière page conservée de notre *De somniis II* amorcera[51] une opposition entre le fleuve d'Égypte et l'Euphrate ou tel autre fleuve sacré (§ 300). Là encore, il s'agit sans doute de faire aboutir une malédiction (le fleuve d'Égypte a des '*lèvres*", organe de la parole inutile ...) à une bénédiction (les frontières d'Israël sont celles de fleuves sans lèvres, symbole de la préférence des "*actions*"). La précaution oratoire du § 301 suffit à souligner l'importance de cette (dernière ?) allégorie.

Le résultat de ces trois usages du même procédé dialectique ou oratoire (le retournement de la malédiction de l'Égypte en bénédiction d'Israël) engage l'intelligence de tout le *De somniis II*, me semble-t-il, et du *De Josepho*, par contrecoup. Le *De Josepho* transporte Joseph en Égypte, et elle en est sauvée; le *De somniis* montre Israël submergé par l'invasion du mal égyptien, mais racheté par la Prophétie et le Culte. En effet, le repentir est possible (§ 292–299), et Philon complète discrètement son évocation claire de Jérusalem par celle des "*supplications et sacrifices*" (§299), qui évoquent le Temple, coeur de Jérusalem, lieu "lévitique" par excellence (désignation explicite : § 271–273).

Les signes synthétiques de la "géographie" morale
Voici d'abord, sous forme d'un tableau parallèle, un résumé éloquent du premier "chapitre", consacré à Joseph.

1) le § 6 réunit d'emblée les deux rêves de Joseph comme synopse du Monde, les "*gerbes*" rappelant la "*terre*", et les "*astres*", le "*ciel*".

2) les deux dernières sections du premier "chapitre", consacré directement à Joseph, se correspondent:

    a. – la "*folie*" des révoltés sous un tyran achevé (§ 80–92)
        mais les "*frères*" du tyran inchoatif le *morigènent*

---

[49] L'*In Flaccum*, § 46, et la *Legatio ad Caium*, passim, parlent de Jérusalem comme d'une capitale, sans allégorie, sur un plan historique.

[50] Je ne peux pas développer ici la dialectique des § 237–299, arcboutés sur Jérusalem, au début, et le Temple, à la fin et au milieu (§ 271–73).

[51] Déjà, le § 255 citait *Genèse*, ch. 15, v. 18, où les fleuves délimitent Israël.

> *durement* et barrent sa *"tyrannie"* (§ 93–109);
>   Joseph, alors, *se convertit* (§ 105–109),
>   échappant au *"fleuve égyptien"* (§ 109).
>   b. – la *"folie"* de Xerxès ... (§ 114–132)
>   mais le *"père"* de Joseph inconscient le *reprend*
>   *doucement* et l'éclaire sur l'*"anarchie"* (§ 133–154);
>   Joseph, alors, *est sauvé*
>   échappant au *"courant"* (§ 151).

Par la mention explicite du *"fleuve égyptien"*, puis l'allusion du *"courant"*, les § 109 et 151, achevant chacune des diatribes, assurent la *géographie* des *frontières*.

Rappelons que le "chapitre" troisième, sur le rêve de Pharaon, achève le mouvement de sublimation commencé avec le premier "chapitre", qui sauvait Joseph. La prétention de Pharaon à posséder la *"stabilité"* divine conduit au contraire à la présence *"stabilisante"* de Dieu; la *"parole"* perverse conduit à la *Parole divine* (§ 241–254); la *"Joie"* (déjà active dans le "chapitre" deuxième, § 160–180) s'épanouit en *"Paix"* avec le nom de Jérusalem (§ 250) et revient à la *"Joie"*, sans doute, symbolisée par l'*"Euphrate"* (§ 255, puis à partir du § 302, vraisemblablement ...).[52]

Ajoutons, et cela intéresse la composition d'ensemble du *De somniis II*, que le thème de la *"stabilité"* donne occasion, à la fois dans le premier "chapitre" (§ 136–154) et dans le troisième (§ 220–236), à un groupement de synonymes ou d'antonymes, comme *histēme, idruō, sterizō, ereidō, pēgnumi* ou *antimetaklinō, anatrepō, huposkelizō, phora, tarachē ex eustatheias*.[53] Ces repères, parmi d'autres, permettent de mesurer l'harmonie du *De somniis II*, sa dialectique.

1) Un premier "chapitre" (§ 6–154) met en oeuvre les rêves de Joseph. Il est le plus enfoncé dans la condamnation du mal. Des diatribes pleines de verve et de complaisance rhétorique présentent une autre version de la dissertation du *De Josepho*, § 127–142. Les perversions que sont la *tyrannie* et l'*anarchie* ruinent toutes deux la précieuse *isotēs* (§ 16, 40, 80).

2) Le deuxième "chapitre" (§ 155–214) présente deux registres contrastés. D'une part, il nous enfonce plus avant dans la ruine de l'âme, puisque l'*orgueil* du premier "chapitre", cette maladie de l'Esprit, voire des étoiles même sur le Zodiaque (§ 114–115a), engendre en fait les vices les plus grossiers, *"ivrognerie et gloutonnerie"* du ventre (§ 157–

---

[52] Voir *Legum allegoriae*, I, § 63–87; *Quis heres*, § 315. Pour le système qui donne un commentaire positif à une donnée négative de l'Écriture, voir par exemple le début du *De migratione*, ou *Quod Deus*, § 140–182.

[53] À noter un emploi également concentré de *histēmi, ereidō* de la notion de stabilité, dans la fin du livre précédent, le *De somniis I* (§ 241–250).

158, selon une relation déjà présumée dans les § 11–16). Mais, en même temps, Philon nous entraîne, à l'opposé, vers la belle *"Vigne"* d'Israël, à partir du vin misérable (§ 164–168, avec une sorte d'hésitation entre les deux voies; et § 169–180, sur le mode de la pure *"Joie"*). Il faut souligner ici que ce passage commente, sans le citer explicitement, *Nombres*, ch. 13–14 : Moïse donne l'ordre d'évaluer le pays de Canaan à partir du point de vue offert par la montagne; les explorateurs rapportent d'immenses grappes de raisin, sans pouvoir transplanter les vignes—ce qui explique le § 171. Le texte des *Nombres* concerne la frontière, le territoire d'Israël—notre thème *géographique*.

Toujours suivant le même système d'abaissement et d'exaltation, la réflexion des § 181–184 (qui excuse l'échanson comme Joseph a précédemment été excusé …) se poursuit par sublimation : il existe un Échanson, le Grand-Prêtre d'Israël; et nous remontons progressivement jusqu'à l'image de la Divinité. Avec ce Prêtre, c'est déjà le Culte, âme de ce Pays moral d'Israël.

3) Enfin, le troisième "chapitre" est fortement lié au deuxième. En effet, les § 205–214, conclusion du deuxième "chapitre", décrivent le rêve du Panetier, mais en des termes tels que le sujet véritable en devient le Pharaon lui-même : ces § 205–214 sont plutôt une transition qu'un second développement qui entrerait dans les limites strictes du "chapitre" deuxième. On peut dire qu'en lui-même, le "chapitre" troisième approfondit l'analyse des folies apparues d'abord en Joseph, au premier "chapitre". Le début du Traité en montrait le *effets*. Ici, nous mesurons la *cause*, en amont, et, en aval, la *finalité* perverses des fumées de l'orgueil où Joseph manqua de se perdre en égyptianisant; ici, nous contemplons en même temps (encore le système d'abaissement et d'exaltation) les sublimités de la *"Parole"*, celles de la *"Paix"*, de *"Jérusalem"*, et surtout de la *"stabilité"* divine, qui est la racine commune de tous les biens précédents, et qui sauve Israël.

On voit que le "chapitre" deuxième tient le milieu logique aussi bien que matériel. Le souci de Philon d'obtenir une cohérence sur tous les plans et de porter son exégèse à la vision de "totalités"[54] est manifeste dans le *De somniis II* comme ailleurs. Ainsi, le premier "chapitre" voit dans les deux rêves de Joseph le couple synthétique de la *"terre"* et du *"ciel"*. Ainsi, le second "chapitre" cherche à marquer le caractère total du vice égyptien (§ 155–158), où la logique des opposés, des couples, des symétries, permet de constituer une sorte de monde, parodiquement aussi unifié que

---

[54] Le réflexe mental de Philon le porte toujours à la "totalité". Les "divisions" qu'il multiplie sans cesse n'ont pas pour finalité l'analyse, mais au contraire la synthèse : deux pôles opposés forment un seul monde.

l'Univers); la suite (§ 159–163 couronne l'exégèse de l'échanson par une analyse des mots *"en face de moi"* qui argumente sur une série d'harmonies du vice : le tout, comme dans une charade, aboutit à une ruine *"totale"* (§ 163). Mieux, le mal introduit par l'échanson a le triste mérite de préfigurer la gloutonnerie, à laquelle c'est le panetier qui pourvoit théoriquement. De même, à la fin, le chiffre *"trois"* qui organise les rêves des deux Ministres, *"trois racines – trois corbeilles"*, représente pour Philon les *"trois parts du Temps"* (§ 195 et 208). Cette plénitude perverse est évidemment proche du blasphème, un blasphème dont le Pharaon du troisième "chapitre" assume la pleine responsabilité. Ajoutons que la cellule centrale du "chapitre" deuxième (§ 169–180) jouit, de façon bénéfique cette fois, d'une belle unité. Trois citations composent un Univers intensif, harmonieux, idéal, où règent symétriquement la *"jubilation"* d'Israël et la *"Jubilation"* divine (§ 170–180). C'est peut-être ici l'axe du *De somniis II*. Israël est le lieu où le *"Logos"* (§ 170s) vient parler à l'Homme. En plein rêve égyptien le principe de réalité éclate par *Israël*.[55] Une simple citation d'*Isaïe*, sans commentaire d'ailleurs, tel le caillou de David frappant Goliath en plein front, fait s'évanouir le faux-semblant du rêve immense de l'Égypte et du monde. Cette citation est au centre du centre du "chapitre" deuxième. Quant au troisième "chapitre", les divisions adéquates qu'il renferme et l'achèvement qu'il donne aux rêves de Joseph montrent assez sa vollonté de clore et de totaliser. Joseph *serait* Pharaon, s'il n'était pas entouré de ses frères; s'il sortait de la famille d'Israël.

Cohérence du rôle de Joseph

Il se définit par ce couple moral : Joseph est un monstre en Israël; il est un Prince éclairé en Égypte. Curieusement, les rêves de la troisième catégorie, envisagés donc par notre *De somniis II*, sont ceux qui ont besoin d'un interprète. Or, les rêves de Joseph ne sont pas exactement "interprétés", mais barrés, volatilisés, éliminés, par les frères de Joseph. Et cela, immédiatement : cette purification immédiate opérée par les fils d'Israël est marquée dans les § 100–109, et en particulier dans les étranges § 101–104. À l'errance, à la fumée, à la folie qui menacent Joseph s'oppose sans délai la *"stabilité"* (§ 102).

Si Philon ne retient pas le rêve de domination en Joseph comme un présage du rôle de Prince qu'il exercera effectivement,[56] c'est qu'il veut stigmatiser les prétentions d'un fils d'Israël à exercer *en Israël*, pays de la naturelle *isotès*, un pouvoir qu'Israël doit exercer naturellement *sur les Nations*, et spécialement sur l'Égypte, le pays le plus éloigné du salut.

---

55 De proche en proche, le Logos ou la Sagesse des § 170s désigne la Tora, cette lecture que le Gouverneur d'Égypte prétendait faire cesser ou moquer (§ 123–132).
56 C'est un ressort dramatique essentiel au récit de la *Genèse*, pourtant.

La réponse brutale des frères de Joseph le convertit (§ 101–109). Mais les signes ou les effets de cette rédemption de Joseph nous conduisent en Égypte : c'est en Égypte qu'il sera "bon"; là, qu'il résistera à la femme; là, qu'il confessera Dieu; là, qu'il souhaitera enfin le reour de ses ossements en terre natale. Comme dans la partie "récit" du *De Josepho*, le Joseph de Philon est saint au-dehors, en Égypte. Mais chez ses frères, chez son père, s'il rêve, s'il est pris de façon prématurée et intempestive par le rêve de la gloire, alors, il devient *au-dedans* le témoin misérable de la folie même qu'il devra soigner *au-dehors*. On pourrait paraphraser Pascal : "Blasphème en-deçà, lumière au-delà …"; ou l'Évangile : "Nul n'est prophète dans son pays".

C'est sans doute le rayonnement de Joseph au-dehors qui est exprimé au moyen de ce procédé majeur de la *sublimation*, à partir du "chapitre" deuxième. L'exégèse tourne de la condamnation à l'exaltation de valeurs propres à Israël. Qu'il s'agisse d'Israël comme tel, derrière un Joseph apparemment oublié dans les deux derniers "chapitres", un signe nous en est fourni par les § 101–104, dont j'ai noté plus haut le caractère étrange. Là, c'est Philon qui se glisse lui-même, comme *fils d'Israël*, comme un ami des fils de Jacob et qui les suit obstinément dans la lecture du "réel", parce qu'ils sont, comme fils d'Israël, comme détenteurs de la Tora malmenée ensuite par le Gouverneur fou, les "*exégètes du Rêve*", les éclaireurs de la nuit qui a pour nom propre l'Égypte et ses fumées. Le tout pourrait se résumer dans ce double théorème :

    o *Joseph, présent en Israël, mais comme fou Égyptien, est sauvé par Israël (ses frères, son père, la vérité de la Tora et de Jérusalem).*

    o *Joseph, présent en Égypte* (De Josepho)—*ou même absent ("chapitres" 2 et 3 du* De somniis II)—*fait rayonner Israël, qui sauve le Monde de la folie égyptienne.*

La "nuit" menace Israël par Joseph; le "Jour" envahit l'Égypte par Israël.

L'effacement de la Politique

Un autre facteur d'unité, négatif, marque le *De somniis II*: la réduction de l'ordre "politique" en symbole de la vie personnelle. Philon nous montre qu'*avant* de réaliser le plus modeste commencement du pouvoir, Joseph est sermonné, rabroué, converti par sa famille; et c'est au comble du pouvoir exercé et de son mauvais usage, et donc en ce sens, *après* cet exercice, que Pharaon est puni de la pire instabilité. Entre les deux positions, l'une de prétendant, l'autre de potentat assis et confirmé, il n'y a pas d'inter-médiaire. Le *De somniis* contourne l'ordre "politique", et c'est à bon escient que le nom, même abâtardi, du *politikos* en est écarté. On n'insistera jamais trop sur ce phénomène, puisque le souvenir de Joseph attire invariablement cet adjectif dans les autres traités, y compris dans le *De somniis I*, aux portes du livre II. Mieux encore: on dirait que Philon s'amuse à "tenter le Diable": l'autre qualificatif appartenant au blason de Joseph, *poikilos*, est employé quatre fois, mais avec une valeur purement descriptive, matérielle (§ 19, 53, 57, 155), et où rien ne perce des prolongements moraux qui ont permis la rédaction des § 189–227 du livre I, par exemple. Rien ne descend dans la pratique; rien sur les régimes divers: la "*tyrannie*" et l'"*anarchie*" populaire sont des images de ce qui trouble l'âme.[57] Pour Philon, Joseph "*a cru voir*" son élévation au pouvoir; Pharaon "*croit*" qu'il est roi (§ 17–20 et § 215–216)—et c'est l'un des détails importants qui rapprochent évidemment Pharaon de Joseph, le "chapitre" troisième du "chapitre" premier … Si Politique il y a, il faut la placer à un niveau transcendantal. Elle se résume, de façon inutile pour l'éducation des futurs princes, dans la relation médicinale d'Israël aux Nations: le médecin guérira-t-il son malade, ou en recevra-t-il la contagion? Joseph joue ce jeu dangereux. Si Philon, qui suggère que l'*isotēs* constitue le trésor qu'Israël apporte aux Nations, montrait aussitôt comment la Loi organise cette égalité, nous entrerions dans l'ordre "politique". Mais il s'en garde bien.[58]

> Sur le plan moral, le projet du *De somniis II* est unifié. Connivence des parties du Texte biblique, puisque les rêves divers, de Joseph, des Ministres puis de Pharaon, deviennent le plan d'une perception de la folie mondaine en face de la stabilité divine; illumination progressive des exégèses, prenant de plus en plus les rêves malsains *a contrario*, tirant vers la conversion, la Joie, la Paix; équilibre et relation interne de l'*isotēs* propre à Israël et revendiqué à ce titre par les frères de Joseph, d'une part ("chapitre" premier), et, d'autre part, sa Cause première, la "*Stabilité*" du Dieu d'Israël (troisième "chapitre") – l'harmonie des deux "chapitres" extrêmes étant complétée par la double symétrie des propos de Philon sur la nécessaire humiliation (§ 23–30 et § 68–77; puis § 265–266 et § 292–299); contournement constant de l'ordre du "politique", par un Joseph, trop tôt découragé de prendre le pouvoir, puis par un Pharaon, trop tard morigéné: tous ces facteurs homogènes ont pour perspective commune la *géographie morale*, d'Israël à l'Égypte.

À titre d'analyse plus concrète du texte de Philon et en même temps de résumé portant sur ma méthode de lecture et sur les signes semés par Philon, voici un tableau qui paraphrase l'exégèse du premier rêve de Joseph, soit les § 21–77:

---

[57] Les folies de Xerxès et du Governeur d'Égypte, par leur excès même, ne sont plus politiques, mais relèvant de la psychologie, de la pathologie, voire de la métaphysique.
[58] Le dernier crime évoqué est celui de Babel (§ 284–291). Il est donné par Philon comme une alternance de la tyrannie affectée à l'anarchie, les deux régimes extrêmes. Mais leur remède ne consiste pas dans une meilleure politique: c'est la religion, la pénitence, le recours au Temple dont nous avons parlé.

§ 21
Il fallait MOISSONNER
"terme" telos ; FIN

§ 77
en Israël, LES MOISSONS
PRÉMICES; *telesphoros "porte
à terme"*

"moissonner la moisson"
est une redondance mystique
comme *"circoncire de circoncision"* ...

*le perverse utilise des
"paires" nocives, l'Arbre aux 2
fruits, pour Adam ...*

DYADE d'HARMONIE
§§ 31 sv.
GERBES DES
VERTUS D'ISRAËL
= *RÉALITÉ* EN ISRAËL

DUALITÉ COUPABLE
§§ 48 sv.
ALIMENTS
SUPERFLUS DE L'ÉGYPTE
= SONGES *ÉGYPTIENS*

§§ *42–47*
JOSEPH:
*et ses titres ou ornements
fallacieux
(char - collier - sceau)*
son NOM = *"addition"*

À gauche, le côté d'Israël; à droite, l'Égypte: entre les deux, Joseph. L'organisation de cette section enferme la "raison" de tout de *De somniis II*, et, par rebondissement, celle du *De Josepho*. Ajoutons que le mot *telos-telesphoros*, qui permet l'inclusion de toute la section, revient à la fin de ce qui nous reste du "chapitre" troisième: les § 271–273 font aboutir ce *telos* à "*moisson*" parfaite, au "*Temple*", aux "*Lévites*", à la joie que "*chante Israël*"."

Conclusion: Moïse, Législation et Mystique

Abraham gouverne sa Maison, qui est bien vite l'univers mystique. Joseph, qui s'est risqué dans le monde intermédiaire de la vraie prise de pouvoir, ne peut l'exercer légitimement que comme instrument du Logos à l'usage des Nations. Reste le troisième Politique de la Torah et de Philon. C'est Moïse. Qu'en pense Philon par rapport à son rôle de Prince, à la politique? Il faudrait citer maintenant le portrait développé que trace de luí la *Vita Mosis*, I, § 150–162.

La grande différence séparant Abraham et Moïse de Joseph, c'est le fait que Joseph s'enfonce en Égypte (physiquement dans le *De Josepho*, et moralement dans le début du *De somniis II*), alors qu'Abraham et Moïse n'y descendent que pour en remonter. C'est ce voyage, cette sortie d'Égypte qu'on peut deviner en fond de tableau dans le parcours moral de ces § 150–162 de la *Vita Mosis* I, un autre "encomion" de Philon. Sans doute Moïse joue-t-il un premier rôle qui aborde la "politique": il encourage les bons et châtie les méchants (§ 154). Mais ce qui retient l'attention dans ce portrait récapitulatif, c'est plutôt la *hâte* de Philon: il tire qu plus vite son héros vers les sphères mystiques. Le *crescendo* part des vertus propres de Moïse (§ 150–154): vite, Moïse dépasse le Peuple, et ce qu'il gouverne, ce n'est plus ce Peuple, mais le Monde (§ 155–157). Vite, il va se retrouver sublimé et porté à l'égal de Dieu (§ 158), modèle, à son tour, "*loi vivante*" (§ 162), alors qu'on attend de lui les lois concrètes, écrites, la sanction, bref une "politique". En trois étapes, Moïse s'est "évadé". Il passe, pour ainsi dire, son temps et son activité à sauver Joseph, à emporter ses ossements d'Égypte. Il ne donne pas poids ou valeur au métier de roi, ce métier pratique et hasardé que Joseph a dû affronter.

Platon laissait au Désir, image parallèle de la sophistique et du politique, une certaine dose de vérité: ce qui en faisait le sujet d'une *longue et lente persuasion de mémoire*, un espace mental donc, où nous pouvions assigner des dimensions à la "politique", justement ... Rien d'analogue, chez Philon. Il est notable que, parcourant la vie de Moïse et son oeuvre de législateur, Philon fuie les détours de la lente persuasion, les détours tout simplement. Il bascule tout de suite vers le parfait, le "donné" déjà, le merveilleux, s'il faut: ainsi, au plus précis des réglements, Philon se réjouit-il de ce que la Loi ne fasse pas de décret sur les poids et mesures, mais qu'elle *invite* chacun[59] à user de poids justes et de justes mesures (*Lois spécifiques*, IV, §§ 193–194, figurant, il est vrai, dans la fin de l'ouvrage, également pressée de mystique ...)! Lorsque Platon annonce que les lois particulières doivent être précédées de "*préambules*" (le thème revient périodiquement dans les *Lois*), il s'agit réellement de préambules. Philon s'y complaît et fait tout dériver vers l'Idée, sans prendre le temps de politiser ...

Le plan de la *Vie de Moïse* illustre cette hâte.

La Vita Mosis

Moïse sera donc roi -mettons. Il le sera au mieux, parce que *législateur, prêtre et prophète*. Législateur? Un espoir se glisse en nous à ce mot concret. Mais, lorsque Philon aborde cette fonction, c'est pour nous prouver que Moïse fut le plus parfait des législateurs, le seul en somme. Et encore la démonstration ne s'appuie-t-elle que sur des *effets* extérieurs: la Loi a perduré sans changement pendant deux mille ans; elle a obtenu le respect universel— les philosophes Grecs ne l'ont-ils pas plus ou moins connue et copiée? Arrivons à son contenu (là, de nouveau, un espoir pour la contingence, le

---

59   Voir *Allégories des Lois*, III, § 80 (cf. Platon, *Critias*, 109c, etc.).

"politique"?), c'est pour déclarer comme il est préférable d'ouvrir une législation par le ... préambule de la Création, des Vies exemplaires des Patriarches ou des récits de châtiments exemplaires, tel le Déluge (tout cela figure dans les débuts[60] de la *Vie de Moïse*, II).

Philon veut arriver rapidement à l'Un, à l'Idée, à la contemplation, que, pour lui, très vite, *chaque* exercice du monde, chaque iota de sa Loi, infiniment divers cependant, appelle et révèle, comme une monade; que, pour lui, *chacun* possède pleinement, pourvu qu'il soit de l'âme israélite-peuple ou personne.

Moïse ou Philon, l'escamoteur
Ce besion d'aller vite vers l'Un, c'est la mystique. Il est toujours actif chez Philon. À supposer qu'on puisse recomposer une doctrine politique de Philon, en isolant des phrases, il faudra cependant interpréter par le mouvement de la page ou du "chapitre" ces quelques aspects concrets. Voici quelques échantillons des détournements opérés par Philon.

1) Si Moïse, disions-nous, est le roi le meilleur, c'est qu'il est législateur parfait. Il est législateur parfait, du fait qu'il est prêtre - ailleurs, Philon explique comment le prêtre est finalement meilleur juge ... (*Lois spécifiques*, IV, §§ 188–192). Ce n'est pas fini: Moïse jouit aussi de la prophétie: et la prophétie servira à escamoter le temps, les obscurités du monde empirique; massivement, elle remplacera la politique, donc, dans la *Vie de Moïse*, II, 187–291. La politique est omise.

2) S'il aborde tout de même les lois, Moïse (ou Philon ...) commencera par la Création, comme Platon; mais Philon aura tendance à réduire le projet complet qui allait du *Timée* au *Critias*, puis à l'examen de la Constitution archaïque d'Athènes. L'ouverture contemplative suffira à Moïse. La politique est omise.

3) Une fois entré dans le détail des prescriptions, Philon envisage par exemple une révolution, une révolte: elle sera réglée soit miraculeusement, soit par suppléance mystique (voir le Veau d'or et Coré, dans la *Vie de Moïse*, II, §§ 270–287). Où est passé le gouvernement? Même dans les *Lois spécifiques*, III et IV, un appel répété se fait entendre à des châtiments directs, issus de la *dikē* suprême. La politique est omise ...

Le De specialibus legibus
4) On peut mesurer la répugnance de Philon a descendre dans la basse-fosse des nécessités humaines en suivant les quatre livres des *Lois spécifiques*. En principe, quand il aborde ce sujet, il a déjà parlé des grandes Lois, c'est à dire du Décalogue. Or, Philon tend à remonter au lieu de

---

[60] Que je reprends ci-dessous, page 57.

descendre. Les lois particulières qu'il peut rapporter tout d'abord au premier volet, à la première Table exactement, du Décalogue, sont traitées comme un nouveau commentaire du Décalogue. Puis arrive la deuxième Table, avec les lois particulières qu'il faut bien leur faire assumer, sur le vol, les sordides calculs, les bassesses de tous les désirs, les pièges, les adultères, les accidents. C'est alors que prend place une réflexion-*off* pour ainsi dire. Philon s'y plaint d'avoir à quitter la philosophie pour les tempêtes des affaires: c'est le célèbre début du *De specialibue legibus*, III, où Philon oppose vie active et contemplation (ce sont les § 3–7). Anecdote ou non, il est certain que cette préface rend parfaitement compte du rôle relatif des deux Tables: Philon essaiera autant que possible de maintenir l'esprit hors du flot, et de conserver au Décalogue le rôle d'une âme par rapport au corps des lois spécifiques, puis de la première Table des Lois spécifiques par rapport aux règles de la seconde Table, grâce au beau principe de "salut" des confins par le centre et l'Unité.

Plus loin, l'exposé du neuvième Commandement et de ses spécifications (sur le faux témoignage) tourne rapidement à un portrait du bon juge (IV, §§ 55–78). Celui du dixième Commandement analyse le Désir, mais s'arrête au désir des nourritures, donnant prétexte à justifier les règles alimentaires juives. Cette justification n'est pas d'abord apologétique: elle débouche bientôt sur un thème qui ornera toute la fin des *Lois spécifiques* de façon sans plus aucune retenue: le refus des mélanges, de toutes hybridations et confusions, nous conduit à la règle mystique de la *simplicité*, de l'UNITÉ. Et, pour clore, l'*isotēs*, patiemment contemplée ... Au passage, l'évocation du Prince d'Israël—personnage à la fois élu et royal, unique, mais décoratif, mis là pour symboliser à jamais en Israël[61] la Monarchie divine. La politique est encore différée, contournée.

5) Enfin la *Vie de Moïse* procède en deux grandes étapes: la première est un exposé "historique"; la seconde fait place à une reprise de type allégorisé, mystique, où le roi s'engouffre dans le prophète—heureux juge qui n'a pas à siéger, à délibérer, à peser, à risquer ... Voici un dernier portrait de Moïse, à la charnière des deux lectures:

---

[61] Selon la formule idéalisée du *Deutéronome*, ch. 17, v. 14s.

[3] "Et si j'ai choisi d'écrire à leur sujet, c'est que j'ai été nécessairement amené à penser qu'elles doivent toutes se combiner dans le même homme. Car Moïse, par l'effet de la providence divine, a éte tout à la fois roi, législateur, grand-prêtre et prophète, et dans chacune de ces fonctions il a remporté la première place. Mais pourquoi elles se combinent toutes dans un même homme, c'est ce qu'il faut expliquer. [4] Au roi il appartient de prescrire le bien et d'interdire le mal; or prescrire ce qui doit être fait et interdire ce qui ne doit pas lêtre, c'est le propre de la loi: d'où il suit que le roi est la loi vivante, et la loi un roi juste. [5] Mais un roi et législateur doit tenir sous son regard non seulement l'ensemble des choses humaines mais aussi des choses divines: car, si Dieu ne leur accorde pas son attention, les entreprises des rois ni celles des sujets ne peuvent être menées à bien. Et c'est pourquoi il faut qu'un tel homme soit le premier parmi les prêtres afin que, grâce à des rites parfaits et à une parfaite connaissance du service divin, il demande à Celui qui veut notre bien et consent à nos prières, d'être préservé du malheur et d'avoir part au bonheur, lui et ses sujets. Car Il exaucera certainement nos prières, l'Étres bienveillant de sa nature et qui accorde ses faveurs à ceux qui le servent sincèrement. [6] Mais, comme une infinité de choses humaines et divines sont invisibles au roi, au législateur et au grand-prêtre – car bien qu'en possession d'un héritage surabondant des dons qui donnent le succès, il n'en est pas moins une créature mortelle –, Moïse eut obligatoirement le don de prophétie afin de découvrir par la providence divine ce qu'il ne pouvait saisir par le raisonnement. Car ce qui échappe à l'intelligence, la prophétie l'atteint tout de suite. [7] Et vraiment, elle est belle et d'une parfaite harmonie, l'union de ces quatre facultés: en effet, enlacées et attachées l'une à l'autre, elles se déplacent en choeur, tour à tour acceptant et rendant des services, semblables aux Grâces qu'une loi de la nature immuable empêche de se séparer. En sorte que l'on pourrait à juste titre dire d'elles ce que l'on dit couramment des vertus: qui en a une les a toutes."

(*Vita Mosis*, II, § 3–6)

L'enchaînement, la hâte, la disparition de toute "sagesse", tout cela ressort du texte. C'est un adieu au monde réel de la politique.

C'est pour tracer la voie d'une étude plus fouillée que je viens de survoler la *Vita Mosis* et les quatre livres du *De specialibus legibus*. On y voit cependant la même tendance de Philon à sublimer la Politique au moment même où les textes de la Bible pourraient l'inviter à la regarder en face. Nous avons vu comment le *De Josepho* et le *De somniis II* ne trouvaient pas leur explication la plus simple dans le problème "politique", mais dans la question bien plus précise, plus "juive", du rapport entre l'Égypte—et derrière elle, les Nations—et un Israël, dépositaire du Logos, et, avec Lui, de la meilleure Législation.

THE BODY AND SOCIETY
IN PHILO AND THE *APOCRYPHON OF JOHN*

KAREN L. KING

For many years, a teacher and his student debated the relative merits of the intellectual endeavors of Philo and Gnosticism. For the teacher's part, the terms of the debate concerned an intellectual system, designed to allow the pursuit of one's faith under foreign domination without violence or bloodshed, versus an aesthetically and ethically unacceptable fantasy, which rejected the world as a whole in order to eliminate its faults. For the student at that time, the terms looked more like an elitist moralism that avoided serious political engagement, versus a profound and sensitive response to human suffering and powerlessness. Though they never came to a complete agreement, the student will always remember these conversations. This essay is dedicated with gratitude and affection to the memory of Horst R. Moehring, a dedicated teacher and a profound scholar.

Introduction

The writings of Philo and the *Apocryphon of John* belong to the same political and intellectual world, the Roman Mediterranean of the first and second centuries CE. Each presents a cosmology and anthropology that draws deeply upon traditions of Middle-Platonic thought and Jewish exegesis. The many profound similarities between Philo's writings and the *Apocryphon of John* therefore come as no surprise. Nor do we need to presuppose any direct literary dependence between them, since access to common cultural traditions is sufficient to account for their similarities.

Yet any student of ancient Mediterranean religion knows that reading Philo and reading the *Apocryphon of John* are quite different experiences. Contrasts in genre, style, and mood are sharp. And it is relatively simple to pick out substantive points where they disagree irreconcilably, for example in their valuation of the creator God. For Philo, the world and humanity are the purposeful work of God's providence; for the *Apocryphon of John,* the existence of the world and humanity's place in it are due to an unfortunate, even tragic error.

How are their differences to be accounted for, given that they share many elements of the imaginative world of Mediterranean culture in the

Roman period? Anthropologists have pointed out that both the body and the cosmos are, so to speak, symbols to think with. What are Philo and the *Apocryphon of John* "thinking about" when they describe creation so differently? What is at stake in their imagination of self and the world?

A comparison between Philo and the *Apocryphon of John* shows up only relative, not absolute differences in the ways in which they address issues about the self and the world. For example, both agree to the following points:[1]

The purpose of life is to attain likeness to God.

The ethical self is a battleground between a higher and lower self.

The soul is utterly dependent upon God's providence and mercy, but is responsible for its choice to accept God's providential care or to turn away from Him.

The true God is utterly transcendent and unknowable, but yet His likeness is present to and in men.[2]

God is completely good; no taint of evil can be said to accrue to Him. The problem of theodicy is addressed at least in part by a multiplication of intermediaries between God and humankind.

These important agreements, however, do not have the same meaning for the two authors. These points will be taken up below under two headings: "Likeness to God" and "The Battleground: Salvation and Ethics." A final section will speculate upon the political implications of their positions.

Likeness to God

By the first and second centuries CE, the identification of the purpose of life[3] had shifted in Middle Platonic thought from the ideal of "life in accordance with nature" to a greater emphasis upon the ideal of achieving "likeness to God."[4] Both Philo and the *Apocryphon of John* reflect this shift.

---

[1] These five topics correspond roughly to those listed by John Dillon as the central issues of ethics and physics under discussion in Middle Platonism: the purpose of life, the value of virtue to happiness, free will and necessity, distinquishing a first and a second God, and the multiplication of intermediaries between God and man. See *The Middle Platonists,* (London, 1977) 43–49.

[2] Although the *Apocryphon of John* shows some indications that women are included in its description of humanity, especially in the Berlin Codex version, the male remains the primary topic of discussion. Philo's consideration of humanity is thoroughly androcentric. The use of the term "man" or "mankind" here is therefore not inclusive, but descriptive of these androcentric perspectives.

[3] Dillon 1977, 43–44.

[4] Plato, *Theaetetus* 176b.

Philo[5] can use either definition of purpose, since in his view to live according to nature[6] is complementary to the desire to achieve likeness to God.[7] Since God has inscribed his Law in nature through the ruling of Logos, to follow nature is in accord with obeying the divine Law.[8] Life in accordance with nature is a task subordinate to pursuit of God. Only the man who sets his hopes on God as the source of life and providence is worthy of praise in Philo's view.[9]

This pursuit is possible because human nature is created by God and the highest part of human nature (called alternatively spirit, mind, or *logos*) is "kindred" to God,[10] itself a mirror of the divine nature in its creative and ruling aspects. For example, in interpreting the meaning of man's "likeness" to God in Genesis 1:26–27, Philo writes:[11]

> Let no one represent the likeness as one to a bodily form; for neither is God in human form, nor is the human body God-like (*theoeides*). No, it is in respect of the Mind, the sovereign element of the soul, that the word 'image' is used; for after the pattern of a single Mind, even the Mind of the Universe as an archetype, the mind in each of those who successively came into being was moulded. It is in a fashion a god to him who carries and enshrines it as an object of reverence; for the human mind evidently occupies a position in men precisely answering to that which the Ruler occupies in all the world.

Assimilation to God is limited, however, by God's transcendence; the divine part of man is formed in the likeness of God's *logos*, not God Himself.[12]

For the *Apocryphon of John*, the situation is a bit more complex. Since the true God is not the creator,[13] a life lived according to nature (creation) does

---

[5] See Dillon 1977, 145–146.

[6] See *Abr*. 4–6.

[7] See *Fug*. 63; *Opif.* 144.

[8] See Dillon 1977, 146.

[9] See *Praem*. 11–13.

[10] See *Opif.* 144.

[11] *Opif.* 69. All English citations of Philo's work are taken from Colson, Earp, and Whittaker in the Loeb Classical Library edition of Philo's works.

[12] See *QG* II, 62.

[13] Although the *Apocryphon of John* does not do so, it is possible for Gnostic thought to embrace the ideal of living "according to nature." To do so would require making a distinction between a person's true spiritual nature and the false, so-called "nature" of matter, a distinction that is foreign to Philo. Other gnostic Christian texts do, however, make just such a distinction. The *Gospel of Mary*, for example, teaches that discovering one's own divine nature within means to abandon the false illusory "nature" of the world. Living according to the "nature of the body" must be denied in order to achieve the realization of one's spiritual likeness to God. See *GosMary* 7.1–21 and the excellent discussion by Anne Pasquier, *L'Évangile selon Marie*. (Quebec, 1983), 48–56.

not directly relate to attaining "likeness to God." As we might expect, the *Apocryphon of John* seldom uses the term "nature" (*physis*), and then only to refer either to the lower nature of the planetary rulers[14] or to the physical body.[15] The more important terminology in the *Apocryphon of John* is that of "likeness." As with Philo, there are direct interpretive references to the creation of humanity in the "image and likeness" of God which are intended to show the "kinship" between the two.

The text's theogony illustrates a direct continuity between the Father and all Gnostics through Man, Adam, and Seth. From the transcendent and unknowable Father, the Invisible Spirit, comes his image (ϩΙΚШΝ), the Mother Barbelo;[16] from her comes forth the Son, Autogenes, according to the Father's likeness (ΕΙΝΕ).[17] From Autogenes comes the First Man (the heavenly Adam) who is the father of the heavenly Seth and the seed of Seth.[18]

When the first Man appears in order to teach, his likeness (ΕΙΝΕ) appears in a male form (ΟΥΤΥΠΟC ΝΑΝΑΡΕΑC).[19] The image of his form (ΠΤΥΠΟC ΝΘΙΚШΝ) is reflected in the waters below matter. When the lower Demiurge and his angels see this form (ϩΙΚШΝ), they create the first mortal man according to the image and likeness of the heavenly first Man.

> The blessed one (the heavenly Man) revealed his likeness (ΕΙΝΕ) to them. And the whole archon company of the seven powers assented. They saw in the water the likeness of the image (ϩΙΚШΝ). They said to one another: 'Let us make a man after the image (ϩΙΚШΝ) of God and his likeness (ΕΙΝΕ).' They created out of themselves and all their powers ... They created it after the image (ϩΙΚШΝ) which they had seen, in imitation of him who exists from the beginning, the perfect Man.[20]

This first mortal man, Adam, also creates a son in his own likeness, Seth.[21] The Gnostics are the offspring ("seed") of Seth, and presumably share in his likeness with the divine Man. They are described collectively as "the substance (ΟΥCΙΑ) which is like (ΕΙΝΕ) him (Seth), after the

---

14 See, for example, *Berolinensis Gnosticus [BG]* 41.6; II, 15.10.
15 See, for example, *BG* 69.17; II, 20.15; 27.13–14.
16 See II, 4.22–5.4; *BG* 27.2, 12, 19.
17 II, 6.14; III, 9.15.
18 *BG* 34.91–36.15; III,12.24–14.9; II, 8.28–9.24.
19 II, 14.24–25.
20 *BG* 48.4–49.6. English translations of the Berlin Codex are taken from Werner Foerster, *Gnosis. A Selection of Gnostics Texts.* ed. R. McL. Wilson, (Oxford, 1972). English translations of Codex II are taken from Frederik Wisse, "The Apocryphon of John" in *The Nag Hammadi Library In English.* Edited by James M. Robinson and Richard Smith. (San Francisco, 1988, 3rd ed.), 104–123. At points I have modified these translations.
21 II, 24.35–25.2.

pattern (TYΠOC)[22] of perfection."[23] Hence there is a relationship of likeness and image which illustrates a direct continuity between the Father
and all Gnostics through Man, Adam, and Seth. Moreover, there is a
likeness between the Gnostics below and the spirits above.[24]

But this likeness is only a part of the story. There is another geneaology
for Gnostic humanity, a story of discontinuity from the true Father. It begins when Sophia, one of the Aeons,[25] wishes to create a "likeness (EINE)
out of herself." But she does so without the patriarchal consent of the
Father or her male consort. The result is a being who was "dissimilar to
the likeness (EINE) of his mother for he has another form" (MOPΦH).[26]
This being is Yaldabaoth, the demiurgic creator of the world below. To
reproduce his own misshapen likeness, the Demiurge "planted in Adam
a desire of seed, which, through marital intercourse, brings forth a
likeness (EINE) from their counterfeit <spirit>."[27] The products of this
counterfeit likeness are contrasted with those formed after the spiritual
likeness. Worse, the counterfeit likeness was devised purposefully to lead
men astray and pollute their souls.[28]

It would be wrong, however, to suppose that the *Apocryphon of John*
envisages two types of humanity: those formed after the likeness of the
first Man and those formed after the likeness of the Demiurge and his
counterfeit. Rather, persons are themselves a mixture. Each person has
continuity to the Father of the All in the spiritual likeness to Man, and is
cut off from that likeness to God by the imprisonment of the Demiurgic
likeness. The likeness to the Father is in a person's spirit; the likeness to
the Demiurge, in one's soul and body.

As was seen above, both Philo[29] and the *Apocryphon of John* use the

---

[22] Similarly, the text distinguishes clearly between this world and the imperishable
Aeon of which it is a pattern (TYΠOC). It also distinguishes between the Demiurge
who is *not* patterned after the spiritual Man (*BG* 37.20) and the Gnostics who are (*BG*
63.19–64.2).

[23] *BG* 63.19–64.2.

[24] The Gnostics below, who are "the seed of Seth," will find their final resting place
with the heavenly seed of Seth in the third aeon. See II, 9.14–17.

[25] *BG* 54.1–2 states that Sophia is of the same likeness (EINE) as the other Aeons.

[26] II, 9.26–10.7. See also *BG* 37.15, 17, 20.

[27] *BG* 63.5–9. Compare II, 24.26–31. See King, "Sophia and Christ in the *Apocryphon of
John*" in *Images of the Feminine in Gnosticism* . Edited by Karen L. King. Studies in
Antiquity and Chrisitanity. (Philadelphia: 1988), 169–171.

[28] See II,29.23–25; compare *BG* 74.12.

[29] But, for Philo, the content of this terminology is described primarily in terms of
the *Timaeus*. Thus, although the language may reflect Genesis, its conceptuality is that
of Plato. David Runia summarizes: "In order to show man's exceptional place in the
structure of the cosmos, Philo *centres his account* around the two primary anthropo-
logical passages of the Mosaic creation story. But in his endeavour to *explain what these*

terminology of Genesis 1:26–27 (LXX), where humanity is said to be created in the "image and likeness" of God (*kat'eikona theou kai kath homoiosin*), to establish a link between God and humanity, and both insist that that link is not with regard to the material body. Both make a distinction between the higher portion of a person which is god-like and the lower portion of a person created by lesser beings. The lower portion is that part of the human being subject to passion and sense-perception.

In taking this perspective, both follow the lead of Plato's *Timaeus*. They both diverge from Plato, however, in explaining why it was necessary to combine the divine part of man with passions and the material body. Plato ascribes a primarily aesthetic reason to his demiurge: it was necessary in order to complete the plentitude of the universe. For Philo and the *Apocryphon of John,* however, the main issue raised by this unfortunate combination is that of theodicy. Clearly both see the mixture of the divine part of the soul with lesser parts and its enclosure in the sense-perceptible body as suspect. Philo gives no reason why God would do such a thing, trusting simply to His providence. His interest is solely to make it clear that God is not responsible for the evil that human beings do. Indeed, in contrast to the *Apocryphon of John,* Philo gives little attention to the creation of the body, except to protect God from implications of evil. This silence seems to obscure a path he will not allow his thought to follow. The *Apocryphon of John* solves the issue in a more straightforward manner by ascribing the wicked deed to wicked powers.

As we have seen, both Philo and the *Apocryphon of John* treat men as composite beings, made up of higher and lower aspects. The higher portion is immaterial, noetic, and spiritual; the lower portion is material and the location of both sense-perception and passion. Only the higher self can possibly achieve likeness to God, although that likeness is limited by the absolute transcendence of God. For both, a mediating figure (Logos or Man) represents the divine aspect attainable by humanity.

The primary difference therefore between the two lies not in their view of humanity's higher nature and its goal, but in their views of humanity's lower nature and its origins. The significance of this observation comes into view when we note that in Philo the divine portion of men

---

texts actually tell us about man's nature he resorts to the two Platonic accounts of man which he knew best, the *Timaeus* and the *Phaedrus* myth. Man is separated from the other earth-bound animals because he possesses a rational soul. It is in the possession of reason that man shows a likeness to God his creator. Man's possession of reason orientates him towards the heavens, and beyond them to God himself. The object of man's existence is to set eyes on God and become like him, and this can only be done with the (mental) eye of the soul." (David T. Runia, *Philo of Alexandria and the Timaeus of Plato.* (Amsterdam, 1983), 328–29).

corresponds to the ruling power of the world. For the *Apocryphon of John,* it decidedly does not; rather the likeness to the world-rulers corresponds to the lower psychic body. For Philo, the lower self is rightly subject to the ruling power of the world; for the *Apocryphon of John,* that subjection signals humankind's doom.

The Battleground: Salvation and Ethics

Does this difference in the relationship of the divine portion of man or humankind to the world-ruler(s) require different strategies in achieving likeness to God? Apparently not. Both Philo and the *Apocryphon of John* agree that the clearest likeness to God[30] is achieved by overcoming the passions and escaping the influence of the body, that is by the attainment of *apatheia.*[31]

Henri-Charles Puech terms the final ideal of the Gnostic an ethic of "resemblance."[32] Michel Tardieu summarizes:[33]

> Le sort final n'est pas lié à un changement de lieu (passer de la terre au ciel) ou à changement d'état (passer d'un corps de chair à un corps de résurrection) mais à l'accomplissement du 'rassemblement' par le triomphe en soi de l'Esprit vivant sur l'Esprit travesti.

This triumph of the true spirit over the counterfeit spirit is essentially the triumph of the divine part of a person over the lower passions and the body. Among the blessed who still reside in the world, this triumph is manifest as a state of *apatheia*:[34]

> Those on whom the Spirit of life will descend and (with whom) the power will be present, they will be saved and become perfect and be worthy of the greatness and be purified in that place from all wickedness and involvements in evil. Then they have no other care than the incorruption alone, to which they direct their attention from here on, without anger or envy or jealousy or desire and greed of anything. They are not affected by anything except the state of being in the flesh alone, which they bear while looking expectantly for the time when they will be met by the receivers. Such then are worthy of the imperishable, eternal life and the calling.

Philo agrees. Although he values both the Aristotelian model of moderation and the Stoic doctrine of *apatheia*, he clearly considers the

---

[30] For Philo, see *Leg.* III.129–132, *Agr.* 10, and *Fug.* 82.

[31] For discussion of Philo's possible ascription of *eupatheia* to God (and the sage who seeks to be in His image), see John Dillon, "The Nature of God in the 'Quod Deus.'" in *Two Treatises of Philo of Alexandria.* Edited by David Winston and John Dillon. Brown Judaic Studies 25 (Chico, 1983), 217–227.

[32] See Henri-Charles Puech, *En quête de la gnose*, II, (Paris, 1978) 255–256.

[33] Michel Tardieu, *Écrits gnostique. Codex de Berlin.* (Paris, 1984) 332.

[34] II, 25.23–26.3.

latter to be the superior course. For example, in comparing Aaron with Moses, Philo opines that Aaron chooses an inferior, albeit good method to deal with the passions. According to Philo, "He curbs and controls it (passion), first by reason, that being driven by an excellent charioteer it may not get too restive; next he employs the virtues of speech, distinctness, and truth."[35] But Moses, says Philo, takes the better method. "He thinks it necessary to use the knife on the seat of anger in its entirety, and to cut it clean out of the soul, for no moderaton of passion can satisfy him; he is content with nothing but complete absence of passion (*apatheian*)."[36]

Another example illustrates Philo's preference for *apatheia* even more clearly:[37]

> ... only could that which is best in ourselves become capable of ministering before Him Who is Best of all Existences, if in the first place the man were resolved into soul, his brother body and its interminable cravings being broken off and cut in twain; if in the next place the soul rid itself, as I have said, of that neighbour of our rational element, the irrational, which like a torrent in five divisions pours through the channels of all the senses and rouses the violence of the passions; if in the next place the reasoning faculty sever and banish from itself that which has the appearance of being closest to it, the word of utterance. All this is to the end that the word or thought within the mind may be left behind by itself alone, destitute of body, destitute of sense-perception, destitute of utterance in audible speech; for when it has been thus left, it will live a life in harmony with such solitude, and will render, with nothing to mar or to disturb it, its glad homage to the Sole Existence.

Attainment to God means to leave behind the body with its senses and irrational passions, and even the capacity for audible speech.

Moreover, both Philo and the *Apocryphon of John* can speak of ethics in terms of combat, so that they have a tendency to treat persons dualistically as composed of a higher and a lower element in battle with each other.

The *Apocryphon of John* distinguishes souls on the basis of how well they succeed in this battle. As was noted above, the most blessed are those who have succeeded in defeating the passions completely.[38] The Berlin Codex notes that the blessed have no concern for the body, although they "make use of it" for a time until they are taken up.[39] But, according to the Berlin Codex, there are clearly others who, while they have not achieved such a perfect state of virtue (defeat of the passions), yet the Spirit has descended upon them. These have received the spirit when they were

---

[35] *Leg.* 128.
[36] *Leg.* 129.
[37] *Fug.* 91–92.
[38] See II, 25.23–26.1; compare *BG* 65.3–66.8. See also the discussion of the creation of the passions (*BG* 65.15–16; II, 18.14–34); Tardieu 1984, 313–316.
[39] *BG* 66.1.

born, but then the counterfeit spirit entered and seduced it so that the soul went astray.[40] These will nonetheless be saved because in the final calculation the power of the Spirit and the intervention of "imperishable oversight" will bring them to the "repose of the aeons."[41]

There are yet others who received the Spirit at birth, but never received any teaching at all about their true origins. In these, the counterfeit spirit has almost full sway: "it weighs down their soul and draws it to the works of wickedness, and thus brings it to oblivion."[42] But even such a soul will ultimately receive knowledge "and so become perfect and saved."[43]

Only those who received knowledge and then turned away, that is to say apostates, will undergo eternal punishment. No repentence is given to these souls, no doubt because apostasy is the ultimate treason.[44] This damnation of the apostate also points toward an interest in the internal order and integrity of the group. That order is based upon the level of spiritual power each person (soul) has achieved, corresponding to a person's virtue, that is, the degree to which each has overcome the passions associated with the body.[45]

Although the struggle of the soul is framed as a cosmic battle between the transcendent divine realm and the lower world, for the Gnostic it is played out primarily on the battleground of ethics. Knowledge of the true nature of oneself, the body, and the world is the basis for this ethical struggle.

At one point, Philo speaks of the soul's ethical struggles, in a manner quite close to that of the *Apocryphon of John,* as a battle of two powers at war in the self.[46]

---

[40] *BG* 67.1–14.

[41] *BG* 68.4–13.

[42] *BG* 69.2–5.

[43] *BG* 69.12–13.

[44] Here the text cites Matthew 12.31 which says that no insult against the Holy Spirit can be forgiven.

[45] Till writes that knowledge (*gnosis*) is the decisive issue. "Die Ethik, das richtige Verhalten, ist etwas Sekundäres, eine Folge der richtigen Erkenntnis, und stellt sich ganz von selbst ein" (Walter Till and Hans-Martin Schenke, *Die gnostischen Schriften des koptischen Papyrus Berolinensis 8502.* Texte und Untersuchungen 60, Berlin: 1972) 50–51. I think this assessment is not really accurate. The point is really that the two are not separable: the purpose of gaining knowledge is to overcome the passions. Yet both versions of the *Apocryphon of John* (*BG* and II) make it clear that even those who have knowledge succeed in their struggle to overcome the passions *only to varying degrees;* virtue does not simply come of itself as a result of correct knowledge.

[46] *QE* I, 23.

In every soul at birth there enter two powers (*dynameis*), the salutary and the destructive. If the salutary one is victorious and prevails, the ‰pposite one is too weak to <attack>.[47] And if the latter prevails, no profit at all or little is obtained from the salutary one. Through these powers the world too was created. People call them by other names: the salutary (power) they call powerful and beneficent, and the opposite one (they call) unbounded and destructive...Now, sometimes the evil becomes greater in this mixture, and hence (all creatures) live in torment, harm, ignominy, contention, battle and bodily illness together with all the other things in human life, as in the whole world, so in man. And this mixture is in both the wicked man and the wise man, but not in the same way. For the souls of foolish men have the unbounded and destructive rather than the powerful and salutary (power), and it is full of misery when it dwells with earthly creatures. But the prudent and noble (soul) rather receives the powerful and salutary (power) and, on the contrary, possesses in itself good fortune and happiness, being carried around with the heaven because of kinship (*syngeneian*) with it.

The similarity of this account to the *Apocryphon of John* is probably due to a common reliance upon traditions of interpretation of Plato's discussion of the soul in the *Laws*. There the Athenian establishes the existence of two souls which rule the universe, one which is beneficent, the other which is responsible for the contrary effect.[48] He identifies the first soul with intelligence; it is supremely good, moving according to one single law and plan. The other soul is its opposite; it results in "motion which has no order, plan, or law" but has "kinship with folly of every kind."[49] The first soul corresponds to wisdom, the second to folly. The text goes on, however, to state that human beings have both kinds of soul within them, although their formation is subject to human volition: a man comes to be just as his desires tend and as the soul conceives those desires.[50] A man's destiny follows as a consequence of his exercise of this free will:[51]

If a soul have drunk still deeper of vice or virtue, by reason of its own volition and the potent influence of past converse with others, when near contact with divine goodness has made it itself especially godlike, so surely is it removed to a special place of utter holiness, and translated to another and a better world, or in the contrary case, transported to live in the opposite realm.

It may be that Philo and the *Apocryphon of John* have both taken an interest in this passage or later interpretations of it. Both see two powers battling in men for governance of their souls, a good and an evil. Both understand the good power to be the divine Spirit. Both agree that these powers enter a

---

[47]   Here I follow the emendation of Ralph Marcus (trans.), *Philo Supplement*, I (Cambridge, MA, 1953) 33 n. a.

[48]   *Laws* 896e.

[49]   *Laws* 898 a–b.

[50]   *Laws* 904a–c.

[51]   *Laws* 904d–e.

person at birth. Both understand a person's destiny to be based upon which prevails. Both see the struggle as an ethical one. And, while both insist that only with the presence and aid of the divine Spirit can a person overcome the power of evil, both agree that human volition plays some role. In this matter, however, neither has worked out a clear formulation of the sticky problem of free will and providence (or determinism). According to John Dillon, this problem is one that all Middle Platonists share:[52]

> The Platonists' position maintained the autonomy of the will, in order to preserve the basis of ethical judgments... But yet every Platonist wished to maintain the doctrine of God's Providence. Without that, one would fall into Epicurean atheism, and once again there would be no objective basis for ethical judgments... The Platonists are thus caught in what is, if not a contradiction, at least a profound tension between free will and determinism.

One of Philo's primary emphases is the responsibility a person bears for his own evil acts; these can never be ascribed to the creator.[53] In *On Fleeing and Finding*, he presents a particularly coherent presentation of this issue. He begins by noting that the plural in Genesis 1:26 refers to agents acting with God in the creation of man. As was stated above, for Plato the Demiurge has the younger Gods help the Demiurge in the creation of man in order that the universe might be filled with every kind of thing. For Philo, as for the *Apocryphon of John*, the function of intermediaries in the creation of man has to do with protecting the highest God from charges of evil; that is, it is a matter of theodicy.[54]

> And He employed the powers that are associated with Him ... because, alone among created beings, the soul of man was to be susceptible of conceptions of evil things and good things, and to use one sort or the other, since it is impossible for him to use both. Therefore God deemed it necessary to assign the creation of evil things to other makers, reserving that of good things to Himself alone.

God himself made the "true man" (*aletheian anthropou*) who is absolutely pure mind (*nous*), while his powers (*dynameis*) made the "so-called" man who has an admixture of sense-perception.[55] It is therefore proper, Philo says, to give God responsibility (and thanks) for the good which humanity may do, but completely wrong to ascribe any responsibility to God for evil acts.[56]

---

[52]   See Dillon,1977, 168.
[53]   See *Deus* 47–48 and the discussion of David Winston, "Freedom and Determinism in Philo of Alexandria." *Studia Philonica* 3 (1974–75), 47–70.
[54]   *Fug.* 70.
[55]   *Fug.* 71–72.
[56]   *Fug.* 76–81.

This discussion elucidates Philo's allegorical interpretation of Moses' decrees about cities of refuge. Philo distinguishes among the souls that take refuge in God at the altar, those that take refuge in God at one of the appointed cities of refuge, and those that flee God.

The first souls are innocent.[57] They are free from even unintentional offense and abide in God alone.[58]

Those souls who take refuge in one of the appointed cities are those who have sinned unintentionally. They blame themselves for their sins, but seek God to purify them from their offenses.[59] Philo notes that there are six cities of refuge, each allegorically corresponding to one of God's powers. A person flees for refuge to these cities according to the person's own strength and receives the due reward.[60] These can be summarized as follows:

GOD'S POWER	REWARD FOR THE SOUL
Word and Wisdom	eternal life
Creator	the knowledge and love of God
Sovereign	fear of God
Mercy	hope of forgiveness
Lawgiver who enjoins duties	happiness
Lawgiver who forbids offenses	the averting of ills

The powers of God are arranged hierarchically, as are the rewards for the soul which takes refuge in them. Only the man who ascribes any evil to God is completely locked out from receiving any of God's gifts. These persons belong to Philo's third group.

The third group of souls are those who flee God, who do not seek any refuge with Him. They blame God for the sins they have themselves intentionally committed. For Philo, the ascription of any kind of wickedness to God is the worst offense possible: "it is a blemish that can hardly, if at all, be remedied, to assert that the Deity is the cause of evil things as of all others."[61] Such souls, says Philo, have chosen death[62] and are deserving of punishment.[63] Philo saves for these people the worst of his invective:[64]

---

[57] *Fug.* 80.
[58] *Fug.* 102.
[59] See *Fug.* 115.
[60] *Fug.* 97–98.
[61] *Fug.* 80.
[62] "And is it not life eternal to take refuge with Him that IS, and death to flee away from Him?" (*Fug.* 78).
[63] *Fug.* 80.
[64] *Fug.* 84.

(Moses) as good as proclaims in a loud voice that no pardon must be granted to a blasphemer against God. For if those who have reviled mortal parents are led away for execution (Exodus 21.15 ff.), what penalty must we consider that those have merited who take upon them to blaspheme the Father and Maker of the universe? And what more foul reviling could be uttered than the statement, that the origination of evil lies not at our door but at God's?

All such characters have made self-love their aim rather than love of God. Let them go forth outside the hallowed precincts, that in their foulness and uncleanness they may not behold even from afar the sacred flame of the soul ascending in unquenchable fire, and with power entire and unimpaired being sacrificed to God.[65]

The interpretation of the cities of refuge illustrates quite well the tension in Philo's thought between free will and God's providence. One perspective emphasizes the dependence of the created mortal upon God and the incapacity of a person to do any good apart from God. On the other hand, the issue of theodicy makes Philo emphasize human responsibility for evil. Even punishment is taken out of God's hands to ensure that no evil touches Him.[66]

An almost equal concern preoccupies the *Apocryphon of John*. There, too, it is emphasized, on the one hand, that the soul requires divine aid to escape evil and suffering. All punishment is administered at the hands of lower powers, the company of the demiurge, Yaltabaoth. The true Father above is protected from any charge of responsibility for evil. On the other hand, souls are held responsible for whether or not they turn away from the true God.

Politics and Power: Some Speculations

Philo and the *Apocryphon of John* are concerned with understanding the goal of humankind, salvation and ethics. In thinking out these issues, they can at points express surprisingly similar views of God,[67] of the

---

[65] *Fug.* 81.

[66] Moses "wishes to teach us that the nature of evil is far removed from the Divine Company, inasmuch as even the good thing which imitates evil, punishment, is ratified by others" (*Fug.* 74).

[67] Pearson has argued that the Gnostics split God into a "transcendent Deity ('Man') and a lower Creator," while, for Philo, "the Biblical God is the One transcendent God, Creator and Preserver of the universe and the only Savior" [Birger A. Pearson, "Philo and Gnosticism," *ANRW* II. 21.1 (1984), 339]. From this Pearson concludes: "Philo adheres to the Biblical view of the 'otherness' of God, whereas God is, for the Gnostics, 'Man' – which is to say that man himself is God!" (339). Here Pearson misunderstands the *Apocryphon of John*. It, too, describes the transcendence of God in terms quite similar to Philo (both are drawing upon similar traditions in Middle Platonism). The divine Gnostic "Man" functions as the perfect and transcendent

human self and the body, of free will and providence, and the need for revelation to aid the soul in coming to know God and obtain a likeness to Him. Their differences are often a matter of emphasis rather than real opposition. The *Apocryphon of John*, for example, is more negative toward the body and the cosmos than Philo. It tends to express its views more in terms of cosmology than ethics, while Philo does the reverse. But one can also point finally to their irreconcilable differences in the valuation of the creator God and Moses. To note such similarities and differences is perhaps simply to catalogue the obvious.

But, as was stated at the beginning, the body and the cosmos can be, so to speak, symbols to think with. What is at stake in the imagination of self and world, in where one locates the causes of human suffering and the paths to human salvation? Whether one chooses to call them philosophers or myth-makers, both Philo and the *Apocryphon of John* are engaged in the imaginative, intellectual enterprise of human culture-making.

In comparing the two, we can really only talk about variations within the complex strategical situation[68] of Hellenistic culture in the Roman colonies. Where to locate the rupture in (divine) order, the upheaval of values, the point where justice is restored, the power of the soul—all these can illustrate variations in strategy, processes of confrontation and resistence to perceived situations of suffering and injustice. The location of rupture and justice articulates strategies in the definition and location of power.

Where does Philo locate a rupture in divine order? With men who cannot rule themselves and who do not submit to God's rule, yet have political power and authority over others. Philo's primary examples are the disordered self, turned away from God and enslaved to its own passions, and particular Roman leaders, especially Flaccus and Gaius. A primary offense of all such persons is their arrogance.[69] Where does he

---

model for man below and is clearly distinquished from the transcendent Father. Hence the difference Pearson discerns between Philo and the Gnostics concerning salvation does not hold: both can refer to the spiritual aspect of man as "divine" (perhaps better translated "god-like") while yet affirming the transcendence of God. Moreover, both Philo and the *Apocryphon of John* affirm that humanity requires aid to discover God. For Philo that aid is given especially in the writings of Moses (given in God's descent on Mount Sinai, which Philo interprets as a special kind of voice in *Decal.* 32–35); for the *Apocryphon of John* it comes in the form of a divine revealer or spirit who descends from above and grants salvation in the form of knowledge inscribed in Gnostic revelation.

[68] The terminology here is that of M. Foucault. See *The History of Sexuality* I, (New York, 1980), 92–102.

[69] See Edwin R. Goodenough, *The Politics of Philo Judaeus. Practice and Theory*. (New Haven, 1938), 33–34.

locate the power for justice? In God's providential care of the cosmos and in the exalted teachings given through Moses.

Where does the *Apocryphon of John* locate the rupture of order? With the arrogant[70] world ruler who disobeys his divine betters[71] and claims to be the sole God, yet who, along with his minions, is illegitimately in control of the higher spiritual beings in the world, the Gnostics. Where does the text locate the power for justice? Beyond the cosmos, in the providential care of God and in the revelations of the saviors He sends into the world.

Philo and the *Apocryphon of John* locate disorder both (potentially) within the self and within the governing structures of the world (whether political or cosmic). Justice (salvation) ultimately derives from the conformity of the self to God and acceptance of his providential care.

What difference does it make where rupture and justice are located? For Philo and the *Apocryphon of John*, it may come down to the identity and the power of the self in the world.

Philo locates the rupture of divine order primarily within the moral order of the self. This position makes the moral self the seat of cosmic order and divine justice—an extremely powerful role for mortals to play. But this position allows him to critique Roman rule only insofar as individual Roman leaders have not achieved virtue and do not exercise justice. There is no place to criticize political power as such, or even Roman governance in general. Philo's view of God as Creator limits the range his political critique could extend. A radical critique would lead to despair, since it would deny Philo's basic premise of hope: that justice is located in God's creation and His care of the cosmos, including human society. The ethical discipline of *apatheia* provides one means whereby the self purposefully affirms that its existence lies in the hands of God and God's justice.

The *Apocryphon of John* achieves a wider and possibly more consistent critique of suffering and injustice, but it does so at the sacrifice of power for the self in the world. Hence, the *Apocryphon of John* speaks less of ethics than Philo, not because it countenances a greater acceptance of moral evil, but because ethics imply a purposefulness and power to human action that the *Apocryphon of John* does not experience. Ultimately, of course, the true spiritual self possesses power vastly beyond that of the limited world rulers. But for this life, the only position is complete rejection, a rejection symboled on the body in the *Apocryphon of John*'s ethic of passionlessness.

One might speculate upon the social location of such views. For Philo, the meaningfulness of existence is experienced within the community of

---

[70]   See *ApJohn* II,10.26; 13.5–9.
[71]   *ApJohn* II,12.9–10.

Judaism, a community that is under the often unjust hegemony of Roman government. The seeming contradictions of Philo's thought, the limits he places upon challenging the goodness of God (for example, in placing the soul in the body or in placing the Jews under Roman power), are congruent with the ambiguous social situation of Philo himself: both leader (within Judaism) and subject (of Roman rule). It is simply not safe to challenge certain locations of power, such as expressing direct opposition to Roman rule. But his intellectual system effectively subordinates Roman power to the Jewish God (and Jewish law)—an effective counter-stroke and point of resistance. Meanwhile, the Jewish community can criticize the Romans, but it must look to a solution within itself, by making itself obedient to God and accepting his providence. In taking this position, Philo locates the power for salvation and justice within the self while at the same time advocating a certain passivity with regard to sometimes less-than-just social-political conditions. The power for true participation in the rule of the cosmos is located, not in political rule, but in the soul turned toward God. Such a position might militate greatly against relative political powerlessness.

For the *Apocryphon of John*, community with others is created through the common rejection of—not merely resistence to—the meaningfulness of existence under the current hegemony, and the utopian desire for unalloyed purity and power. This text takes a decidedly more critical and more intellectually negative stance toward the world of power and politics than does Philo. We can speculate that its description of the powerlessness of the self in the face of illegitimate oppression expresses accurately how the Gnostics of the *Apocryphon of John* perceived their situation.

In the end, we learn perhaps little about the social realities of life in the Roman world by reading Philo or the *Apocryphon of John,* for they have overlaid their desires and their complaints upon the face of the world and the body. Yet their intellectual endeavors show us the importance of the religious imagination and the moral life in working out the integrity and power of the self in situations of ambiguity and powerlessness.

THE CATEGORIES OF BEING IN MIDDLE PLATONISM:

Philo, Clement, and Origen of Alexandria

ROBERT M. BERCHMAN

Introduction

1. *The Problem*

The categories may justifiably be regarded as among the Cinderellas of Platonic studies. Clothed in the unattractive terminological garb of absolute and relative, essential and accidental, necessary and contingent, they cannot meet the attractions of their more glamorous sisters, the first principles and the ideas. So in practice they have been relegated to the kitchen of scholarly enterprises.

This is a great pity. Certainly, even in the unlikely event that the fairy godmother should wave her wand and the categories should find their place in the palace alongside noetic triads and divine ideas, the desultory form and arcane procedure of their presentation would remain a drawback. Nonetheless, the categories have an intrinsic value of their own. It is gradually emerging that they provide us with important information on a constellation of concepts and problems in later Platonic metaphysics.

In recent years there has been a growth of interest in the category theories of Hellenic Platonism.[1] Most of this interest has focused on the fragments of Xenocrates and Hermadorus[2] and the writings of Seneca,[3] Plotinus, Porphyry, and Boethius.[4] Little interest has been

---

[1] It is W. Theiler who deserves credit for bringing the categories to the attention of students of the history of philosophy: *Die Vorbereitung des Neuplatonismus* (Berlin, 1930) and *Die Forschungen zum Neuplatonismus* (Berlin, 1964). Also see J. Dillon, *The Middle Platonists* (London, 1977).

[2] Dillon, *op. cit.*, 8; R. Heinze, *Xenocrates. Darstellung der Lehre und Sammlung der Fragmente* (Leipzig, 1892) fr. 12; Simp., *In Phys.* 247.30 ff. Diels.

[3] S. Gersh, *Middle Platonism and Neoplatonism: The Latin Tradition* (Notre Dame, 1986) 181–188; cf. E. Bickel, "Senecas *Briefe* 58 und 65. Das Antiochus-Posidonius Problem," *Rhein. Mus.* 103 (1960) 1–20; Theiler *op. cit.* 1932 and 1964; G. Scarpat, *La Lettera 65 di Seneca* (Brescia, 1970) 103 ff. Dillon, *op. cit.*, 135 ff. ap. Seneca, *Ep.* 58, 65.

[4] The bibliography on Plotinus, Porphyry, and Boethius on the categories is immense. See R.E. Witt, *Albinus and the History of Middle Platonism* (Cambridge, 1932), 38 ff.; A. Graeser, *Plotinus and the Stoics: A Preliminary Study* Philosophia Antiqua 22

shown in the category theories of Christian Platonism.[5]

The present study intends to examine a series of category theories from Hellenic and Christian Middle Platonism. A glance at the remains of these later Platonisms shows that a comprehensive discussion of all the aspects of this theme would far exceed the limits set for such a paper as this. Consequently, we shall bring only so much material as seems necessary to establish our thesis.

The thesis of this study is that shifts in Platonic interpretations of the Aristotelian and Stoic categories begins in earnest with Antiochus, Eudorus, Seneca, and Philo Judaeus. It culminates with Clement and Origen. Their acceptance of the efficacy of these categories is based to a high degree on attempts to solve a series of metaphysical problems.

For our purposes it must suffice that one problem be introduced and a representative sample of solutions be presented. The results gained permit us to draw some general observations about later Platonic category theory and to propose some specific conclusions about the categories in Christian Middle Platonism.

2. *Method*

To understand the thought of a thinker, to penetrate to problems and to grasp arguments used to solve problems, it is necessary to choose a method to guide us. This can be done straightforwardly. John Passmore has provided us with a concise methodological model. It is called "problematic elucidation".[6]

The "elucidatory problematic" of the categories was generated by a series of paradigmatic postulates from the *Timaeus*[7] and the first two hypotheses from the *Parmenides*.[8] Wide ranging and comprehensive discussions circled around the paradigmatic theology and cosmology and the question of ontological unity and plurality.[9]

(Leiden, 1972); C. Evangeliou, "The Ontological Basis of Plotinus' Criticism of Aristotle's Theory of Categories" in *The Structure of Being: A Neoplatonic Approach* ed. by R. B. Harris, (New York, 1982), 73–82. Ap. Plotinus, *Enn.*, 6.13; Porphyry, *In Cat.*, 64–67; *Isagoge.*, passim; Simplicius, *In Cat.* 1.19 ff.; cf. 402.12 ff; 156.16 ff; 388.4 ff; Boethius, *In Cat.*, passim.

[5] See R.M. Berchman, *From Philo to Origen: Middle Platonism in Transition*, Brown Judaic Studies 69 (1984), s.v. categories.

[6] See J. Passmore, "The Idea of a History of Philosophy," *History and Theory* Supplement 5 (1965) 1–32. This approach has been applied to Christian Platonism. Cf. E.F. Osborn, *The Beginnings of Christian Philosophy* (Cambridge, 1981). For critique of this method see D.T. Runia, *Philo of Alexandria and the Timaeus of Plato* (Amsterdam, 1983) 46.

[7] Cf. *Tim.* 27d–28e; 29b; 48e.

[8] Cf. *Parm.* For the first hypothesis see 137d–e; 138a; 139b–c; 140b, d; 141a, e. For the second hypothesis see 144b; 145a, b, e; 146a.

[9] A glance at any index of the use of Platonic passages from Middle and Neoplatonic

These passages raised the issue of the relation between an uncreated
God and a created universe, between a perfect unitary God and an imper-
fect, pluralistic cosmos.[10] Moreover, they compelled Platonists to address a
constellation of related issues. Chief among these was the relationship
between first principles; between first principles and intelligibles; and
between intelligibles and sensibles.

A. Hillary Armstrong provides us with a concise historical assessment
of this "elucidatory problematic" in later Platonism.[11] He shows that one
controversy dominated later Platonic metaphysics. Controversy circled
around the issue of theological *apophaticism* and *kataphaticism.*

Armstrong points out that Platonists before Plotinus did not make full
use of an *apophatic* theology which proposes a God beyond being and
intelligence.[12] Although the transcendence of God is stressed, a purely
apophatic theology of a God beyond being *and* intelligence is rarely
utilized. Rather a *apophatic-kataphatic* theology is stressed which associates
God with being and intelligence.

Some Platonists cast their demiurgic theologies in apophatic form,
relating God to cosmos paradigmatically—as creator to created, as image
to copy. However, for other Platonists an *apophatic* theology runs the risk of
severing God from creation, thereby establishing a *chorismos* between
deity and cosmos. Conscious of this risk they were adverse to a purely
apophatic theology. In its place they proposed an *apophatic-kataphatic*
theology. This insured a *methexis* between deity and cosmos.

3. *The Evidence*

A comprehensive discussion of all the evidence related to these issues
would far exceed the limits set for this paper. Nonetheless, it is helpful to
sketch a typology of Middle Platonisms and Middle Platonic positions on
the relation between first principles, intelligibles, and sensibles.

First, there was Reinforced Platonism with its *apophatic* metaphysic.
Neopythagoreans and Gnostics postulated a radically transcendent God,
distinct from the universe. They saw the universe as the creation of a

---

sources illustrates that these passages were widely discussed. Cf. E.R. Dodds, "The
Parmenides of Plato and the Origin of the Neoplatonic One," *CQ* 22 (1928) 129–142,
on the use of the *Timaeus* and the *Parmenides* by later Platonists to construct first principles and a cosmology.

[10] See Cornford, *Plato's Cosmology: Plato's Timaeus* (New York, 1952) 110–111; 160–161;
243.

[11] Following A.H. Armstrong, "Beauty and Discovery of Divinity in the Thought of
Plotinus" *Kephalaion. Studies in Greek Philosophy and its Continuation offered to C.J. de Vogel.*
ed. J. Mansfield and L.M. de Rijk (Assen, 1975) 77–89.

[12] *Ibid.*, 77–80.

lower God or as a cosmos formed from a substance distinct from God. Their goal was to disassociate the eternal and the immutable from the temporal and mutable. There was no direct relationship between an uncreated God and creation, between an absolute and derivative reality.

Second, there was Modified Platonism with its *apophatic-kataphatic* metaphysic. Stoicizing and Peripateticizing Platonists postulated a transcendent God likened to the universe. They saw the universe as the creation of this God or a lower God and as a cosmos formed from either an analogous substance or from the same substance as God. Their goal was to associate the eternal and the immutable with the temporal and the mutable. The relationship between an uncreated God and creation was one between an absolute and a dependent reality.

Reinforced Platonists postulated two basic categories. The Absolute and the Relative categories functioned to divide two distinct degrees of reality. The Peripatetic and Stoic categories have no referential efficacy to Absolute being. They only have reference to Accidental becoming. Hence, there are only accidental categories.

Reinforced Platonists proposed a *choristic* categorical *realism, nominalism,* and *conceptualism.* The categories refer to sensible things; they refer to words which signify sensible things; and they refer to words which signify sensible concepts about physical things. The categories never refer to first principles, or to intelligibles, or to uncreated things. They refer only to sensibles and to matter, to created things.

Modified Platonists postulated two basic categories. The Absolute and Relative categories functioned to divide two analogous degrees of reality. The Peripatetic and Stoic categories have referential efficacy to Absolute and to Relative being. Hence, there are both essential and accidental categories. Therefore, Modified Platonists held a *pragmatic* interpretation of the categories.

Modified Platonists were proponents of categorical pragmatism. They proposed a *methetic* categorical *realism, nominalism,* and *conceptualism.* The categories refer to intelligible and sensible things; they refer to words which signify intelligible and sensible things; and they refer to concepts which signify intelligible and sensible things. The categories refer to first principles and to intelligibles, to both the uncreated and created realms.

Each trajectory proposes a category theory. Each category theory is formulated within the context of a distinct metaphysical model. Between the first century B.C.E. and the third century C.E. Platonists debated a problem and their use of the categories elucidates our problematic.

The chief means of access to this debate is through an examination of the evidence culled from Xenocrates, Aristotle, and the Stoa. Next, Eudorus, Seneca, and Philo provide us with examples from early Middle Platonic

category theory. Finally, we conclude with an examination of the later
Middle Platonic category theories of Clement and Origen of Alexandria.

Such an agenda requires a brief summary of the character and development of category theory and interpretation before Middle Platonism.

I

The Categories in Early Platonism

How the categories were interpreted by Platonists has a long history.[13] In a
complex tradition such as Platonism we encounter not merely one attitude
towards the categories or even a consensus about their meaning and
function. Indeed, between Xenocrates and Porphyry arose an extended
range of subtle category interpretations.[14]

We must differentiate between distinct epochs, schools. We must
attempt to clarify the thematic relationship between the Platonic doctrines
of the categories and other concomitant doctrines concerning reality and
knowledge. As a starting point for our inquiry, it is useful to begin with
Plato and his cosmological and epistemological observations. From this
beginning we can trace a map of a philosophical system's understanding
of the meaning and function of the categories.

Although there is little evidence that Plato proposed a theory of the
categories, his dialogues were mined by his students to build such a
theory.[15] From the paradigmatic epistemology and cosmology of the
Timaeus early Platonists constructed a variety of category theories.[16] Most
likely Platonic category doctrine emerged in the Old Academy as a
response to doctrines proposed by the Lyceum and the Porch.[17] From the
five genera of the *Sophist*, Platonists, beginning with Plotinus, would build
new category theories. Neoplatonic category doctrine emerged as a
response to doctrines proposed by Plotinus and Porphyry.[18]

Hermadorus claims such a theory for Plato.[19] He says Plato operated
with the basic categories of Absolute and Alio-Relative with the latter
category being subdivided into Opposite and Relative, which were

---

[13] See Dillon, *op. cit.*, 8, 37, 133 ff., 178 ff., 180, 226, 234 ff., 262, 279, 342–343.
[14] See Theiler, *op. cit.* 1932 and 1964; Witt, *op. cit.* ; H. J. Kraemer, *Der Ursprung der
Geistmetaphysik.* (Amsterdam, 1967); T. A. Szlezak, *Platon und Aristoteles in der Nuslehre
Plotins.* (Basel, 1979).
[15] See Evangeliou, *op. cit.* 1982, 73–75.
[16] *Ibid.*, 73–82. Also see Dillon, *op. cit.*, 9.
[17] See Theiler, *op. cit.* 1932 and 1964, 3–15; Bickel, *op. cit.*; Scarpat, *op. cit.*, 103 ff.;
Dillon, *op. cit.*, 8, 135–137; Gersch, *op. cit.*, 181–188.
[18] Evangeliou, *op. cit.*, 73–82.
[19] Ap. Simplicius, *In Phys.*, 247.30 ff. Diels.

subdivided into Definite and Indefinite. He does not base his claim on the evidence of the dialogues but asserts these categories can be discerned by a careful reading of the master.[20]

Xenocrates recognizes two basic categories.[21] They are the Absolute and Relative. The categories Absolute and Relative rest on a distinction between degrees of knowing and degrees of reality which Xenocrates infers from the paradigmatic epistemology and cosmology of the *Timaeus*.

Xenocrates frames his theory in the context of Aristotelian category theory. This appears highly probable since he concludes his discussion by claiming the two categories of Plato render the ten categories of Aristotle nugatory.[22] Why this is so, at least from a Platonic perspective, will be examined shortly. In the interim we shall examine the category theories of the Lyceum and the Porch. For Academic category theory emerges as a response to definitions and classifications of reality, know-ledge, and logic implicit in these Aristotelian and Stoic doctrines.

Aristotle introduced a list of categories and developed the first doctrine of categories in ancient philosophy. Later Xenocrates, Hermadorus, Zeno, Chrysippus, and Cleanthes proposed different lists of categories. Moreover, they developed a distinct categorical doctrines from those of the Peripatos. Consequently, as a starting point for our inquiry, then, we begin with a brief sketch of category theory in the Lyceum and the Stoa.

Aristotle proposed ten categories and his use of them includes logical, linguistic, and ontological functions.[23] The categories are being, quantity, quality, relation, place, time, position, possession, activity, and passivity. They represent an exhaustive classification of the ways in which we think, speak, and refer to things. In the Old and New Lyceums the categories maintain these interpretations and functions.

The basic ideas of Aristotle's *Categories* can be stated simply. First, there are individuals such as person, horse, or house. Such individuals are primary substances. Second, these individuals have qualities. These qualities are present in primary substances.

To predicate a quality of an individual requires terms which are general. They cannot exist independently or apart from individuals. Thus, we have a distinction between primary substances and accidents, viz., substances and qualities "present in" substances. It is also a distinction between subjects and predicates, things we say of subjects.

---

[20] See Dillon, *op. cit.*, 8.
[21] Cf. R. Heinze, fr.12.
[22] Cf. Dillon, *op. cit.*, 37.
[23] Following J. Owens, *The Doctrine of Being in Aristotelian Metaphysics* (Toronto, 1951) for Aristotle. For the New Lyceum, see P. Moraux, *Der Aristotelismus bei den Griechen: von Andronikos bis Alexander von Aphrodisias* (Berlin, 1973–1984).

Individual or particular substances not only have qualities but they can be grouped into kinds of substances. What is predicated of individual substances tell us what kind of individual substance a particular substance is. The idea of kinds of substances is absolutely vital to his category theory.

For Aristotle the word genus is derived from genesis, meaning birth, so that the source of secondary substances is related to kinds of things which are generated or created. The most important things predicated of an individual are its genus and species. This gives us its essence. They tell us what an individual is; they tell us what kind of individual it is. The other things we predicate of a primary substance do not tell us what kind of thing it is. So there are two types of predicates; (1) those which tell us the kind of thing each individual thing is; and (2) those which do not. Secondary substances tell us what a thing is essentially; the other predicates tell us what a substance is accidentally.

Following Aristotle we have a major distinction between substances and accidents— between individuals and what is present in them. We have a distinction between substances themselves: individual substances (primary substances) and kinds of substances (secondary substances). Genera and species which group individual substances into various kinds of substance and accidents are predicated of primary substances. But only genera and species give us what is essential to a primary substance—that is what a primary substance must have in order to be that particular kind of reality.

There are ten categories. Primary and secondary substances make up the first of the ten categories. Those attributes which are present in primary substances are grouped into nine categories according to their similarities. The nine categories are the most general kinds of predicate terms or classes of predicates. Thus, Aristotle makes the distinction between that which is essential and that which is accidental.

In the *Metaphysics* Aristotle says that the categories are the senses in which a thing may be said to be. For example, a substance means an individual substance; in another sense, substance means what a thing is; in still another sense it means a thing is of such and such a quality, quantity, relation, etc. However, to be an individual (primary) substance is the fundamental sense of being. There are kinds of substances only because there are individual substances: and good or sitting must be said of what is good or sitting. Consequently, that which is primarily and simply is primary substance.

The four Stoic categories represent a series of headings for analyzing and describing the two constituents of reality—*pneuma* and *hyle*, as well as their interrelations.[24] Substance, form, variety, and variety of relation are sufficient for the definition of things and the words which signify things.[25]

The first category is substrate or substance and it refers to matter. The second category is qualification. Matter always exists with qualification, since it is permeated by *pneuma*. Being and qualification are general predicates which characterize anything that exists. These categories refer to the permanent substrate and qualification of a thing.

The third category, being in a certain state or disposition, describes any differentiation as *pneuma* in a certain state. This category refers to the temporary and not the permanent characteristics of a thing. Disposition describes a material object at a certain time and place as being somewhere, at sometime, acting, having a certain size or color.

The fourth category is relative disposition. It refers to the properties a thing has in reference to another thing. It is used to analyze the extent to which one thing is different from or is dependent upon something else. Since all parts of the universe are related to one another by the *pneuma* which pervades them, it appears that relative disposition describes the working of cosmic sympathy in things. In a system where all things are interdependent the definition of specific relationships and dependencies is an important categorical function.

The Stoic categories refer to things and the words which signify things. Whether the categories refer to concepts is not altogether clear. Thus, in the early Stoicism the categories have an ontological and a logical function.

The study of the meaning and function of the categories in Aristotelianism and Stoicism stands apart from a study of Platonic category theory. Nonetheless, how Platonists interpreted these categories requires examination.

Early Platonic assessments of the meaning, function, and value of the Peripatetic and Stoic categories rest on Plato's judgement in the *Timaeus* that there are two realms of reality, intelligible being and sensible becoming,[26] and two categories that refer to these degrees of reality—one Absolute and the other Relative.[27] Absolute Being is devoid of all

---

[24] Stoic category theories are difficult to reconstruct. See, J.M. Rist, *Stoic Philosophy* (Cambridge, 1969) 152–172. Cf. P. De Lacy, "The Stoic Categories as Methodological Principles," *Proceedings of the American Philological Association* 76 (1945), 146–163; B. Mates, *Stoic Logic* (Berkeley, 1953) 32 ff.; M. Reesor, "The Stoic Categories," *AJP* 78 (1957), 63–82.

[25] Cf. Rist, *op. cit.*,152–172.

[26] Cf.*Tim.*, 27d–28e; cf. 29b; 48e.

[27] Cf. Xenocrates, fr. 12 Heinze.

categorical reference. Relative Being is not. Consequently, Platonists subsumed the Peripatetic and Stoic categories under the category of Relative Being. They refer to the sensible world, not to the intelligible world.

Since early Platonists worked largely from the *Timaeus* to build a category theory, reality is divided into Being and Becoming and the two realms are related to each other as pattern (*paradeigma*) to image (*eikon*). Xenocrates rigorously maintained this ontological distinction to argue that the categories are applicable to things in nature alone. They have no reference to being or to anything beyond being.[28]

In summary, early Platonists generally promote a rigorous ontological interpretation of the categories. They assume the categories refer to things alone. They reject the view of Peripatetics and Stoics that the categories also refer to things which may be known and classified, or to words which signify things.

This is clear from Xenocrates. He divides knowledge into three types— *episteme, aisthesis,* and *doxa*—relating knowledge to the apprehension of the ideas, perception to the grasp of sense objects below the moon, and opinion to the cognition of sense objects in the celestial realm.[29] Consequently, categorical knowledge and classification yield a knowledge of the sensible things alone. Such knowledge is merely aesthetic or doxastic. It is not epistemic and could never lead to an apprehension of intelligible things.[30]

II

The Categories in Early Middle Platonism

Andronicus of Rhodes in the first century B.C.E. presented a new edition of the Aristotelian writings. Shortly after its appearance numerous commentaries emerged devoted to a criticism of Aristotle's *Categories.* Platonists were at the center of this category debate. Platonic category theory takes two trajectories.

The first is a negative, hostile reinforced Platonic position which admits an ontological function for the categories but no epistemological or logical reference for the categories. The "Pythagorizing" Platonist Archytas maintains this realist attitude towards the categories.[31] Later Nicostratus

---

[28] See Dillon, *op. cit.,* 8.
[29] Cf. Aristotle, *De Anima,* 1.2, 404b16 ff.; cf. *Laws,* 10.894a.
[30] See Dillon, *op. cit.,* 6.
[31] H. Thesleff, *The Pythagorean Texts of the Hellenistic Period* (Abo, 1965), 22.31; 31.5. Cf. T.A. Szlezak, *Pseudo-Archytas Uber die Katagorien* (Berlin, 1972).

and Plotinus will argue the *realist* thesis that the categories have referential efficacy to the sensible world alone.[32]

The second is a positive, constructive "modified" Platonic position which proposes not only an ontological function for the categories but also an epistemological and logical reference for the categories. The "Pythagorizing" Platonist Eudorus and the "Stoicizing" Platonists Seneca and Philo Judaeus maintain this pragmatic attitude toward the categories.[33] Later Clement and Origen of Alexandria will argue the *pragmatic* thesis that the categories have referential efficacy to the intelligible and sensible worlds.[34]

The "problematic elucidation" of the meaning and function of these category doctrines is important for understanding developments in later Platonic theology and physics.[35] *Pragmatic* category theories form the basis of the *apophatic-kataphatic* metaphysics and epistemology of much of Hellenic, Latin, and Christian Middle Platonism, and Latin Christian Neoplatonism, while *realist* category theories form the basis of the *apophatic* metaphysics and epistemology of much of Hellenic Neoplatonism and Christian Neoplatonism.

Christian Platonists were involved in the "problematic elucidation" of the categories in the Middle and Neoplatonic periods. Indeed, Christian category theories were instrumental in the formulation of an *apophatic-kataphatic* metaphysical trajectory for Platonism from late antiquity through the middle ages in the Greek East and the Latin West.

The origins of this *pragmatic* trajectory lies in the early Middle Platonic metaphysics of Eudorus of Alexandria and Seneca. It is to these figures we now turn.

Eudorus of Alexandria

The best entrance, perhaps, into Eudorus' doctrine of categories is through his first principles. For in his theoretic he postulates three principles and employs the terms unqualified and qualified as classificatory markers to distinguish the principles from one another.[36]

Eudorus postulates three principles: The One, the Monad, and the Dyad. The One is above all qualification, the Monad is qualified, and the Dyad is

---

[32] See Dillon, *op. cit.*, 133–135; 233–236. ap. Simpl., *In Phys.*, 206.10 ff; 248.2; cf. Nicostratus, ap. Simpl., *In Cat.*, 1.19 ff.; 156.16 ff.; 402.12 ff.; 429.13 ff.

[33] For Seneca see P. Hadot, *Porphyre et Victorinus* (Paris, 1968) 156–163. Cf. Gersch, *op. cit.*,181–186. For Eudorus, see Dillon, *op. cit.*, 133–135.

[34] See Berchman, *op. cit.*, s.v. categories.

[35] Following Dillon, *op. cit.*, 126 ff.

[36] See Dodds, *op. cit.*, 135 ff. Cf. Dillon, *op. cit.*, 126–129.

unqualified. The One is an Intellect beyond intellection; the Monad is a thinking intellect; and the Dyad is non-intellective matter.[37]

Eudorus makes the first One the causal principle of Matter and of all created things.[38] The second One is the archetype of Form or Limit, the Dyad the archetype of Matter or Unlimit. The first One employs the second One as a demiurgic instrument who works upon Matter to produce the transcendent ideas which, as reason principles, create the material universe.[39]

This *kataphatic* theology and cosmology is a most fruitful development for later Platonism.[40] Not only is the first One the cause of all things (the second One, the maker of all things, and the Dyad, the material of all things) but each of the principles has categorical reference. The first One represents substance; the second One quality and relation; and the Dyad is equivalent to quantity.

For the first time in Platonism the categories are associated with first principles and the ideas immanent in the physical world. However, this association is a nominalist not a realist association.

The *kataphatic* association between principles and categories is clearly a logical one.[41] For in his rearrangement of the Aristotelian categories Eudorus puts quality after substance, then quantity, and then 'where and when' which he associated with space and time.[42] This association has the following structure:

First One	=	Substance
Second One	=	Quality, Relation
Dyad	=	Quantity
Ideas	=	Where, When, Space, Time, etc.

The One represents substance and the Monad and Dyad quality and quantity. Quality refers to Form (Logos) which imposes itself on quantity (Matter) to create the ideas and the cosmos. Relation refers to Form (Logos) immanent in the world.[43] Consequently, the causal, demiurgic,

---

[37] Ap. Simpl., *In Phys*, 181.10 ff. Cf. Syrianus, *Com. In Metaphys.*, 112.14 Kroll.

[38] This is shown in his emendation to Aristotle's *Met.* 988 10–11 where he makes the One the cause of matter as well as the ideas. Cf. Dillon, *op. cit.*, 128, n. 1.

[39] Eudorus' doctrine of ideas is not recorded. Some have argued his doctrine is derived from Arius Didymus, cf. H. Diels, *Doxographi Graeci.* (Berlin, 1892), 447. If so, the Idea is an eternal substance, cause and first principle of each thing as it is; it has reference to natural entities not to artificial creations. Cf. ap. Eusebius, *PE* 11.23. For a critique of this interpretation see, Dillon, *op. cit.*, 128 n. 2.

[40] It is reproduced by Albinus, see, *Did.*, 12. Cf. Dillon, *op. cit.*, 269.

[41] Eudorus holds an animus against a *realist* use of the Aristotelian categories. Cf. ap. Simplicius, *In Cat.*, 174.14 ff. ad *Cat.*, 6a 36.

[42] Cf. ap. Simplicius, *In Cat.*, 206.10 ff.

[43] *Ibid.*, 135.

and formative activities of the first principles are definable through a logical use of the categories.

Although the categories have no ontological reference beyond the sensible realm, they have logical reference to the intelligible and sensible realms. Although Eudorus' first principles are not associated with qualified existence in any *realist* sense, they are associated with the qualified existence in a *pragmatic* sense.[44]

By combining *apophatic* realism with *kataphatic* pragmatism Eudorus is able both to distinguish and to link an uncreated God with a created universe. This is accomplished through an intermediary—the Form or Logos—who creates, informs and sustains matter. This principle stands as intermediary between unqualified and qualified existence, and unqualified non-existence. The *apophatic* dimensions of his category theory requires clarification.

Although Eudorus' categorical *pragmatism* is decidedly *kataphatic* his categorical *realism* is clearly *apophatic*. He makes an ontological distinction between an unqualified, first noetic One, a qualified second noetic One, and unqualified matter. Unqualified being characterizes the first One, qualified being characterizes the second One, and unqualified non-being characterizes dyadic matter.[45] The structure of Eudorus' first principles is the following:

Monas (*apoios*)

Monad (*poios*)

Dyad (*apoios*)

It is possible that Eudorus is influenced by the first two hypotheses of the *Parmenides* and that this dialogue frames the context of his first principles.[46]

Eudorus adopts the Old Academic categories of the Absolute and the Relative.[47] Unqualified being is subsumed under the category of the Absolute, qualified being under the category of the Relative and unqualified matter under non-Being.[48] Until matter is qualified by form the categories have no reference to the Dyad. Matter initially refers to non-being and

---

[44] See Dillon, *op. cit.*, 133 ff.
[45] Cf. Simpl. *In Phys.*, 181.10 ff. Here Eudorus, at least according to Simplicius, postulates a first One and below that a pair of opposites called Monad and Dyad. The Monad represents Form, the Dyad Matter. This first One is both the causal principle of matter and created things, that is, of the dyad and the monad.
[46] Cf. Dodds, *op. cit.*, 135 ff.
[47] Cf. Xenocrates, fr. 12 Heinze.
[48] Cf. ap. Simplicius, *In Cat.*, 174. 14 ff.

has no categorical reference. Once it is formed, matter has reference to the relative categories. Consequently, the structure of Eudorus' reality system is:

Absolute Being

Relative Being

Non-Being

Eudorus makes a distinction between absolute being, relative being, and non-being. The dividing line in this degree of reality system is between "bare existence" on the one hand, and "qualified existence" and "unqualified-nonexistence" on the other.

This means that reality is tri-partite and this division is represented by subsuming "unqualified existence" under the category of Absolute being, "qualified-existence" under the category of Absolute being, "qualified-existence" under the category of Relative being and "unqualified non-existence" under the category of Nonbeing.

Absolute Being
(Intelligibles)

Relative Being
(Sensibles)

Nonbeing
(Matter)

In this scheme the Peripatetic categories do not refer to the first One, absolute being for it is beyond qualification. They refer to Form and Matter, relative being for it is qualified. They do not refer to Matter or non-being. Thus, the ten categories have no real reference to the intelligible or meontic realms. They only have real reference to the sensible world:

Absolute Being

Relative Being
(10 Peripatetic Categories)

Nonbeing

Although Eudorus' category scheme reflects premises formulated in Early Platonism, it also reflects developments common to Middle Platonism.

First, he maintains the Old Academic categories of the Absolute and the Relative.

Second, he asserts that the Peripatetic categories have no efficacy to Absolute being but he admits their efficacy to Relative being. Both postulates are linked to his classificatory distinction between unqualified and qualified being and unqualified non-being.

Third, this distinction permits a use for the Peripatetic categories in a Platonic reality system. This is clearly a new development in Platonic category theory, which points toward the possibility for a wider logical use of the categories.

In summary, Eudorus is an advocate of a *realist* approach to the categories. He is representative of a "Reinforced" Platonic interpretation of the categories. However, his category theory also suggests a *pragmatic* use of the categories which is representative of a "Modified" Platonic interpretation of the categories reflecting the *apophatic-kataphatic* mixture of an emerging Middle Platonic category theory.

He argues that there are two distinct degrees of reality. The categories have no reference to unqualified being. Thus they cannot be used to analyze and classify Absolute Being.

He proposes that the categories have reference to qualified being. Thus they can be used to analyze and classify Relative Being.

However, he also associates his first principles with the categories: Monas with substance; Monad with quality and relation; and the Dyad with quantity. Furthermore, the ideas-numbers, once instantiated in matter, permit the definition and classification of the sensibles through the use of the remaining categories.

It is a short step from Eudorus to invest the categories with wider pragmatic efficacy and to imbue them with greater pragmatic significance. Since this new category configuration emerges in Seneca and finds acceptance in Philo, Clement, and Origen, it deserves attention.

Seneca

The category scheme of Epistula 58 is important.[49] Seneca begins by exploring the possible Latin translations of the Greek terms *ousia* and *on*.[50] The first he translates as a substantive—*essentia*; the second into the verbal

---

[49]   For a discussion of Seneca's category theory see Theiler, *op. cit.* 1932, 1964; Bickel, *op. cit.*, 1–20 ; Hadot, *op. cit.*, 156–163; Scarpat, *op. cit.*, 94–101; Dillon, *op. cit.*, 135–139; Gersch, *op. cit.*, 181–186.

[50]   Cf. *Ep.*, 58, 6–8.

form—*quod est*. *Essentia* refers to the substratum which underlies all material things. *Quod est* refers to a six-fold classification of genus and species, and *quid* refers to the most generic category.

Seneca begins by discussing the meaning of the terms genus and species.[51] This is accomplished by ascending from the lowest species to the highest genus or from highest genus to lowest species. Next he comments that certain Stoics postulate another genus prior to those mentioned in his illustrations. This is *quid = ti* , which for some Stoics precedes the genus *quod est = on*. This addition has important significance.

Seneca uses the Stoic categories *quid, quod est,* and *essentia* for a definition and classification of being.

Quid refers to the most generic something beyond qualification;[52] *quod est* refers to the qualification of *esssentia* into genus and species.[53] For Seneca these categories are a series of headings for analyzing and describing the constituents of reality and their interrelations.[54]

This is clear from his use of the term *quod est.* He informs us that Plato understands it in six ways.[55] It signifies: (1) "that which is generic," such as universal man; (2) it means "that which stands out and surpasses everything else," such as Homer among poets and God among the class of existents; (3) "things really existing," which refer to the transcendent ides; (4) "forms," which refer to the immanent ideas; (5) "things which exist," such as men, cattle, property; and (6) "things which are quasi-existent," such as void and time.

It appears that class (i) refers to the Stoic category "most generic", this means to universal concepts such as man or God which are apprehended by thought alone; class (ii) refers to the Stoic category "substratum" wherein individual things correlate to their generic universals, and where thought relates a universal, e.g., poet, to a specific poet, viz., Homer; class (iii) refers to the Stoic category "quality" or the transcendent forms; class (iv) refers to the Stoic category "state" or the immanent forms; class (v) to the Stoic category "relation" or the relation of immanent forms to their transcendent archetypes; and class (vi) refers to things which are "quasi-existent," such as void and time, which are clearly the Stoic incorporeals (*asomata*).[56]

Seneca's category theory represents more than another ontological interpretation of the categories. In the context of later Platonism it

51   *Ibid.*, 58.8–12, 14–15.
52   *Ibid.*, 58.16.
53   *Ibid.*, 58.17.
54   *Ibid.*, 58.18–19.
55   *Ibid.*, 58.16–20, 22.
56   Following Hadot, *op. cit.*, 156–163.

represents the first sustained attempt to argue for an epistemological and logical reference for the categories.[57] His use of the categories rests on the Stoic practice of understanding the categories as words which signify things. Next Seneca couples the Platonic ideas, which refer to a knowledge of things incorporeal and corporeal, to the Stoic categories, which refer to words which signify concepts. Consequently, he gives a categorical efficacy to knowledge and to logic.[58]

Seneca renders nugatory the Platonic distinction between different degrees of reality and knowing. He argues that category analysis yields a generic epistemological and logical classification of all things intelligible and sensible.

Nonetheless, Seneca maintains the Platonic ontological distinctions between degrees of reality. The categories do not really refer to "that which stands out and surpasses everything else".[59] They only refer to those subsumed below being *par excellence.* Consequently, his degree of reality model has the following structure:

$$\frac{\text{Quid}}{\begin{array}{c} \text{Quod Est} \\ (\text{Essentia}) \end{array}}$$

$$\text{Quid}$$
$$+$$
$$\text{Quod Est}$$

Seneca's use of the Stoic categories has wide and important implications. His rendering of the categories must be seen in connection with his metaphysics. The term *quod est* is a genus consisting of a number of species represented by six classes.

If the most generic is taken to represent being, its specific divisions are being, god, the transcendent ideas, the immanent ideas, physical individuals, and the receptacle. His division of things that are has the following structure:

---

[57] This is explained by Gersh, *op. cit.*, 187–188.
[58] Cf. Hadot, *op. cit.*, 157–160.
[59] See *Ep.* 58.17. Cf. Dillon, *op. cit.*, 136.

Most Generic	(Quid)
Genus	(Quod Est)
Species	
i. The Intelligible	(quod generaliter est)
ii. Being	(quod eminet et exsuperat omnia)
iii. The Ideas	(ea quae proprie sunt)
iv. The Ideas	(idos)
v. The Existents	(ea quae communiter sunt)
vi. The Quasi-Existents	(quae quasi sunt)

In summary, Seneca is an advocate of a *pragmatic* approach to the categories and is representative of a "Modified" Platonic interpretation of the categories. Being *par excellence* maintains its *apophatic* character.[60] But being in its other five modes has a *kataphatic* character. Finally, since concepts and words refer to things, the categories for Seneca have tridimensional reference—to things, to concepts, and to the conceptual classification of things.

This suggests that his approach and interpretation of the categories represents a apophatic-kataphatic interpretation of reality and a conceptualist and nominalist interpretation of the categories which yield a knowledge and classification of reality.

First, all things are subsumed under a single most generic something. All things are known and classified from genus to species through six specific modes of classification. The categories refer not only to things in nature but to things in the intelligible world and to the divine itself.

Second, the generic content of all divisions and classes of things is of a Stoic nominalist as well as a Platonic realist kind. Not only do the categories have reference to natural things, they also have reference to intelligibles. Furthermore, they refer to things as they are known and classified from the most generic something to its specific classifications.

The whole scheme is coherent. It represents a mixture of Platonic and Stoic elements. It is novel because before Seneca Platonists only stressed the material realism and nominalism of the categories. With Seneca a categorical conceptualism begins to emerge. This three-fold view of the categories has important consequences for later Platonism. To view this perspective further we turn to Philo Judaeus.

---

[60] Cf. *Ep.*, 65.3 ff. Cf. Gersh, *op. cit.*, 187–190.

Philo of Alexandria

Philo continues and expands the *pragmatic* approach to the categories evident in Seneca.[61] He maintains a logical and ontological reference and use for the categories. The categories refer to words which signify immaterial and material things and to all things in nature.[62]

The four Stoic and the ten Peripatetic categories are employed by Philo in a novel way. No longer are they subsumed under the category of Relative being. Some are subsumed under Absolute being. They have logical reference to the words which signify intelligible and material things, and ontological reference to material things.

He employs the Stoic category being (*on*) to refer to God.[63] He uses the Stoic categories most generic (*to genikotaton*) and most generic something (*ti*) to refer to the Logos and the ideas contained within the divine intellect.[64]

He employs the Peripatetic categories quality, place, and relation to refer to the Logos and the transcendent ideas.[65] The Stoic and Peripatetic categories also refer to the words which signify sensible things.[66]

His category theory can be summarized as follows:

1. The category being (*on*) refers to that which is above qualification—God. Deity is above genus, species, and differentia.

2. The most generic categories refer to that which is most generically qualified—the Logos and transcendent ideas. The Logos and the transcendent ideas are a kind of primary genus.

3. Within the most generic category some of the ten Peripatetic and four Stoic categories refer to the Logos and the transcendent ideas. The Peripatetic categories of place and relation and the Stoic category of quality refer to the transcendent ideas and the Logos respectively. However, in this context the categories refer to the words which signify intelligible things.

4. Under the category substance (*ousia*) the ten Peripatetic and four Stoic categories refer to words which signify sensible things as well as to things in nature.

5. At the center of Philo's theory stand the Stoic categories of being, most generic, and something. God is associated with *on*, while the Logos is associated with *to genikotaton* and *ti*. Moreover, the trans-

---

61 This is likely because both employ common *fontes*, cf. Theiler *op. cit.*, 37 ff.; Dillon, *op. cit.*, 135–137; cf. 178 ff.

62 Cf. e.g., *Decal.*, 30. For Philo on the categories, see Berchman, *op. cit.*, 23–53.

63 Cf. *Deus*, 62.

64 Cf. *Leg.* , 2.86, 175; *Det.*, 118.

65 Cf. *Opif.* 24–25, 36, 129; *Sacr.* 83; *Conf.* 172; *Her.* 280; *Plant.*. 50; *Ebr.* 133.

66 Cf. *Deus*, 62.

cendent ideas are the most generic figures and are associated with *to genikotaton* and *ti*. Finally, the sensibles are the specific figures of the most generic forms. They are associated with the four Stoic and ten Peripatetic categories—the natural categories.

6.   The significance of this model is that all reality is subsumed under a single genus. The intelligible categories relate God, the Logos, and the ideas; the sensible categories relate the physicals to the Logos and the ideas.

Philo's category scheme may be illustrated as following:

God (*on*)

Logos (*to genikotaton, ti*)
(place, relation, quality)

Nature (the ten Peripatetic categories
and four Stoic categories)

No longer are Stoic and Peripatetic categories considered relative or accidental. Some of them have referential efficacy to the things of the intelligible realm. Consequently, Philo proposes a typology of categories.

The categories are divided into those which have reference to the intelligible realm and those which have reference to the sensible world. First, there is the unqualified intelligible category—being. Second, there are the qualified intelligible categories—most generic, something, quality, place, relation. Third, there are the qualified-sensible categories, the four Stoic and ten Peripatetic categories that refer to nature.

The intelligible categories number six. The unqualified category, being, refers to God. The qualified categories are the generic categories : most generic, something, together with the specific categories of quality, place, and relation. They refer to the Logos and the ideas.

This category scheme must be seen in connection with his metaphysics.

First, being refers to a transcendent first principle, God the Father. Second, most generic and something refer to a transcendent and immanent second principle, his Logos. Third, quality and relation refer to the transcendent Logos and the Logos immanent in the world. Fourth, quantity refers to the substance or matter of the world. Fifth, quantity is formed by the Logos in its role as divider (*tomeus*). Sixth, once formed, quantity is defined and classified through the four Stoic and ten Peripatetic categories. Seventh, the generic forms employed to qualify matter paradigmatically are the transcendent ideas. Eighth, the specific forms employed to qualify matter immanently are the immanent ideas.

This scheme requires elaboration, for logic is closely linked to metaphysics.[67]

The Alexandrian divides reality between unqualified and qualified existence.

God, as being, is above genus, species, and differentia. Hence, deity is unqualified. He is called bare existence (*hyparxis*).[68]

The Logos and the transcendent ideas are generically qualified (*to genikotaton*).[69] The intelligible world, thus, is the generically qualified existence.

Nature is specifically qualified (*poiotes; poia eide*). The sensible world, therefore, is specifically qualified existence.[70]

The dividing line in Philo's reality model is a *diairesis* between *hyparxis* and *poiotes*. Unqualified refers to God alone, while quality refers to the most generic figure, the Logos, the generic figures contained in this divine intellect, and to the specific things of the material realm.

Philo's degree of reality metaphysic has the following categorical structure:

God (*hyparxis*)

———————

Intelligible World (*poiotes*: generic)

———————

Sensible World (*poiotes*: specific)

The categories refer to things, to words which signify things, and to words which signify concepts which signify things. They function in a *realist, nominalist,* and *conceptualist* manner. To bring category functions together in this manner suggests Philo's *pragmatic* use of the categories.[71]

God is above all qualification. He is bare existence.[72] Whereas nothing can be said of the Father, his Logos is the highest genus of the universe and of logical division.[73] Through his Logos, deity is in contact with his universe because the Logos functions as the primary, generic something

---

67 Cf. *Fug.* 12–13.
68 *Op. cit.,* cf. *on=hyparxis.*
69 Cf. e.g., *Leg.* 2.86; 3.175; *Det* . 118.
70 Cf. e.g., *Spec.* 3.73; 206; cf. *Post.* 48, 168; *Abr.* 31, 163.
71 This clear from *Fug.* 12–13 and *Decal.* 30.
72 Cf. e.g. *Deus.* 62.
73 Cf. e.g., *Leg.* 2.86; 3.175.

of the universe.[74] The Logos as divider (*tomeus*) defines and classifies all reality—both intelligible and sensible.[75]

Philo associates categories and ideas. The Logos, as the sum-total of the ideas, is the most generic entity.[76] The ideas are placed in the mind of God.[77] They have reference to the Logos.[78] They are genera of all species and differentia; of all the shapes and figures of things in the sensible world.[79] This *tertium quid* is important. The categories are concepts which yield knowledge about reality.

In summary, a mixture of Platonic, Stoic, and Peripatetic elements forms the background of Philo's theory. His categorical realism, nominalism, and conceptualism help maintain a rigorous theological *apophaticism*. They also sustain a powerful metaphysical *kataphaticism*.

The results of his experiment are fresh and innovative. Philo's category theory maintains: (1) the Platonic ontological distinction between Absolute and Relative being. Yet, he divides reality between unqualified and qualified being: (2) the Platonic logical divisions between Absolute and Relative being. Yet, he proposes a nominalist net which encompasses unqualified and qualified being: and (3) the Platonic epistemological distinction between paradigm and image. Yet, he offers a conceptualist link between knowledge and perception.

This is clear from his philosophical theology, his first principles. God is a bare existence who cannot be compared with anything else. He transcends genus and species because they are divisions of created things. Nothing positive can be said of his essence, quality or state of movement. Nonetheless, deity is a being. Through his Logos he is the primary, generic something of the universe and through his ideas he knows his universe.

The categories stand at the center of his theoretic. They separate and link types of existence. They bridge degrees of reality and knowledge. Distinctions between an uncreated God and a created cosmos, a divine intellect and its thoughts, and transcendent forms and immanent images, are linked categorically.

Philo's category theory points backward and forward.

It represents the *apophatic-kataphatic* theories we have associated with the

---

[74] Cf. e.g., *Det.* 115–116 where the Logos described as the mother of all things and nurse is also presented as manna or the something (*ti*) of the universe.

[75] See Philo's use of *tomeus* in *Her.* 133–236. Here the Logos brings mathematical and proportional equality to the world, cf. 221–223.

[76] Cf. *Leg.* 2.86; 3.175; *Det.* 118.

[77] Cf. *Opif.* 20, 24–25; *Conf.* 172; *Somn.* 1.62; *Cher.* 49; *Her.* 188; *Fug.* 110–112.

[78] Cf. *Opif.* 24–25; *Conf.* 172; *Somn.* 1.62.

[79] Cf. *Opif.* 32, 97.

Modified Platonisms of Eudorus and Seneca. Philo rejects both the strict apophaticism characteristic of Archytas and the rigorous *kataphaticism* characteristic of Antiochus.[80]

It prefigures the pragmatic *apophatic-kataphatic* theories of the second and third century Modified Platonisms of Clement, Albinus, and Origen. It is to these we now turn.

III

Later Middle Platonism

Clement of Alexandria

Clement is knowledgeable of both Stoic and Aristotelian category theory.[81] He employs such knowledge to define the nature of his noetic triad; the relationship between the noetic triad and the intelligibles, and the relationship between the noetic triad, the intelligibles, and the sensibles.

Although Clement's category theory is difficult to reconstruct,[82] it nonetheless signals a series of important shifts in later Platonic category theory.[83] The Alexandrian employs the Peripatetic categories in a manner unprecedented in later Platonism.[84] His *kataphatic* emphasis in philosophical theology, physics, logic, and epistemology is unknown in earlier Platonism.[85] This paradigm shift in Middle Platonic metaphysics can be summarized as following:

1. All reality is subsumed under a single substance, the Logos. The use of the term *ousia* rather than *on* for substance is novel in Platonism. Before Clement *ousia* refers to *hyle*, the material substrate of the sensible world. The category is never used to refer to anything in the intelligible world.

2. Substance (*ousia*), previously assumed to be a relative or accidental category, now is assumed to be an absolute or essential category.

---

[80] *Apophatic* or reinforced early Middle Platonism finds its representative in Archytas, cf. ap. Stobaeus, *Anth.*, 1.41.2; Simplicius, *In Phys.*, 181.10 ff. *Kataphatic* or modified early Middle Platonism finds its representative in Antiochus, cf. ap. Cicero, *Ac. Post.*, 27 ff.; *Par. Or.*, 139. See Dillon, *op. cit.*, s.v. Archytas and Antiochus.

[81] Cf. Witt, *op. cit.*, 36 ff.; Moraux, *op. cit.*, 176 ff.

[82] Clement did not write a commentary on the categories. He offers a doxographical account of Middle Platonic category theory, cf. *Strom.*, 8.8.23 ff. He also associates the categories with his metaphysic through a metaphysic of prepositions, cf. *Strom.*, 7.9.2 ff.

[83] Little work has been done on Clement's theory. For a recent appraisal, cf. Berchman, *op. cit.*, 63–81.

[84] Cf. Witt, *op. cit.*, 36–38, 60, who argues for a connection between Clement's category theory and those of Boethius of Sidon, Antiochus, and Andronicus.

[85] Berchman, *op. cit.*, 63 ff.

However, substance does not refer in the same way to the Logos and Holy Spirit as it does to the sensibles. The substance of the Logos and Holy Spirit is a primary substance (*prote ousia*) while the substance of the sensibles is a secondary substance (*deutra ousia*).

3. All reality is subsumed under a single genus, the Logos. The use of the term *ousia* rather than *to genikotaton* and *ti* is novel in Platonism. Before Clement *ousia* refers to *hyle*, the *hypokeimenon* of the sensible world. The category was never used to refer to a primary genus or to the most generic something under which reality is subsumed.

4. The Father, Son, and Holy Spirit are distinct and irreducible to one another. Substance does not refer to God. He is above genus, species, and differentia. He is "unqualified". Substance refers to the Logos as primary genus. He is "qualified". Substance refers to the Holy Spirit since it participates in the form of the Logos.

5. Substance refers to the intelligibles. They are the thoughts of the Logos which participate in a single form, sharing a common nature with the Logos since they participate in the forms.

6. Reality is known and classified through the ten Peripatetic categories. Substance, quality, relation, and place refer to Absolute being. The nine categories refer to sensible being. Hence, Clement has a *nominalist* and *conceptualist* use of the categories as well as a *realist* one.

Even though one must interpret Clement's category scheme within a Platonic degree of reality metaphysic and within a Platonic understanding of common natures in which particulars participate in a single form, his doctrine represents a turn to a *kataphatic* metaphysics. Consequently, his category scheme requires further elaboration.

First, Clement makes the categories of the Absolute and the Relative his two basic categories.[86] Second, he subsumes the ten Peripatetic categories under these two Academic categories.[87] Consequently, substance refers to both Absolute and Relative being. The remaining nine categories refer to Relative being alone.

This signals a significant shift in Platonic category theory. First, all reality is subsumed under a single *ousia*. Second, each degree of reality shares a common set of categories.

From a *realist* perspective the category substance refers to Absolute being while the remaining nine categories refer to Relative being.

Clement's distinction between types of substance is intended to keep us from using the term substance interchangeably.

The substance of absolute reality is primary. That of relative reality is

---

[86] Cf. *Strom.* 8.8.23 ff.
[87] *Ibid.*

secondary. Hence, the way Clement uses substance for sensibles is only an analogy for their use with theologicals and intelligibles.

The substance of the Logos and the ideas is a primary substance. In the case of intelligibles substance refers to a generic unity, so it is the unity (*homoousia*) of substance that is affirmed. They *are* the same *ousia*. They do not *have* the same *ousia*.

The substance of sensibles is a secondary substance. In the case of sensibles substance refers to a specific unity, so that it is the likeness or co-equality (*homoiousia*) of substance that is affirmed. They *are* not the same *ousia*. They *have* the same *ousia*.

Clement's category scheme has the following structure:

Absolute (*ousia kath' hauto*)
(substance)

Relative (*ousia pros ti*)
(the Peripatetic categories)

From a *realist* perspective the category substance refers to Absolute being while the remaining nine categories refer to Relative being. From a *nominalist* and *conceptualist* perspective, however, some of the nine Peripatetic categories have reference to intelligibles as well as sensibles. These categories are quality, relation, and place.

As we shall see Clement uses the terminology of unqualified (*apoios*), qualified (*poiotes*) and generated (*genetos*) to make nominalist and conceptualist distinctions between the hypostases of the noetic triad, intelligibles, and sensibles. To grasp this aspect of Clement's category theory it is necessary to examine his first principles and doctrine of ideas.

Clement's first principles are based upon the first two hypotheses of the *Parmenides*.[88] He postulates two Ones, God and Logos, that have aspects in common with the first principles of Philo, Nicomachus and Numenius.[89]

God is eternal, ungenerated, and unqualified. He is called a One (*hen*), the good (*agathon*), measure (*metron*), and the number of all things (*arithmos ton panton*). The Father is an intellect (*nous*) at rest. He is also beyond genus, species, and differentia and is not a countable unit.[90]

The Logos is the first being created by God. He is called One (*monas*) and a unity in plurality (*panta hen*). The Logos is an intellect (*logos-nous*),

---

[88] Cf. Dodds, *op. cit.*, 129–142.

[89] See S. Lilla, *Clement of Alexandria: A study of Christian Platonism and Gnosticism* (Oxford, 1972) 204–209; cf. Berchman, *op. cit.*, 64 ff.

[90] Cf. *Prot.* 10.98.4; 6.92.2; 2.875.2; *Strom.* 4.25.162.5 ff.; 5.12.82.1; 7.17.107; 5.6.38.

and is the place of the ideas (*chora ton ideon*). Since the Logos is *monas* and *panta hen*, he is a countable unit and not beyond genus, species, and differentia. Thus, the Logos is qualified and is the first principle (*arche*) of all being and thought.[91]

The Logos is the paradigmatic monad who contains the ideas within his intellect.[92] The transcendent ideas are the genera, the intelligible models of all the species of the sensible world.[93]

The Logos is also the immanent monad who is the point upon which the sensible universe is grounded. The immanent ideas are reason principles, the sensible forms of all the species of the sensible world.[94]

The Logos is the creator and sustainer of the universe. It shapes unformed matter on the patterns of its ideas and matter sustains form through the power of its ideas dispersed throughout the cosmos.[95]

Clement distinguishes between an unqualified and a qualified first principle:

God (*apoios*)

———

Logos (*poios*)

And between unqualified and qualified being:[96]

God-Hen (*apoios*)

———

Logos-Monas (*kosmos noetos*)
Ideai (*noema-gene*)
(*poios*)

———

Logos-Panta Hen (*kosmos aisthetos*)
Eide (*logoi spermatikoi*)
(*poiotes*)

———

Dyas-Hexas (*apoios*)

---

91 Cf. *Strom.* 5.14.94.1; cf. 4.25.155.2; 5.3.16.3; 5.11.73.3.
92 *Ibid.*, 5.14.93.1; cf. 4.15.156.1 ff.
93 Cf. *Prot.* 9.88.2; *Strom.* 4.23.151.3; 152.1; 4.25.175.2.
94 Cf. e.g, *Prot.* 5.2; *Strom.* 4.156.1–2; 5.104.4.
95 For Clement's paradigmatic cosmology, cf. e.g., *Strom.* 5.94.1–5, 93.4; 5.16.5; for his immanentist cosmology, cf. e.g., *Prot.*, 5.2; *Strom.* 5.104.4.
96 For the connections between Eudorus, Philo, and Clement, see Berchman, *op. cit.*, 63 ff.

The categories refer to things, to words which signify things, and to concepts which signify things. How the Peripatetic categories function is best approached through Clement's Logos doctrine.

The Logos has three aspects.

As the intellect of God it exists *intra mentem dei*. In this aspect it exists within the mind of the divine intellect and is indistinguishable from the divine intellect.[97] Within the mind of God the Logos is a mind at rest and the place of the ideas. *Intra mentem dei* the Logos is called *patrikos logos*, an intellect identical with the mind of God and the place (*chora*) of the divine ideas (*logoi*).[98]

As an intellect distinct from God it exists *extra mentem dei*. In this aspect it exists outside the mind of the divine intellect as a second divine intellect.[99] Outside the mind of God the Logos is an active intellect and the place of the ideas. *Extra mentem dei* the Logos is called *nous*, an intellect distinct from the mind of God, a mind which thinks (*noesis*) the divine ideas (*noema*).[100]

As transcendent Logos it contains the intelligible world within itself. It is the totality of the ideas and powers of God. In this aspect the Logos is the intelligible world, a mind which thinks the *kosmos noetos*.[101]

As immanent Logos it creates a sensible world on the patterns of the transcendent ideas and sustains a sensible world through the ideas immanent in the universe.[102] It is the power which creates and holds the physical world together, penetrating it from one extremity to the other as the mind of the sensible world. In this aspect the Logos is the harmony or law of the sensible world, a power which sustains the *kosmos aisthesis*.[103]

The Logos is the principle which connects the degrees of reality to each other. Through the Logos a transcendent God is connected to the different degrees of reality. In the Logos different degrees of reality find a common locus. This interrelationship is expressed by Clement through the categories.

When identical with the mind of God, Clement employs the categories place (*chora*) and relation (*pros*) to describe their relationship. The place of the Logos is in the mind of God. The Logos is related to God as first One to second One, as unqualified principle to qualified principle and as uncreated principle to created principle.

---

97 Cf. *Strom.* 5.16.3.
98 *Ibid.*, 4.155.2; 5.73.3.
99 *Ibid.*, 5.93.4, 16.3; 4.155.2; 5.73.3.
100 *Ibid.*, 4.155.2, 156.2; 5.14.94, 73.3.
101 *Ibid.*, 5.14.94; 4.25.155; cf. 5.3.16.
102 *Ibid.*, 8.9.27.
103 Cf. e.g. *Prot.* 5.2; *Strom.* 5.104.4.

When distinct from the mind of God and in its transcendent aspect, Clement uses the categories substance (*ousia*) and quality (*poios*) to describe the Logos, place (*chora*) to describe the locus of the ideas in the divine intellect, and relation (*pros*) to describe the relationship between the intellect and its thoughts.

When distinct from the mind of God and in its immanent aspect, Clement uses the ten Peripatetic categories to define and classify the variety of ways in which the sensibles as copies of the transcendent ideas are a combination of substance (*ousia*) and matter (*posotes*).

Clement introduces a theory of equivocals, univocals, and paronyms in connection with the categories.[104] Indeed, equivocals, univocals, and paronyms are expressed grammatically through the categories. The categories are terms which signify things.

Equivocals are things which have one name in common but different definitions. Univocals are things which have a common name and definition. For example, the term animal signifies man and ox. Paronyms are things which are denominated by different names. A grammarian receives his designation from grammar, the brave are named from bravery.

For Clement things are signified through the categories. Nominally, the categories serve to define the relationship between first principles, intelligibles, and sensibles. Within the limited scope of this study it is instructive to focus on Clement's theory of equivocals and his equivocal use of the categories. This course is followed because the context of Platonic discussions of equivocals arose within debates concerning the first two hypotheses of Plato's *Parmenides*.[105] Clement appears to use a theory of equivocals to define the relationship between his first principles.

Equivocals are things which have one name in common but different definitions are denoted by the name. There are two types of equivocals. Those of common origin (*aph'henos*) and those by reference (*pros hen*).

Clement uses these two notions to define the relationship of God to the Logos. God and the Logos are equivocal by common origin and by reference. The terms *logos* and *nous* express these types of equivocity.

The Logos, *intra mentem dei*, is one and the same with the mind of God. The term, *logos*, signifies this equivocity. The Logos is equivocal with God "as the same from the same" (*apo tou autou kai pros tou autou*).[106] From the identity of the term *logos*, Clement postulates the identity of God and Logos. They are equivocal from common origin. The categories place and relation are terms which signify this type of equivocity.

---

104 Cf. *Strom.* 8.8.24.1.

105 Cf. Cornford, *op. cit.*, 110–111; 160–161; 245.

106 *Strom.* 8.8.24.8–9.

The Logos, *extra mentem dei*, is distinct from the divine intellect since it proceeds (*proelthon*) from it. The term, *nous*, signifies this equivocity. The Logos is equivocal with God "from resemblance" (*homioteta*).[107] From the identity of the term *nous*, Clement postulates the resemblance of God and Logos. They are equivocal from reference. The categories substance, quality, place, and relation, signify this type of equivocity.

God and Logos are things with one name in common but different definitions are denoted by the terms *logos* and *nous*.

Working with the categories as signifying equivocals, univocals and paronyms, Clement systematically works out similarities between first principles and classes of intelligible and sensible things. He understands similarity as imitation, correspondence, and analogy. It is the task of *diairesis* to determine the relations between degrees of reality.[108]

As primary genus, the Logos not only creates and sustains existence. He is also the agent of all division and classification. Therefore, through the nominal procedure of division and classification he knows the universe through the categories.

As noted Clement rejected the notion that Aristotle's substance (*ousia*) must be rejected on the ground that intelligible and sensible reality cannot be subsumed under a single genus.[109] Consequently, Clement subsumes the ten Peripatetic categories under the two Academic categories and uses them to define and classify all modes of being.[110] The Logos and the ideas straddle Absolute and Relative. Through the ideas the Logos knows the genera and species of creation. Moreover, his division and classification of universals and particulars is accomplished, at least partially, through the categories. Therefore, the categories have a *conceptualist* function.

The categories are concepts which signify things. Consequently, the identity, similarity, and difference either between classes of things or things themselves is known through the ten Peripatetic categories.

The transcendent ideas have place. They are in the mind of the Logos. They have relation. They are thoughts of an intellect. They have quality. They are the genera of the created universe. Finally, the transcendent ideas have substance. They are the thoughts of the divine intellect.

The immanent ideas have place. They are in the mind of the Logos and in the world. They have relation. They are thoughts of an intellect and are instantiated in matter. They have quality. They are the genera of

---

[107] *Ibid*, 8.8.24.8.
[108] Clement's model has affinities to Speusippus: ap. Iamblichus, *Theol. Arith.*, 82.8–9; 43–60. Cf. Aristotle, *Metaphysics*, 1028b15–17. See Berchman, *op. cit.*, 76 ff.
[109] See Theiler, *op. cit.* 1964, 6 ff.; Witt, *op. cit.*, 38 ff.
[110] Cf. *Strom.* 8.24.1.

the created universe and the cosmos they refer to the species of all created things. They have substance. They are the thoughts of the divine intellect and the reason principles which inform matter. Finally, since the immanent ideas are in matter they also express the time, position, possession, activity, and passivity of matter.[111]

Clement's categorical scheme has the following structure:

God
Logos-Ideai (place, relation)

Logos-Nous-Noema-Kosmos Noetos (substance, quality, place, relation)

Logos-Eide-Logou-Kosmos Aisthetos (substance, quality, quantity, place, relation, time, position, possession, activity, and passivity)

The Logos is the key to Clement's category theory. It is the point which thinks, defines, and classifies all the entities of the universe. All genera, species and differentia are known, defined and classified through the Logos and the ten Peripatetic categories which have reference to the divine intellect and its thoughts.

As primary genus, with the ideas its genera, and the universe created and sustained into species and differentia on the pattern of its thoughts, the Logos is a common categorical net which envelopes all of reality.

The categories of substance, quality, quantity, relation, and place have reference to the intelligible world. These categories in addition to time, possession, position, action, and suffering have reference to the sensible world.

For Clement the categories refer to things, to words which signify things, and to concepts which signify things. This is evident in his use of the categories to refer to intelligibles and sensibles, to the words which signify the classification and definition of intelligible and sensible things, and to the concepts which signify intelligible and sensible things. These postulates are explained below.

1. Substance refers to all intelligibles and sensibles. The remaining nine categories refer to the arrangement of substance in the intelligible and sensible worlds.

2. Words signify intelligibles and sensibles. Equivocals, heteronyms, specific heteronyms, polyonyms, and paryonyms signify the meanings of intelligibles and sensibles. The ten categories linguistically signify the status and arrangement of things.

---

[111] Material things are called *poia* by Clement. They are informed by the immanent ideas and sustained by the Logos. Cf. *Prot.* 5.2; *Strom.* 5.104.4; 7.5.4.

3. Concepts signify intelligibles and sensibles. There is a correlation between a *nomen* which has reference to *lekta*, between *noemata* which have reference to *nomen*, *lekta*, and *pragmata*, and *pragmata* which are impressed upon the mind in a *nomen*, in *lekta*, and in *noemata*. Since *pragmata* are impressed upon the mind in *noemata* and *noemata* have categorical reference, the ten categories signify the conceptual status and arrangement of things through the words which signify things in concepts.

4. The categories are about words which signify things by way of signifying concepts. It is through concepts that the mind receives impressions of things and interprets their meaning through the study of language. This turn to questions of the relationship between objects, language, and thought is one of the more significant aspects of Clement's category theory.

Clement's use of the categories is novel.

First, he subsumes all qualified reality under a single substance (*ousia*). For the first time in Platonism substance refers to intelligible and not merely to sensible being.

Second, the Peripatetic categories have reference to all degrees of qualified existence. Five Peripatetic categories refer to being in its intelligible mode of classification and ten Peripatetic categories refer to being in its sensible mode of classification.

Third, Clement's understanding and use of the categories illustrates *realist, nominalist,* and *conceptualist* approaches to the categories. This telescoping of Platonic, Stoic, and Aristotelian category theories is a proleptic move which does not attain full expression until Porphyry and Boethius.

In summary, Clement continues a *pragmatic* approach to category theory common to some traditions of "Modified" Middle Platonism. This is illustrated by his expanded use of the categories in their realist and nominalist aspects and by his conceptualist approach and use of the categories.

Clement proposes an *apophatic-kataphatic* theoretical model. God is unqualified. Neither genus, species, or differentia, he is above space, time, and place. Nonetheless, through a primary genus, the Logos, God is linked to qualified creation. The theoretic which accompanies Clement's category theory shows a movement towards the adaptation within a Platonic context of an Aristotelian metaphysic.

This later configuration crystallizes in Origen's category theory. It is to this we now turn.

Origen of Alexandria

Among Christian Platonists few have experienced such a wide range of treatment by later generations as Origen of Alexandria.[112] Because his category theory is difficult to reconstruct,[113] it has been largely neglected.[114]

Although it would be highly desirable to make a detailed analysis of his category theory in each of his writings, this is not possible within the limited scope of our study. For our purposes it must suffice that a representative sample of the evidence be presented. The results gained will permit us to draw some general conclusions about Origen's category doctrine and its relation to his first principles and metaphysic.

Origen is among the "Modified" Platonists. He approaches the categories from a *pragmatic* perspective. He employs the categories in their *realist, nominalist,* and *conceptualist* modes to propose an *apophatic-kataphatic* metaphysic.

However, Origen takes a series of steps which are novel within the *pragmatic* trajectory of Platonic metaphysics. They may be summarized as follows:

1.　God the Father is a substance (*ousia*). All reality is subsumed under this substance (*ousia*). The Logos, Holy Spirit, intelligibles and sensibles are substance in one or more of nine modes of being.

2.　The substance of the Father is a primary substance (*prote ousia*). The substance of the Son, Holy Spirit, intelligibles and sensibles is a secondary substance (*deutra ousia*).

3.　There are two divisions of reality—the Absolute and the Relative. The Peripatetic categories refer to Absolute and Relative being. Substance refers to God. Substance, relation, and quality refer to the Logos and the Holy Spirit. The remaining seven Peripatetic categories refer to the intelligibles and the sensibles.

4.　There are two types of essence and existence. There is subsistent and inherent essence and essential and accidental existence.

5.　Only God subsists and exists essentially. The Logos and the Holy Spirit inhere essentially but exist accidentally.

6.　The intelligibles and the sensibles inhere and exist accidentally.

This category theory can be reconstructed from Origen's theoretic. We turn, therefore, to his first principles to begin our reconstruction. This

---

[112] For a complete bibliography up through 1969 see H. Crouzel, *Bibliographie critique d'Origène* (Paris, 1969).

[113] See Berchman, *op. cit.,* 121–164.

[114] See H. Koch, *Pronoia und Paideusis: Studien Uber Origenes und sein Verhaltnis zum Platonismus* (Berlin, 1932) and Berchman, *op. cit.*.

much of Origen we can easily follow. His first principles parallel most Platonic degrees of reality metaphysical models.

Origen postulates two first principles. These are God and Logos. They are arranged in a hierarchy of Ones.[115] The first One is called *monas, henas, hyperousion hen* and *ousia*.[116] God the Father is an eternal, ungenerated intellect. He is an intellect (*nous*) at rest.[117] That Origen calls his first principle substance (*ousia*) is unprecedented in later Platonism. That Origen calls God intellect is not uncommon in Middle Platonism.[118]

By *hyper ousion hen* Origen means that God is beyond the type of being, existence, and intellect that characterizes all generated and related things. He does not mean that God is neither being or intellect.[119]

The second One is called *monada, henada,* and *ousion hen*.[120] The Logos is an eternally generated intellect (*noesis*).[121] He contains the intelligible world in his intellect as the prefiguration of the sensible world. Once created, the intelligible and sensible worlds exist outside of the mind of this intellect.[122]

As active intellect, the Logos is the demiurge and sustainer of the universe.[123] Here Origen reduplicates the paradigmatic cosmology so common to Middle Platonism to explain creation.[124]

The Logos created the universe. He gives form to matter for his reason principles (*logoi*) penetrate the material substratum unceasingly. The Logos introduces differentiating quality to the physical world. The genera and species of the formed universe are known, defined, and classified through the categories.[125]

The created world contains both intelligibles and sensibles.

In Origen's system all created beings are to some degree corporeal. Like formed matter, intelligibles and sensibles are known, defined, and classified through the categories.[126]

Below these Ones is Spirit (*pneuma*). Called *ousia*, the Holy Spirit is the

---

[115] Cf. e.g., *De Princ.* 1.3.5 Cf. ap. Jerome, *Ep. ad Av.*, 2=Migne 22.1061. On Origen's first principles see Koch, *op. cit.*, 146 ff.; Berchman, *op. cit.*, 123–134.

[116] Cf. *De Princ.* 1.1.6; cf. *C. Cels.* 1.24.

[117] Cf. *Cat. In Jh.* 4.495.20, 24.

[118] Cf. Berchman, *op. cit.*, 123–126.

[119] Cf. *C. Cels.* 8.38; 4.14; *De Princ.* 1.1.6; cf. 1.1.5. and 1.1.7.

[120] Cf. *De Princ.* 1.1.2; *C. Cels.* 6.64; *Com. in Jh.* 1.119.113 f. Cf. ap Justinian, *Ep. ad Men.*=Mansi, 9.528.489d.

[121] Cf. *Com in Jh.* 1.24; *C. Cels.* 6.64; Cf. 3.64; 2.135; *De Princ.* 1.2.30; 1.4.5.

[122] Cf. *De Princ.* 1.2.12; 1.4.3.

[123] Cf. *C. Cels.* 4.54; *De Princ.* 1.4.5; *Com. in Jh.* 1.1.20.

[124] Cf. e.g., *De Princ.* 1.2.12.

[125] Cf. *C. Cels.* 4.54; *De Princ.* 1.4.5; *Com. in Jh .* fr. 1.

[126] Cf. *C. Cels.* 5.39; 43; *Com. in Jh.* 1.1.24; 13.21; *De Princ.* 1.2.2.

first generated intellect.[127] Properly speaking the Holy Spirit is not a metaphysical principle but a soteriological principle. But with the inclusion of the Holy Spirit Origen's noetic triad is complete.

Origen's theoretic has the following structure:

ABSOLUTE BEING
(*kath'hauto*)

God (*hyperousion hen*)

———————————

Logos (*ousion hen*)

———————————

Spirit (*pneuma*)

———————————

RELATIVE BEING
(*pros ti*)

Intelligibles (*noeta*)

———————————

Sensibles (*aistheta*)

Origen folds an Aristotelian category theory into this degree of reality metaphysic. The results are the following:

He accepts the Peripatetic categories as Platonic and subsumes them under the two Academic categories—Absolute and the Relative. Within each degree of reality there are levels of being. Even if we interpret Origen's degree of reality metaphysic along Platonic lines, we still see a series of distinctions based on Aristotle's categories.

He makes distinctions between substances and accidents (between individuals and what is present in them) and between substances themselves (individual or primary substances) and kinds of substances (secondary substances).

He knows that genera and species group primary substances in various kinds of substance and that accidents are predicated of primary substances. He knows that only genera and species give us what is essential to a primary substance. They tell what a primary substance must have in order to be that kind of reality.

The *ousia* of God is a primary substance. It *is* the same *ousia*. The *ousia* of all other existents is a secondary substance. They *have* the same *ousia*.

---

[127] *De Princ.* Pr. 4.; 1.2.3; *Com. in Jh.* fr. 1; 2.10; cf. Epihanius, *Haer.* 64.5; Justinian, *Ep. ad Men.* = Mansi 9.528.489; Jerome, *Ep. ad Av.* 2 = Migne 22.1060.

Only for the Father are *ousia* and *hypostasis* used interchangeably. They are of the same substance (*homoousioi*). For all others *ousia* and *hypostasis* are not used interchangeably. They are of like substance (*homoiousia*).

One of these junctures is well illustrated by Origen's terminology. The Father is a primary substance, that is beyond genus, species, differentia— a *hyper ousion hen*. The Son is the secondary substance, that is a genus—an *ousion hen*, an *ousia ousion* or an *idea ideon*. The intelligibles are a secondary substance, that is universal genera and species. The sensibles are a secondary substance, that is specific genera and species.

Origen does not apply the terms *ousia* and *hypostasis* to God in precisely the same way he does to the Son, the Holy Spirit, and to the intelligibles and sensibles. Indeed, the Father, Son, and Holy Spirit are distinct and irreducible to one another.

Origen makes the distinction between individuals and the nature they share in order to show that *ousia* and *hypostasis* do not mean the same thing when they refer to God as they do when they refer to all other things.

His stress on the distinction between *ousia* and *hypostasis* when dealing with all existents save the Father is intended to keep from using these terms interchangeably; for if used interchangeably, we are led to deny the distinction between deity and creation.

He does this to keep us from using each term interchangeably in speaking of each individual within his noetic triad and from using substance interchangeably in speaking of each degree of reality. Consequently, substance and individual do not mean the same thing when speaking of Father, Son, and Holy Spirit, nor do they mean the same thing when speaking of intelligibles, and sensibles.

In Peripatetic fashion substance refers to all levels of reality in its many variations. In Platonic fashion each particular participates in a common substance and form; each is but a reflection of a higher substance and form.

Even if one interprets his model within a Platonic context of common natures in which particulars participate in a single form (so that the unity between individuals is greater than that found among Peripatetics), Origen clearly believes that the unity of genera and species is but a reflection of the unity and oneness of the Logos, which is but a reflection of the oneness of the Father.

With this established, Origen's metaphysic is more intelligible.

Only one entity in Origen's system is substance *kauth'hauto* (*per se*). This is God the Father. This is because Origen interprets the phrase in I Samuel 1.11:

... non est praeter te ...

(there is none besides you)

to mean:

... nihil eorum, quae sunt, hoc ipsum, quod sunt, naturaliter habent ...

(nothing save the Father is by virtue of its own nature)[128]

This is because the Father is the only non-generated, non-created principle.[129] He is the only principle whose essence and existence are identical. Moreover, he is the only existent whose existence is subsistent and not inherent.

The Son and Holy Spirit are also substances *kauth'hauto* (*per se*). Yet, unlike the Father who is eternal and ungenerated, they are eternally generated or generated substances. The Son is the eternal impress of the Father.[130] The Holy Spirit participates in the Father through the agency of the Son.[131]

The Logos and Spirit are principles whose essence and existence are not identical. Consequently, the Son and Holy Spirit are existents whose existence is not subsistent. Rather it is inherent.[132] Their nature is "not by virtue of their own nature".

Only God the Father has a unity of substance and existence (*homoousia*). The distinction between substance and existence for the Logos and Holy Spirit means a likeness or co-equality (*homoiousia*) between them and God the Father.

In the case of the intelligibles and sensibles we encounter created entities which are substances that exist *kata symbebekos (per accidens)*.[133] For Origen this means their essence is accidental and their existence is inherent.

Origen's use of the Peripatetic categories clarifies his degree of reality metaphysic. We have a major division between primary and secondary substances—between individual substance and kinds of substances. We have major divisions between substance and accidents—between substance which yields what an individual is and the predicates which yield what kind of individual it is.

For Origen there is only one primary substance—God the Father. We know this because only *ousia* refers to him. Secondary substances tell us

---

128 See *In Lib. I Sam.*, 1.11; cf. *De Princ.* 1.2.9.
129 Cf. *De Princ.* 1.2.6; 1.3.3; 1.3.5; *Com. in Jh.* 2.10.65. Cf. Jerome, *Ep. ad A.* 2 = Migne 22.1061.
130 Cf. *De Princ.* 1.2.6; 1.2.6; 1.2.8; 4.4.1.
131 *Ibid.*, Pr. 4; cf. Justinian, *Ep. ad Men.*, = fr. 9 Koe.
132 Cf. *De Princ.* 1.2.6, p. 36.7 ff.; Koe.
133 Cf. *De Princ.* 1.2.13; *Com. in Jh.* 2.18.

what *ousia* is essentially and predicates tell us what an *ousia* is accidentally.

For example, the categories of place, relation, and quality refer to the Logos and the Holy Spirit. This is because the Logos is a primary genus that groups genera and species into various kinds of substance and accidents.

These levels of being are arranged through the categories. Origen's category scheme has the following structure:

ABSOLUTE BEING
(*kauth'hauto*)
God (*ousia*)

Logos (*ousia, pros, poiotes*)
Holy Spirit (*ousia, pros, poiotes*)

RELATIVE BEING
(*pros ti*)
The Intelligibles and Sensibles
(the Ten Peripatetic categories)

Since all reality is subsumed under a single substance (*ousia*), Origen provides a typology of categories. Three categories have reference to Absolute Being and ten categories that have reference to Relative Being. Substance refers to God, while substance, relation, and quality refer to the Logos and the Holy Spirit. All ten categories refer to the intelligibles and the sensibles. Origen's distinctions between modes of being and existence are presented through the categories.

The ontological fault-line of Origen's degrees of reality rests on the distinction between essential being and accidental being and between subsistent assistance and inherent existence. This division into types of being and modes of existence requires further elaboration.

The classificatory markers distinguishing modes of existence are four. They are between ungenerated being, eternally generated being, first generated being, and created being.[134] The categories function to mark these modal distinctions.

---

[134] According to a number of sources Origen understood the Son and Holy Spirit to be *egenethe* and *ktisma*. Cf. *De Princ.* 4.4.1; *In Jerem. Hom.* 9.4. Also see Justinian, *Ep. ad Men* = fr. 32 Koe.= Mansi 9.525.489b.

OUSIA KATH'HAUTO
God (*ousia agenetos*)

Logos (*ousia egenetos*)
Holy Spirit (*ousia prote genetos*)

OUSIA PROS TI
(KATA SYMBEBEKOS)
All Created Entities (*ousia genetos*)

At the core of Origen's theoretic lies a distinction between uncreated and created being.

These distinctions mark boundaries between the type of being and existence of the three hypostases.[135] Only God the Father is necessary being and has necessary existence. In God being and essence are one.[136] For example, God's being is necessary and his existence is eternal and ungenerated.[137]

Only God's existence is subsistent for he is the only non-generated and non-created entity. Moreover, nothing existed before him or is co-eternal with him.[138]

The Logos and Holy Spirit are necessary beings but their existence is derivative. Their being and existence are not one. For example, their being is necessary but their existence is either eternally generated or generated.[139]

The existence of the Logos and the Holy Spirit is inherent. The substance of the Logos is the impress or image of God's substance.[140] Moreover, the substance of the Holy Spirit is the copy of the substance of the Logos.[141] The existence of the Logos and the Holy Spirit is each contingent, because neither exists by virtue of its own nature.

All created beings are accidental beings and their existence is generated. For example, their being is accidental, and, since their existence is generated, it is accidental.

---

[135] Cf. *De Princ.* 1.3.5. God extends to all things, the Son to rational things, the Holy Spirit to the saints alone.
[136] Cf. *In Lib. I Sam. Hom.* 1.11.
[137] Cf. e.g., *De Princ.* 4.4.1.
[138] *Ibid.*, 1.2.6; 1.3.3; 1.3.5; *Com. in Jh.* 2.10.65.
[139] Cf. e.g., *De Princ.* 1.3.5; 1.2.6; *Com. in Jr.* fr. 1 Koe.
[140] Cf. *De Princ.* Pr 4; 1.2.6; 1.3.5. Cf. Jerome, *Ep. ad av.* 2 = Migne 22.1060; Hieron, *Ep.* 92 = Migne 22.762.
[141] Cf. e.g., *Com. in Jh.* 2.10; *De Princ.* Pr. 4; Justinian, *Ep. ad Men.*, = fr. 9 Koe.= Migne 22.1060.

The existence of the intelligibles and sensibles is also inherent. Their particular substances receive their form from the Father through the Logos. All generated existence is contingent because it does not exist by virtue of its own nature.[142]

Origen's model, at least within Platonism, is novel. He postulates an essential unity among hypostases but an existential distinction between hypostases.

He accomplishes this by applying the Aristotelian categories within the context of a Platonic degree of reality metaphysic. This application requires explanation.

Origen postulates three hypostases in descending order of energy, power, and value.[143] This is not novel. However, although the three hypostases are fully subsistent, they exist in different ways. This is novel.

Origen postulates three levels of existence and a level of non-existence.[144] His model has the following structure:

EXISTENCE
(*Kauth'hauto*)
(*ousia*)
God the Father

EXISTENCE
(*Pros Ti*)
(*ousia, pros, poiotes*)
Logos and Holy Spirit

EXISTENCE
(*Kata Symbebekos*)
(Ten Peripatetic Categories)
The Intelligibles and Sensibles

NON-EXISTENCE
(*Me-On*)
Matter

This model requires further clarification.

---

[142] Cf. e.g., *De Princ.* 2.1.5; *Com. in Jh.* 2.18.75.

[143] Cf. *De Princ.* 1.3.5; Jerome, *Ep. ad Av.*, 2 = Migne 22.1061.

[144] Cf. *Com. in Jh.* 1.17; cf. *De Princ.* 2.1.5. Matter (*hypokeimenon*) is a kind of non-being: *ex ouk onton*.

Origen assumes the "Father is by virtue of his own nature".[145] God is the only substance whose existence is given by none. He never received any beginning of being. His existence and essence are identical. This is why, categorically, substance refers to God alone.

God is the only necessary existent hypostasis. Origen illustrates this categorically. Only the category substance has referential efficacy to God the Father. Consequently, his existence is necessary existence.

Universality and necessity belong to God alone. He is the first principle and cause of all things. He pertains essentially to himself, to the Logos and the Holy Spirit, and to all rational beings. God is the cause of rational being in all its types, generated and created.[146]

Origen assumes the Logos and Holy Spirit are not by virtue of their own nature.[147] When he refers to the Logos and the Holy Spirit their essence and existence are not identical. Their existence is based on a nature prior to their own. This is why, categorically, not only substance but relation and quality refer to the Logos and the Holy Spirit.

Universality and necessity belong to the Logos. The Logos is the creator of all things.[148] He pertains essentially to God, and all things pertain to him. The Logos is the sustainer of all types of being.[149]

Particularity and necessity belong to the Holy Spirit. The Holy Spirit is the sustainer of the "saints".[150] He pertains essentially to God the Logos and only the saved pertain to him. The Holy Spirit is the sustainer of certain types of rational being.[151]

Particularity and contingency belong to the created intelligibles and the sensibles. They subsist and exist differently than God, the Logos and the Holy Spirit. They are dependent for their substance on God, for their existence on God through the Logos, and for their salvation on God and the Logos through the Holy Spirit.

Their essence and existence are not identical. They exist by virtue of natures prior to their own.[152] Origen pictures this categorically. All the categories have referential efficacy to created substance and existence. Consequently, their essence and existence are accidental.

---

[145] Following *In Lib. 1 Sam. Hom.*, 1.11.
[146] Cf. e.g., *De Princ.* 1.2.2; 1.2.4; 1.2.8; cf. *In Jerem. Hom.* 10.7; *Com. in Jh.* 20.18; *De Princ.* 4.4.1.
[147] See nn. 136, 138.
[148] Cf. e.g., There was no time when he was not, cf. *De Princ.* 4.4.1. He also gives existence to all things, cf. *De Princ.* 1.5.5.
[149] Cf. *De Princ.* 3.1.2 where the Logos is the efficient and instrumental cause of created things.
[150] Cf. e.g., *De Princ.*, Pr. 4; *De Princ.* 1.2.3.
[151] Cf. *Com. in Jh.* 2.10.
[152] They are and exist *kata symbebekos*, cf. *Com. in Jh.* 2.18.75.

In summary, Origen's degree of reality metaphysic has two aspects. One is Platonic, the other is Peripatetic. First, his distinctions between first principles, intelligibles, sensibles and matter are expressed through the paradigmatic terminology of Platonism. Second, his distinctions between modes of essence, existence, and non-existence are defined through the *realist* categorical terminology of Aristotelianism.

Origen employs Platonic and Peripatetic models to distinguish between an eternal paradigm and its image; an eternally generated paradigm and its images; as well as to distinguish absolute from relative being; and necessary from contingent existence.

The Academic categories function to divide being into its absolute and relative degrees: eternal and ungenerated, eternally generated, first generated, and created. The Peripatetic categories function to define being and existence in its different modes. First, the variety of meanings being has, that is, subsistent and inherent being. Second, the variety of meanings existence has, that is, necessary and contingent existence.

For Origen the categories refer to things. They, however, also refer to words which signify things and to concepts which signify things. Thus, he held a *nominalist* and a *conceptualist* approach to the categories. To conclude our study, we turn to these aspects of his category theory.

Origen uses dialectic to uncover the meanings of words in scripture and the meaning of words which signify things in nature.[153] He calls such words "signs" (*semeia-dicta*) which present "common notions" (*koinai ennoiai*) to the mind.[154]

Signs are of two kinds—commemorative and indicative.[155] Scriptural words are indicative signs which yield to the mind knowledge of immaterial things. Natural words are commemorative signs which yield to the mind knowledge of material things.

Knowledge is presented to the mind through language and the meaning language conveys. Since words signify things and present notions to the mind, language and its concepts have categorical reference.[156] The categories are about words which signify things by way of signifying concepts. Consequently, they are utilized by Origen to define and classify the substance and accidents of things grammatically and conceptually.[157] Nominally and conceptually the categories inform the intellect about the meaning of words as they refer to things.

---

[153] Cf. *C. Cels.* 6.7; *Com. in Jh.* 20.43.
[154] Cf. *C. Cels.* 7.34.
[155] On Origen's theory of signs, see Berchman, *op. cit.*, 209–214.
[156] This notion is presented by Origen at *De Princ.* 4.4.6.
[157] See *Com. in Jh.* 2.18; *De Princ.* 4.4.6.

This use has importance because it is through logical and conceptual analysis that Origen defines and classifies first principles and classifies the degrees of reality.

When the categories are employed in this manner Origen is able to demonstrate that categorical reference yields knowledge about the essence and existence of things.

For example, since the Father is neither genus, species, or differentia, he is beyond knowledge, classification and definition. He is known to the Son alone.[158]

Only substance has reference to the Father. We only know what he is not. We know he is without quality, place, and so on. The categories perform an important role in the epistemological and logical *apophaticism* of Origen's philosophical theology.

The Son, the Holy Spirit, and created things are knowable. They are defined, classified and known through the categories.

For example, the Son is known through the categories which have reference to him. He is a qualified substance in relation to the Father, Spirit, and cosmos. He is the place of the genera and species of creation. The categories play a large role in the epistemological and logical *kataphaticism* of Origen's metaphysic.

For Origen the Logos is a primary intelligible. He is called the "idea of ideas" (*idea ideon*).[159] He contains within his intellect the prefigurations of all the genera and species of the intelligible and sensible worlds.[160]

When the Logos created the universe, these prefigurations became the formative principles of the universe[161] These *eide-logoi* are the shape or form of matter.[162]

Through the categories Origen is able to classify, and define created reality according to genus, species, and differentia.[163] He is able to know the types of essence and existence equivocally, univocally, and analogically. He is able to know what existents are essential and necessary and which are accidental and contingent.

In summary, Origen's theoretic and category theory exhibits the *apophatic-kataphatic* mixture we have come to expect from Platonism before Plotinus. However, how this mixture is presented is quite different. Origen's *apophaticism* and *kataphaticism* is largely expressed through a new, bold Platonic-Aristotelian synthesis.

---

158   Cf. *De Princ.* 1.1.9.
159   Cf. *C. Cels.* 6.64.
160   Cf. *Com. in Jh.* 1.24; 19.22; cf. Justinian, *Ep. ad Men.* = Mansi 9.528.
161   Cf. *C. Cels.* 5.39, 43; cf. 5.24.
162   *Ibid.*
163   Cf. *Com. in Jh.* 13.21.

He postulates a radically transcendent God whose Logos is the mere image and impress of the Father and whose Holy Spirit is the image and impress of his Son. He underscores this by distinguishing a subsistent and necessary God, with a inherent and contingent existence. His *apophaticism* is unparalleled in its Platonic rigorousness.

He also postulates a God who imparts his being and existence to the Logos and through the Logos and the Holy Spirit to creation. Eternal being and existence imparts being and existence to a whole universe. Both are sustained through his Logos and Holy Spirit. His *kataphaticism* is unparalled in its Platonic inclusiveness.

Conclusion

This partial, yet it is hoped, representative survey of Middle Platonic category theories, does not yield firm conclusions about their use. The full extent of its use and function can be drawn only when all the evidence has been collected and analyzed. Nonetheless, it is possible to draw a few preliminary conclusions:

1. Philo, Clement, and Origen make extensive use of Stoic and Peripatetic category theory. They apply them to an Academic context. Their category theories form an integral part of the "Modified" trajectory of Platonic *apophatic-kataphatic* metaphysics between Eudorus and Origen.
2. Philo, Clement, and Origen employ *pragmatic* category theories to explain the relationship between deity and cosmos and between first principles, first principles and intelligibles, and intelligibles and sensibles.
3. For Philo, Clement, and Origen the categories have *realist, nominalist,* and *conceptualist* functions which serve to establish a *methexis* between deity and creation, first principles and intelligibles, and intelligibles and sensibles.
4. Philo, Clement, and Origen use of the categories permits us to make two main points:
    a. The categorical distinction between God the Father and creation permits each to maintain an epistemological *apophaticism.*
    b. The categorical relation between God the Father, Logos, and creation permits each to assert an ontological *kataphaticism.*

The categories, then, are a valuable tool for interpreting a constellation of problems that dominated later Platonic metaphysics. Philo, Clement, and Origen were not only receptive to a Modified Platonic solution to these problems. They were at the center of elucidating solutions to them. Therefore, their writings are important and independent contributions to the history of Platonic metaphysics. Indeed, to view their writings from this perspective is to connect them with their proper contextual world—the world of later Hellenistic metaphysics.

If this study has shed some light on this world and stimulated others to investigate these connections further, it will have more than fulfilled its purpose.

ARITHMOLOGY AS AN EXEGETICAL TOOL IN THE WRITINGS OF PHILO OF ALEXANDRIA

Horst R. Moehring

Introduction

This paper represents a stage in the development of a study of arithmology in Philo, which has been undertaken as part of the effort of the Philo project research team under the leadership of Burton Mack at the Institute for Antiquity and Christianity at Claremont, California.[1] To keep this paper within appropriate limits and yet show the range of functions which arithmology as an exegetical tool performs in the works of Philo, the discussion will concentrate on only one number within the decade, namely seven. This is not the most significant number within the Pythagorean system of arithmology, but for obvious reasons it has a special appeal for Philo. The paper will attempt to demonstrate the arithmological use of the number seven as an integral part of the exegetical arsenal employed by Philo, and it will try to indicate the type of world view Philo seeks to develop, among many other methods, with the help of arithmology. Such an agenda will require a brief summary of the character and development of arithmology in antiquity.

Recent study of arithmology

The study of the use of numbers in the exegetical writings of Philo, on the whole, has been rather accidental. Many authors speak of a Pythagorean influence on Philo, e.g., Henry Chadwick:

> Pythagoreanism was probably liked by Philo for its cryptic symbolism, its allegorical interpretation of poetic myth, its gnomic morality, and above all its speculations about the mysterious significance of numbers, notably the number seven, which played so important a role in sabbatarian Judaism.[2]

---

[1] I wish to thank Burton Mack and the other members of the team for their valuable critique of my preliminary report and the instructive discussions in general.

[2] Henry Chadwick, "Philo," in A.H. Armstrong (ed.): *The Cambridge History of Later Greek and Early Medieval Philosophy* (Cambridge U.P., 1970) 141. Chadwick also stresses Philo's dependence upon Plato. In an author of the first century, it is not easy to separate all strands of tradition that may have influenced him.

Richard A. Baer speaks of the "extremely complex issue of the philosophical (especially Neo-Pythagorean) background of Philo's use of numbers to describe reality."[3] Frank E. Robbins thinks that Philo's lost work, περὶ ἀριθμῶν, "was not an element of arithmetic, but an arithmology, in which were collected Pythagorean topics that appear in the extant works, and more."[4]

Erwin R. Goodenough, on the other hand, doubts that we have sufficient information to assign specific passages in Philo to the influence of either Pythagoras or Plato:

> The difficulty is that when we compare Philo with the neo-Pythagorean fragments we are without any criterion to determine how much of what resembles Platonism in them has been brought into Pythagorean tradition from Plato's teaching, and how much of it is early genuine Pythagoreanism which Plato knew.[5]

John Dillon devotes a chapter to Philo in his work on the Middle Platonists, and in his list of characteristics of Middle Platonism, he mentions as the fifth and last item, "vivid interest particularly in mystical numerology."[6]

Although he does not specifically refer to Philo, Martin P. Nilsson has some interesting comments on the symbolic use of numbers:

> Besonders bezeichnend für den Pythagoreismus ist die Zahlensymbolik... Die Zahlensymbolik hat an sich keine große religiöse Bedeutung, besitzt aber, wie sich noch in unserer Zeit zeigt, eine eigentümliche Anziehungskraft auf gewisse Gemüter. Auch die Arithmetik hat ihre Mystik.[7]

The only monograph ever written on our topic developed out of a doctoral dissertation submitted to the *philosophische Fakultät* of the University of Tübingen by Karl Staehle: *Die Zahlenmystik bei Philon von Alexandreia.* [8]

---

[3] Richard A. Baer, Jr., *Philo's Use of the Categories Male and Female*, Arbeiten zur Literatur und Geschichte des hellenistischen Judentums III (Leiden: E.J. Brill, 1970) 16, n. 3.

[4] Frank E. Robbins, "Arithmetic in Philo Judaeus," *Classical Philology* XVI (1921), 345–361, 360.

[5] Erwin R. Goodenough, *An Introduction to Philo Judaeus* (New Haven: Yale U.P., 1940; repr. Oxford: Basil Blackwell, 1962) 111.

[6] John Dillon, *The Middle Platonists* (Ithaca, New York: Cornell U.P., 1977) 114.

[7] Martin P. Nilsson, *Geschichte der griechischen Religion,* Handbuch der Altertumswissenschaft V.2.1–2 (München: Verlag C.H. Beck, 2nd ed., 1961) II, 417. Nilsson also has a low opinion of what he calls *Zahlensymbolik*: "[Sie] imponierte der großen Menge durch ihre Schwerverständlichkeit und Spitzfindigkeit, sie verschaffte den Pythagoreern den Ruf, geheimes Wissen zu besitzen" [*ibid.*]

[8] Leptzig und Berlin: Teubner, 1931. Staehle tries to reconstruct Philo's lost work περὶ ἀριθμῶν. He gives a brief survey of arithmology before Philo and reaches this verdict on Philo's accomplishment: "Philon ist in allen Dingen so sehr Pythagoreer und weicht in der Methode der vorgelegten Zeugnisse so wenig von ihnen ab, daß man

Definition of terms

The quotations adduced from the authors just named not only illustrate the fact that modern scholars are encountering difficulties in classifying so complex an ancient author as Philo (a rather common phenomenon in the study of figures from late antiquity), but also that there exists a pronounced and confusing lack of agreement in the use of terminology connected with the study of Philo's use of numbers.[9] While Philo was certainly no mathematician and can hardly be accused of consistency in his voluminous writings, the lack of a generally accepted terminology among modern scholars will only make any comprehensive study of Philo even more difficult than it already is.

The expression "number mysticism" ("*Zahlenmystik*") suffers from the lack of any clear definition of "mysticism" in connection with number. Until the question has finally been solved whether the writings of Philo actually reflect a mystic form of Judaism,[10] it would appear advisable not to confuse the issue through the use of an ambiguous and probably misleading term. Philo's main purpose in his use of numbers as an exegetical tool is to demonstrate that God's creation is orderly and in

---

seine Schrift περὶ ἀριθμῶν beinahe als ein pythagoreisches Lehrbuch bezeichnen könnte, und zwar als eines der umfangreichsten und ältesten, die wir kennen denn alle die Werke, aus denen ich Parallelen gegeben habe, sind später und stammen aus dem 2. bis 6. nachchristlichen Jahrhundert. Philons Werk aber geht hinauf bis in die frühe Kaiserzeit" (11). Staehle's comments on the importance of Philo's arithmological passages are essentially correct. This means that, quite apart from their value as a source for the study of Philo's exegetical methods, they possess an intrinsic value of their own and should be of interest to any student of late antiquity.

[9] E.g., H. Chadwick: "speculations about the mysterious significance of numbers;" F.E. Robbins: "arithmology;" John Dillon: "mystical numerology;" M.P. Nilsson: "Zahlensymbolik," "Mystik der Arithmetik;" K. Staehle: "Zahlenmystik."

[10] See especially Erwin R. Goodenough, *By Light, Light* (New Haven, 1935; repr. Amsterdam: Philo Press, 1969) and *Jewish Symbols in the Graeco-Roman Period* (New York: Bollingen Foundation 1953–68). In X, 72 Goodenough refers to Scholem's work on Jewish mysticism and adduces some instances in which numbers form part of the mystical speculations and then states that this shows "definitely the influence of late hellenistic or Neoplatonic number mysticism, but all integrated quite securely with Jewish conceptions and the Hebrew alphabet. In this mysticism one does not ascend to the throne, ... , but one performs a symbolic act by putting on a special garment in which the name of God had been woven." It is possible that the use of numbers in the Jewish mystical work *Sefer Yetsirah* (a hundred years ago dated around the eighth century, now placed by Scholem somewhere between the third and sixth centuries, *Kabbalah* (Jerusalem: Keter Publishing House, 1974; 27) may have influenced Goodenough to assign numbers a similar function in earlier sources. As will be shown below, only one or two passages in Philo can be regarded as showing numbers with a mystical significance; Philo also states explicitly that the numbers do not permit man to achieve anything like a union with God.

harmony with certain numbers and numerical relations. But at the same time he repeatedly insists that the orderliness and harmony of the cosmos must not mislead the observer into confusing the creation with the creator: that is the serious mistake made by the "Chaldaeans":

> The Chaldaeans were especially active in the elaboration of astrology and ascribed everything to the movement of the stars, guided by influences contained in numbers and numerical proportions. Thus they glorified visible existence, leaving out of consideration the intelligible and invisible. But while exploring numerical order as applied to the revolution of the sun, moon, and other planets, and fixed stars, and the changes of the yearly seasons and the interdependence of phenomena in heaven and on earth, they concluded that the world itself was God, thus profanely likening the created to the Creator.[11]

In a similar vein: "These men [i.e., the Chaldaeans] imagined that the visible universe was the only thing in existence, either itself being God or containing God in itself as the soul of the whole."[12]

In the light of such passages it would probably be easier to argue that Philo used numbers to stress the impossibility of reaching God even through the purest and most abstract thought processes than to demonstrate some form of number mysticism in any meaningful sense of this term.

The expression "number symbolism" is less misleading than number mysticism. It quite correctly describes the fact that many numbers, in addition to their purely numerical value, possess a symbolic meaning or, very frequently, several symbolic meanings. Greek mythology, Greek philosophical writings and poetry, the biblical text used by Philo, not to mention popular lore, all abound with references to the symbolic meanings of various numbers. Philo was aware of that and made use of many such statements. He incorporated them into his own system of using numbers as an exegetical tool. And for this very reason the term "number symbolism" is inadequate to describe the phenomenon in Philo: it is too restrictive and describes only one of the bases on which Philo developed his own method. The symbolic value assigned by Philo to various numbers is invariably part of an ancient tradition that he found at hand and put to his own particular use.

Whereas "number symbolism," within its strict limitations, correctly describes one part of Philo's exegetical use of numbers, the term "numerology" is definitely misleading. Numerology is usually understood as "the

---

[11] *Abr.* 69. English translations of Philonic passages are taken from the Loeb Classical Library translations provided by F.H. Colson, G.H. Whitaker, and, in the case of the *Quaestiones et Solutiones,* Ralph Marcus.

[12] *Migr.* 179.

study of the occult significance of numbers," with the stress clearly on "occult."[13] This is almost the exact opposite of Philo's concern. Philo uses numbers in order to demonstrate what is accessible to any one who cares to look; he does not use them to reveal anything that is not accessible to the unaided human intelligence. In this connection it is important to note that the entire corpus of Philonic writings does not contain a single instance of *gematria*. There is nothing esoteric about Philo's use of numbers.

The term "arithmology" stresses the fact that the procedure involves a systematic attempt to demonstrate the λόγος-character of the use of numbers. The term was adopted by Frank E. Robbins, who quotes the following definition of it by A. Delatte:

Arithmology is "ce genre de remarques sur la formation, la valeur et l'importance des dix premiers nombres, où se mêle la saine recherche scientifique et les fantaisies de la religion et de philosophie.[14]

Arithmology deals not only with individual and specific numbers, but also, and at least as importantly, with the various relationships existing among numbers. These relationships, on the whole, are expressed in a mathematically correct manner. The numbers themselves and their interrelationships are taken seriously and allowed to stand on their own. There may be a symbolic meaning behind the primary sense, but the mathematical value of a number is hardly ever ignored or shunted aside, as so frequently happens to the literal meaning of a text at the hands of the more extravagant exegetes.[15]

All this does not mean that arithmology would give unalloyed pleasure to a specialist in pure mathematics. Aristotle was biting in some of his criticism of some of the Pythagorean procedures and doctrines, especially on the nature of the exact relationship between numbers and reality, including geometric reality.[16] But it does mean that what we have in Philo is a serious attempt to relate the cosmic order to a rational system— expressed in numbers—and thereby to reach an understanding of the

---

[13] See *Webster's New International Dictionary of the English Language,* 2nd ed., unabridged (Springfield, Mass.: G.& C. Merriam, 1969) *s.v.*

[14] Frank E. Robbins: "Posidonius and the Sources of Pythagorean Arithmology," *Classical Philology* XV (1920) 309, n. 1, quoting from *Bibl. de l'École des Hautes Études,* fasc. 217 (Paris, 1915) 139.

[15] In the specific case of Philo, then, one could say that in his arithmology, as in his exegetical methods generally, he follows a middle course between literalism and total disregard for the literal meaning of the text.

[16] *Metaphysics* XIV.6 (1093a): "If all things must share in number, it must follow that many things are the same, and the same number must belong to one thing and another. Is number the cause, then, and does the thing exist because of its number, or is this not certain?"

universe within thought categories that are available to any and all. It was exactly the mathematically universal character of arithmology which Philo found so attractive for his exegetical work: it could help him to explain the sacred texts of the books of the law in terms that were universally understood, even though not universally accepted. Philo's concern for the mathematical soundness of his procedure can be recognized in the fact that he hardly ever tires of repeating the basic arithmetical definitions of the various numbers he adduces.[17]

For these reasons the term "arithmology," among the many designations in use, would appear to be the most appropriate one to describe the phenomenon of Philo's use of numbers. It shall be used in this paper, except, of course, in quotations from authors who use a different term.

Arithmology before Philo

We can distinguish at least three stages in the development of the use of numbers before the period of late antiquity. The history of this development is extremely complex and, to a high degree, remains obscure. Our main key, and perhaps the only one, seems to be the structure of the numerical system within a given language or family of languages. We can recognize various stages of development from such things as the number that is equated with "many" (e.g., forty) or "innumerable" (e.g., ten thousand). Numbers which form the basis for the development of larger systems, like the decimal or the duodecimal, usually achieve a position of special prominence within a language (e.g., the common use of "a dozen" in modern English).

It is the acquisition of special prominence by a given number which constitutes the decisive step to the belief that such a number possesses some extraordinary significance. Thus, if "three" is used, not merely to describe that quantity which is larger than that represented by two and smaller than that signified by four, but also to express the concept of "many" or "innumerable," and thus also of "complete," the word "three" will have acquired—and retain—a position of prominence within the numerical system of that language even long after a larger and more complex system is developed. The residual use of the word "three" (and the number designated by it) is then frequently given a symbolic meaning.

---

[17] Although he occasionally simply omits such definitions, only once does he explicitly refuse to repeat one. The reason given should amuse any reader of Philo: "Many a time has much been said about the number ten in other places, which for those who wish to prolong the discussion it would be easy to transfer here. But brevity of speech is liked by us, and it is timely and sufficient that whatever has been said be remembered" (QE 2:84). Note the incidental remark about his working habits.

Such use of numbers is ancient and seems to be universal. Any given number may thus acquire a symbolic meaning or several. Sometimes these symbolic meanings might be contradictory in character, at least to some other, occasionally logical, way of thinking. The symbolic meaning of numbers may then lead to their association with supernatural beings, and thus with myths, sacred places, liturgical instruments, sacred days or periods, persons, animals, plants, or the cosmos as a whole and in its constituent parts.

The extent and complexity of such number symbolism was carefully studied by scholars of previous generations. In 1903 Hermann Usener published a major article on the number three.[18] He not only collected an amazing amount of detailed information from every conceivable ancient source, he also followed the history of "*three*" and "*Dreiheit*," paying close attention to their many ramifications. For Usener, "three" represented an important and long stage in the history of the Indo-European languages and the attempt of the Indo-European speaking peoples to come to terms with numbers, whereas "five" did not achieve such prominence, at least among the Greeks:

> Unsere Völkergruppen [i.e., the Indo-Europeans] müssen sehr lange auf der Stufe verharrt haben, die alle ihre Zahlen noch an den Gliedern eines Fingers abzählen konnte, wo drei und vier einerlei war. Der Fortschritt zur 4 und 5 und zum dekadischen System muss dann sich rasch und unaufhaltsam vollzogen haben. Die zwei und drei hatten sich zur Vorstellungsform gestalten können: die Periode in der man bis 5 gelangt war und noch nicht die Finger der beiden Hände arithmetisch überschaute war zu kurz um sich dem Volksgeist einzuprägen.[19]

We need not accept Usener's theory about the history of numbers among speakers of Indo-European languages in order to appreciate his documentation of the widespread use of the number three in all areas of life, and particularly in the religious sphere. This use antedates by many centuries later attempts to organize the various symbolic meanings into some kind of pattern.

Of particular interest to the student of Philo is the investigation of the number seven, which played an important role in sabbatarian Judaism and, consequently, was of special importance to our author.[20] Even the most cursory survey reveals that the number seven played an important role in the lives, not only of the Hebrews or the Semites generally, but of many nations of different backgrounds, including the Greeks.

---

[18] Hermann Usener: "Dreiheit," *Rheinisches Museum für Philologie*, N.F. XXVIII, 1–47, 161–208, 321–362.

[19] *Ibid.*, 361.

[20] See note 2.

W.H. Roscher published several articles on the importance of the numbers seven and nine.[21] He clearly demonstrated that the number seven was sacred in the oldest forms of the Greek cults and myths. In the index to his 1903 article he listed over a hundred different functions of the number seven (or its multiples), and these functions reach all the way from the cult of Apollo to the use of seven black beans for magic purposes and in connection with the cult of the dead.

If numbers are important and influential, we must not be surprised that at an early stage some of them were not only sacred to certain divinities, but actually divine in their own right or, at least, identified with certain gods. Thus "seven" was given divine characteristics: ἔστι γὰρ ἡγεμὼν καὶ ἄρχων ἁπάντων, θεός, εἷς, ἀεὶ ὤν, μόνιμος, ἀκίνητος, αὐτὸς ἑαυτῶι ὅμοιος, ἕτερος τῶν ἄλλων.[22] This possibility of deifying numbers was to be exploited later by the members of the Pythagorean school. For Philolaos, "seven" is identical with Athena, and in Nicomachus of Gerasa we shall find a whole system of identifications: numbers are identified with those gods whose characteristics appeared similar to those ascribed to the numbers, thus:

Monas	—Styx, Apollo
Dyas	—Rhea, Artemis, Aphrodite, Dione
Trias	—Lato, Thetis, Harmonia, Hecate, etc.[23]

All of this, we must not forget, is deliberate creation and has nothing to do with the earlier stages in the development, when numbers had been part of the unconscious thought pattern of the people. Hermann Usener expressed this difference pointedly:

Niemand wird leugnen, dass die Pythagoreer, als sie Maass und Form der Dinge in der Zahl erkannt hatten, wie von einem Rausch ergriffen bewusst willkürliche Zahlensymbolikübten;... Aber was verwirrte Wissenschaft und was Afterweisheit ersinnen, liegt weit abseits von den einfachen und unwillkürlichen Gadankengängen des Volkes. Es ist ein offerbarer Missgriff, in den massenhaften Zahlenanwendungen, die sich in Sage und Brauch des Volkes finden, Symbolik zu suchen.[24]

---

[21] "Die enneadischen und hebdomadischen Fristen und Wochen," *Abhandlungen der philologisch-historischen Klasse der Kgl. Sächsischen Gesellschaft der Wissenschaften*, Band XXI, Nr. IV (Leipzig, 1903); "Die Sieben- und Neunzahl im Kultus und Mythus der Griechen," *ibid.* XXIV/I, 1904; "Die Hebdomadenlehre der griechischen Philosophen und Arzte," *ibid.* XXIV.2/VI, 1906; "Planeten," in his *Lexikon der griechischen und römischen Mythologie*, n.d.

[22] Hermann Diels: *Die Fragmente der Vorsokratiker*, 4th ed. (Berlin: Weidmann, 1922) 257.

[23] Quoted by Photius: *Bibliotheka*, cod. 187.

[24] Hermann Usener, *op. cit.*, 348.

With arithmology we enter into a different world. Here numbers are used neither for their traditional symbolic value, nor in the ancient unconscious and spontaneous manner of which Usener speaks. Now numbers are manipulated because of their arithmetical properties and proportions. All these are explored and used as clues for the investigation of the universe: number has become a heuristic principle. The men who worked in this field were not mythographers or obscurantists; they were people with a scientific bend of mind. A man like Pythagoras grew up in a world full of symbolic numbers. In his native Ionia the number seven was held in particular awe, and this number was important also to the Orphics and the Delphic cult of Apollo. An intelligent and alert mind simply could not escape the influence of numbers upon every sphere of life. We do not know exactly what Pythagoras adopted from Babylonia, what he himself discovered and what was attributed to him by his immediate and later disciples. He was the founder of a school that combined scientific inquiry with a common way of life based upon strict and ascetic rules. The school acquired great political influence, especially after Pythagoras' emigration to Magna Graecia. Among the characteristics of the Pythagorean school in its later forms is one of special interest to us: the production of a number of pseudonymous writings attributed to the founder. There can be no doubt that the combination of intellectual activity and communal life, all, of course, within the context of cultic practices, was to be one of the main reasons for the reawakening of interest in the Pythagorean tradition and its teachings during the Graeco-Roman period.

The foundation of the mathematical work done by the Pythagoreans was the exploration of the numbers of the decade and their interrelationships. Smaller and higher numbers were put into a relationship to ten, before they were analyzed any further. Thus, four is important, because it is potentially what ten is in actuality. Thirty, to give another arbitrary example, will be analyzed as 3 x 10. In reading about these ancient Greek studies of arithmetic, the important thing to keep in mind is that the Pythagoreans did all this work visually: numbers were represented by pebbles, and the structure of numbers was made visible through the arrangement of these pebbles in certain patterns, so that the Pythagoreans were able to speak of triangular, square, or pentagonal numbers—and this was meant in a literal sense. A basic illustration of this principle is the representation of the τετρακτύς, the arrangement of the numbers 1, 2, 3, and 4:

.

. .

. . .

. . . .

The sum of 1 + 2 + 3 + 4 is 10, and, as is obvious from the illustration, ten is a triangular number.

We must further keep in mind that what the Pythagoreans did was not computation (which was left to slaves), but the development of a theory of numbers. When they worked on problems of geometry, they used such terms as point, line, or surface as neutral concepts which have no dimension beyond the purely mathematical one. The pebbles on the ground, in their precise arrangement, merely served as aids for the abstract mental operation. This method has one great and important advantage, namely the gain of generality.

The philosophically most important discovery associated with the name of Pythagoras was the recognition that the musical consonants of octave, quint, and quart can be expressed through the numerical proportions of 1:2, 2:3, and 3:4. The conclusion drawn from this observation was that number is the force that ordered the world, both the macrocosmos and the microcosmos. This principle can be extended to the point where it means that the cosmos is numbers.

> These thinkers [i.e., the Pythagoreans] also consider that a number is the principle both as matter for things and as forming both their modifications and their permanent states, and hold that the elements of number are the even and the odd, and that of these the latter is limited, and the former unlimited; and that the One proceeds from both of these (for it is both even and odd) and number from the One, and that the whole heaven is numbers.[25]

It is not clear what made possible the claim that "heaven is numbers." It could have been the Babylonian recognition of seven planets which then led to the doctrine of the harmony of the spheres. It could also have been the result of a dynamic reinterpretation of the static cosmology developed by Anaximander.[26] Such sweeping claims for the all-pervading importance of numbers evoked the scorn of an empiricist like Aristotle, but they had great influence upon Plato, whose *Timaeus* (but not only this dialogue) is heavily indebted to Pythagorean thought.

For the study of cosmogony and cosmology from the fourth century B.C. on, the *Timaeus* proves to be the starting point, whether for assent or dissent. A scholar like A. Schmekel even argued that the main source from which the Pythagorean and Pythagorizing authors of the Roman

---

[25]   Aristotle, *Metaphysics* I, 986a 15–21.
[26]   On Anaximander's cosmology, see G.S. Kirk and J.E. Raven, *The Presocratic Philosophers* (Cambridge U.P., 1957, repr. 1971) 131–142; W.K.C. Guthrie, *A History of Greek Philosophy, vol. I: The Earlier Presocratics and the Pythagoreans* (Cambridge U.P., 1962) 89–115; W.L. West, *Early Greek Philosophy and the Orient* (Oxford: Clarendon Press, 1971) 83–97.

period drew their knowledge of Pythagorean arithmology was the (lost) commentary on the *Timaeus* by Poseidonius.[27]

Plato formulated two concepts in the *Timaeus* which turned out to be important for Philo's interpretation of the account of creation in Genesis: the existence of a world of being above our world of becoming, and number as the basic component of, and the key to, the universe:

> What is that which is existent always and has no becoming? And what is that which is becoming always and never is existent?[28]

> Before that time,... all those things were in a state devoid of reason, but when the work of setting in order this universe was undertaken, fire and water and earth and air, although possessing some traces of their own nature, were yet so disposed as everything is likely to be in the absence of God; and inasmuch as this was their natural condition, God began by first making them out into shapes by means of forms and numbers.[29]

With Plato, then, the decisive step had been taken. Philosophers were to continue to argue whether Plato ever came to identify the numbers with the ideas,[30] or debate the question of how mathematical abstracts can influence the material cosmos—nevertheless, a model for the understanding of the universe had been established that was to exercise profound influence far beyond the confines of the Academy and its derivative philosophical movements and schools.

The history of Pythagoreanism and its development into—or according to Eduard Zeller, its new start as—Neopythagoreanism, is a highly complex problem. Walter Burkert has analyzed the modern study of this question and distinguishes three basic positions.[31]

---

[27] A. Schmekel, *Die Philosophie der mittleren Stoa in ihrem geschichtlichen Zusammenhange dargestellt* (Berlin, 1892) 403ff. The view developed by Schmekel became very influential and led Roscher to attempt a reconstruction of portions of Poseidonius' commentary from Philo's *De Opificio Mundi* ("Die Hebdomadenlehre ...," 112–127). For an alternate view (accepted by Staehle), see F.E. Robbins, "Posidonius and the Sources of Pythagorean Arithmology." On completely different grounds, classical scholars like Wilamowitz had denied the existence of such a commentary by Poseidonius.

[28] Plato: *Timaeus* 27D (Bury's translation in the LCL).

[29] *Ibid.* 53B.

[30] Cf. the instructive work by Julius Stenzel, *Zahl und Gestalt bei Platon und Aristoteles* (Leipzig: Teubner, 1924). This work is probably more faithful to Plato's thought than Eva Sachs, *Die fünf platonishchen Körper, Zur Geschichte der Mathematik und der Elementenlehre Platons und der Pythagoreer,* Philosophische Unterschungen, 24. Haft (Berlin, Weidmann, 1917).

[31] Walter Burkert, "Hellenistische Pseudopythagorica," *Philologus* 105 (1961), 16–43, 226–246; cf. the debate between Burkert and Thesleff in *Pseudepigrapha I,* Entretiens Fondation Hardt 18 (Geneva, 1972); Burkert, *Weisheit und Wissenschaft Studien zu Pythagoras, Philolaos und Platon,* Erlanger Beiträge zur Sprach- und Kunstwissenschaft 10, (Nürnberg: Carl, 1962); Kurt von Fritz, "Mathematiker und Akusmatiker bei den alten Pythagoreern," (SB München, philologische historische Klasse, 1960) Heft XI.

(a) Eduard Zeller argued that the old school of Pythagoreanism died out soon after the middle of the fourth century B.C.[32] A Pythagorean school of philosophy did not come into existence again until the end of the second century B.C.[33] This means that between the Pythagoreanism of the old school and Neopythagoreanism there existed a gap of over two centuries.

(b) Zeller was criticized for failing to take into account the fact that, according to an ancient source preserved in Iamblichus,[34] the Pythagoreans were divided into two groups: the "mathematicians" and the "acusmatics." The "mathematicians" were the scientists, representatives of a *rational nuchtern* wing,[35] whereas the "acusmatics" represented the *mystisch-magische* wing of the movement, who were mainly interested in maintaining the old taboos and religious doctrines of the school.[36] Zeller also ignored the existence of the Pythagorean pseudepigrapha. Some scholars, particularly Carcopino,[37] argued that the mystical wing of the Pythagoreans never ceased to exist and became the nucleus of the Neopythagorean movement. By playing down the distinctions between the "mathematicians" and the "acusmatics," one could finally argue, in complete contrast to Zeller, that the Pythagorean school enjoyed an uninterrupted existence from the days of its founder till the end of Neopythagoreanism.

(c) Burkert, finally, tried to do justice to both the existence of the Pythagorean pseudepigrapha and the statements in ancient authors that after an interval of several centuries, Pythagoreanism had a fresh start during the Roman period.[38] He argues that the kind of non-rational

---

[32] Eduard Zeller, *Die Philosophie der Griechen in ihrer geschichtlichen Entwicklung*, 6th ed. (Leipzig, 1919, repr. Darmstadt: Wissenschaftliche Buchgesellschaft, 1963) I, 426. Zeller, however, makes two important qualifications: "Die bakshisch-pythagoreischen Orgien" continued, and the Pythagorean school survived in Italy.

[33] *Ibid.* III/2, 103: "...fehlt es bis zum Ende des zweiten Jahrhunderts an jedem Beweis für das Fortleben einer pythagoreischen Philosophenschule, und von den Schriftstellern der folgenden Jahrhunderte können auch solche, denen jede Spur ihrer Fortdauer willkommen gewesen wäre, von derselben noch nichts gewußt haben, da sie ihr zeitweiliges Erlöschen unbedenklich berichten."

[34] *Vita Pythg.* 81, 87–89.

[35] Kurt V. Fritz, in the "Discussion of 'Doric Pseudo-pythagorica'" in *Pseudepigrapha* I, 88.

[36] V. Fritz, *loc. cit.*; "Generally, the latter group claims to have preserved without change the original teaching of the master, whereas the former do fresh research and publish it under their own names."

[37] Carcopino, *Le mystère d'un symbol chrétien* (Paris, 1955) esp. 40ff.

[38] Cf. Cicero's statement on Publius Nigidius Figulus (98–45 B.C.) in the introduction to his translation of Plato's *Timaeus*: "He was not only versed in all the other arts which are proper to a gentleman, but was also a keen and diligent investigator of those things that lie hid in nature. Last, but not least, it was he, in my judgment, who, following on those noble Pythagoreans, whose system of philosophy, after

thinking found in some forms of Pythagoreanism continued to exist "underground" even after the demise of the Pythagorean school.[39] The "surface" of intellectual life was dominated by "rational" thinkers, but below the surface, interest in everything mysterious, Oriental, and ancient continued unabated. Figures of the distant past were credited with arcane knowledge, one of these figures being Pythagoras. Only during the last century B.C. did this type of thinking once again become respectable and thus enabled to surface: "Darin also liegt der nicht zu leugnende Neubeginn des Pythagoreismus im 1. Jh. v. Chr.: was zuvor literarisch war, wird ins Leben zurückgerufen, an Stelle der Pseudopythagorica treten wieder die Pythagoreer."[40] At the same time, Burkert passes judgement on the intellectual value of Neopythagoreanism: Greek science in the first century was in a state of decay, and the return to the name of Pythagoras was not a return to science. The new cosmology was more religious than scientific in character, and it pretended to offer more than science is ever able to give.

The interest in Pythagorean thought and arithmology, however, was by no means restricted to Greek and Roman thinkers. Philo is the obvious and most important evidence that this type of thinking also appealed to Jews, but he is neither the only nor even the first Jewish author who can be cited in evidence for this.

Nikolaus Walter, in his monograph on Aristobulus, has a chapter on "Aristobulus und die Angänge eines jüdischen Pythagoreismus."[41] Walter assumes the existence of a Pythagorean (or Pythagoreanizing) *florilegium* in which had been collected from various poets many passages that lent themselves to number speculations. This collection would have contained references to all the numbers within the decade. An Alexandrian Jew then extracted all those passages which dealt with the number seven. Walter speculates that the motivation may have been a desire to collect evidence for the universal character of the commandment to observe the seventh day as a holy day. This unknown Jewish excerptor spared no pains to prove his point, "wobei er sich nicht gescheut hätte, auch in jenem echten Homervers die Vier in eine Sieben zu ändern (um so eine wirklich überraschende Parallele zum jüdischen Schöpfungsglauben zu erhalten) und weitere Verse dazuzuerfinden, bzw. zu

---

flourishing for a number of centuries in Italy and Sicily, was somehow extinguished, arose to revive it." Quoted by John Dillon, *The Middle Platonists*, 117.

[39] Burkert borrows his analogy from Erwin Rohde, *Psyche*, 9th–10th eds., Tübingen, 1925, II, 296.

[40] Burkert, *op. cit.*, 235.

[41] Nikolaus Walter, *Der Thoraausleger Aristobulus*, Texte und Unterschungen 86 (Berlin: Akademie-Verlag, 1964) 166–171.

bearbeiten."[42] Although, Walter argues, the Neopythagoreans quite generally tended to establish a connection between numbers and the cosmos, a Jewish writer, and especially one of the diaspora, would have concentrated on the link between the number seven and creation. It is important to note that Walter thinks that this development of a Jewish Pythagoreanism had its beginnings before Aristobulus, who merely is our oldest extant source. The main contribution made by Aristobulus would have been his claim that the Greek poets whose verses he quotes stood in a relationship of literary dependence upon Moses.

When we finally come to Philo, then, Pythagorean arithmology would not have been anything strange and unknown to him. It had begun to "resurface" among the Greeks and had even made its first impressions on Jewish exegetes of the Torah.

The number seven in the writings of Philo

Whenever Philo introduces a topic with a preliminary statement about its richness, importance, and difficulties, the reader is warned to expect a large amount of diverse materials collected from different sources. The *Opificio Mundi* contains one hundred and seventy-two sections, of which forty, or 23.26% are devoted to a discussion of the many aspects of the number seven.[43] Philo supplies the reader with the following introductory remarks:

> I doubt whether anyone could adequately celebrate the properties of the number seven, for they are beyond all words. Yet the fact that it is more wondrous than all that is said about it is no reason for maintaining silence regarding it. Nay, we must make a brave attempt to bring out all that is within the compass of our understanding, even if it be impossible to bring out all or even the most essential points.[44]

These forty sections on the number seven give most of the arithmological interpretations possible, with much of the material being repeated in *Leg.* 1: 8–16. A few points about this section are worth noting:
It contains only three short passages of unmistakably Jewish content:

    a. 89:   creation of the world in accordance with the properties of the number six, a perfect number;

    b. 116: the law enjoins the keeping of the greatest national festivals at the time of the equinoxes, both of which fall into a seventh month;[45]

---

[42] *Ibid.*, 167.
[43] *Opif.* 89–128.
[44] *Opif.* 90.
[45] On this seeming paradox see below.

c. 128: Moses exceeded the scientists among the Greeks and other peoples in
according honor to the number seven by incorporating it into the Law
and by ordaining the observance of the seventh day as holy.[46]

In contrast to these sparse references to the Jewish tradition, which
could be excised without any effect on the section as a whole, Philo
brings, in addition to the straightforward arithmological statements, a
number of interesting quotations from Greek authors and allusions to
Greek institutions. These form an integral part of the section and cannot
be deleted without violating the structure of the whole. The most obvious of
these passages are the following:

a. 100: Some philosophers liken seven to the motherless and virgin Nike,[47]who
is said to have appeared out of the head of Zeus; the Pythagoreans, on the
other hand, liken seven to Zeus, on which Philo quotes the Pythagorean
Philolaus:[48] "There is a supreme ruler of all things, ever one, abiding,
without motion, himself (alone) like unto himself, different from the
others."
b. 104: Long quotation from Solon's poem on the seven ages of man.
c. 105: Quotation from Hippocrates on the seven ages of man.
d. 119: Reference to Plato's *Timaeus* 75D: through the mouth mortal things have
their entrance, immortal things their exit.[49]
e. 124: Reference to Hippocrates for the time needed for the solidification of the
seed and the formation of the embryo.
f. 126: Reference to the seven vowels of language (appropriate for Ionian).
g. 127: Etymologies for both the Greek and Latin words for seven, which prove
that seven is a holy number.
h. 128: The most approved mathematicians and astronomers among the Greeks
and other peoples pay honor to the number seven.

A similar, detailed summary of the properties of the number seven is to
be found in *Legum Allegoriae* 1: 5–18. In the paragraph preceding this
section, Philo states the purpose of his arithmological speculations, which,
of course, he ascribes to Moses himself: "Moses' wish is to exhibit alike the
things created of mortal kind and those that are incorruptible as having
been formed in a way corresponding to their proper numbers."[50]

---

[46] Even in this perfunctory bow to Moses, Philo describes the purpose of the sabbath
observance in purely universalistic and philosophical terms: "giving their time to the
one sole object of philosophy with a view to the improvement of character and
submission to the scrutiny of conscience."
[47] Athena.
[48] Fifth century B.C. But see below on *Leg.* 1:15.
[49] Plato actually establishes a contrast between ἀναγκαῖα and ἄριστα.
[50] *Leg.* 1:4. The passage is important for the understanding of the entire system of
arithmology in Philo.

This discussion of seven includes a quotation from Euripides,[51] in which the author stresses the integral link between birth and death, an idea Philo will put to use in his discussion of the relationship between the numbers one and seven.

The section closes with a reference to Gen. 2:2, so that the predominantly Greek main part of the section is, as it were, framed by two specific references to things Jewish.

A quick summary of the purely arithmological statements on the number seven, without any specific application to biblical texts, would have to include the following items. They constitute the basic material which Philo uses in his exegetical application of arithmology.[52]

Opif. 91	1.	There are two types of "seven:"
		a. within the decade—consists of seven units and is determined by the seven-fold repetition of the unit;
Opif. 92–94		b. outside the decade: starting from one, it is obtained by seven fold doubling, tripling, etc.; e.g., $64 = 1, 2, 4, 8, 16, 32, 64$ $729 = 1, 3, 9, 27, 81, 243, 729$
Opif. 92		Type (b) is superior: the seventh term of any regular procession, starting from unity and with a ratio of 2, 3, or any number, is both a cube and a square, combining both the corporeal and the incorporeal substance.[53]
Opif. 99–100	2.	The hebdomad within the decade is neither product nor factor. For this reason some people have likened it to the motherless, ever virgin Athena.
Leg. 1: 15		
Mos. 2:210		
QG 2:12		
Spec. 2:56		
Her. 170 216		
Contempl. 65		
Praem. 153		
Decal. 102		

[51] Fragment 839:   Naught that is born does ever die,
                                   Its severed parts together fly,
                                   And yield another shape.

[52] For a schematic presentation of the Greek text and brief references to similar passages in ancient authors, see K. Staehle, *Die Zahlenmystik* ..., 34–50. Since Staehle is interested in reconstructing Philo's lost work on numbers and the history of Neopythagoreanism, he omits from his work all specifically Jewish data (p. III).

[53] In other places (e.g., *QG* 1:77), Philo will argue that the ones are prior to the tens both in order and in power, so that seven is more archetypal and elder than seventy.

Opif. 100	3.	Other writers liken it to Zeus.[54]
QG 2:12		
Leg. 1:15	4.	For this reason the hebdomad is related to the
Deus. 11, 13		monad.[55]
Opif. 95, 96	5.	All partitions of the hebdomad produce musical harmony:

7 = 1 + 6 (6:1 = greatest distance from highest to lowest note)

= 2 + 5 (5:2 = fullest power in harmonies, almost like diapason)

= 3 + 4 (4:3 = first harmony, the sesquitertian or diates saron).

Opif. 107–110	6.	The hebdomad is absolutely harmonious, the source of the most beautiful scale, which contains all the harmonies:

that yielded by the interval of 4

that yielded by the interval of 5

that yielded by the octave.

Opif. 97	7.	In the right-angled triangle, 3 and 4 (components of 7) produce the right angle.
Opif. 98, 106, 102	8.	The hebdomad is the starting point of all plane and solid geometry, or: the hebdomad is the starting point of all things corporeal and incorporeal.
Opif. 101	9.	The hebdomad serves as a symbol in both the intelligible and the sensible world:

a. in the intelligible world it is a symbol for "that which is exempt from movement and passion;"

b. in the sensible world, the hebdomad is a most essential force [in the movement of the planets], from which all earthly things derive advantage.

Opif. 112	10.	Heaven is girdled by seven zones.
Opif. 113	11.	There are seven planets.[56]
Leg. 1:8		
Spec. Leg. 2:57		
Decal. 102		
QE 2:78		

---

[54] Note that seven is likened to Athena or Zeus no fewer than eleven times. The use of motifs from Greek religion is obviously not a problem for Philo.

[55] The affinity between one and seven plays an important role in Philo. He proves it on the basis of the biblical text. For detailed discussion, see below.

[56] In *Spec.* 1:16, Philo comes close to the basic principle of astrology, when he speaks

Opif. 114	12.	Ursa major consists of seven stars.
Opif. 115	13.	The Pleiades consist of seven stars.
Opif. 116	14.	The two equinoxes are seven months apart.[57]
Opif. 101	15.	The phases of the moon last seven days.
Leg. 1:8		
Spec. 1:178		
Spec. 2.56f.	16.	Because of its influence upon the stars the hebdomad is called καιρός
Opif. 124	17.	Semen solidifies in seven days.[58]
Opif. 124	18.	Menstruation lasts at most seven days.
Opif. 124	19.	Seven months' children survive.
Leg. 1:9		
Opif. 104	20.	There are seven stages of ten years each in a man's life.
Opif. 104	21.	There are seven ages in a man's life.
Opif. 105	22.	Man's life can be divided into stages of seven years each.
Leg. 1:10	23.	The irrational part of the soul has seven components.
Opif. 117	24.	The body consists of seven inner and seven outer parts.
Leg. 1:11		
QG 2:12		
Opif. 119	25.	The head has seven essential parts.
Leg. 1:12		
Opif. 120	26.	There are seven things that can be seen.
Opif. 121	27.	There are seven different intonations of the voice.
Leg. 1:14		
Opif. 122	28.	There are seven types of motion.
Leg. 1:12		
Opif. 128	29.	There are seven bodily excretions.
Leg. 1:13		
Opif. 125	30.	Illnesses reach their κρίσις on the seventh day.
Leg. 1:13		

---

of the sun, the moon, and the other stars "in accordance with their sympathetic affinity to things on earth acting and working in a thousand ways for the preservation of the All." At the same time he warns against "supposing that they alone are gods."

[57] As indicated above, this is one of the three passages in *Opif.* 89–128 in which Philo introduces a clearly Jewish element. He actually says that "each of the equinoxes occurs in a seventh month." This allows him to adduce the sacred character of the hebdomad as a reason for the dates of the highest Jewish festivals.

[58] Points 17, 18, 19, and 21 are attributed by Philo to Hippocrates.

Opif. 126	31.	The lyre has seven strings.
Leg. 1:14		
Opif. 126	32.	There are seven vowels.
Leg. 1:14		

A number of observations can be made about this list.

1. Philo almost certainly took it over from some Neopythagorean work either on arithmology in general, or on the number seven. The Greek origin of the list is obvious from the references to Greek mythology and the quotations from Greek authors.

2. Although Philo has collected in the list a veritable armory of data, a glance at the list of the passages in which any of the items re-occurs outside the lists themselves in *De Opificio Mundi* and *Legum Allegoriae*, indicates that he actually made very little use of this material in his own exegetical work. Only items nos. 2, 3, 4, 11, 15, 16, and 23 occur in any of the other treatises of the Philonic corpus. Among these, the most frequently used statement is one of Greek provenance: the number seven can be likened to the goddess Athena. The rest of the repeated items all refer to the seven planets in general or to the moon in particular.

3. These observations seem to justify the conclusion that Philo occasionally introduced arithmological statements for their own sake, without putting them to work as exegetical tools in connection with specific biblical passages.[59]

4. The shorter list of statements on the hebdomad in the *Legum Allegoriae* is based upon the longer one in the *Opificio*. Not only do many of the items occur in the same sequence, but even the transitional clauses are strictly parallel:

Opif.	101	par.	*Leg.*	1:8	transition to sensible world
	117	par.		1:9	transition to man
	126	par.		1:14	transition to sciences

The only exception to this pattern is the transitional clause introducing the hebdomad within the decade, which is found only at *Opif.* 95.[60]

A very important aspect of Philo's understanding of the number seven appears only as a subsidiary consideration in the list of arithmological

---

[59] It should be noted, however, that this is more obvious in the case of the hebdomad than with any other number, if for no other reason than that for no other number does he introduce so long and detailed a list of statements as he does in connection with the number seven.

[60] The introductory statement on the hebdomad quoted above also has no parallel anywhere in Philo.

statements given above: because seven has been likened to Zeus, it is related to the monad. And yet it is this peculiar relationship between one and seven that gives Philo an opportunity to interpret a number of biblical passages according to his own allegorical method.

In *De Posteritate Caini* Philo discusses the superiority of soul over body[61] and the precedence of Israel, though by birth the younger son, over the others, so that he even can be called "firstborn."[62] He who sees God is truly "the earliest offspring of the Uncreated one"; he is the true firstborn, and the law of Dt. 21:7 applies to him, that he should be given a double portion. From this allegorical interpretation of the law of inheritance, Philo moves on to a discussion of the superior position of the number seven, which "takes precedence of every number, in nothing differing from one."[63] Philo invokes Moses himself to supply proof for this seeming paradox. By looking at the seam between the Yahwist and the Priestly accounts of creation and by reading Gen. 2:4, not as an introduction to what follows, but rather as a summary of the preceding account, he reaches the interpretation he wants:

a. Philo quotes Gen. 2:2f.: "And God rested on the seventh day from all his works which he had made; and God blessed the seventh day and hallowed it, because in it God rested from all his works which God had begun to make."

b. He then continues his quotation with Gen. 2:4: "This is the book of the creation of heaven and earth, when it was created, in the day in which God made the heaven and the earth."

c. Philo now harmonizes Gen. 1:1 and 2:4: "Now these things were created on the first day [τῇ πρώτῃ], so that the seventh day is referred back to one, the first and starting point of all."

d. With this equation of one and seven, Philo has accomplished what he had set out to do; he closes this section by expressing satisfaction that the discussion of an opinion held by Cain has been fully treated. Thus the elaborate working-out of the equation, in this context, performs no more than a subsidiary function. In the process of it, Philo casually ignores fine points of exegesis upon which he had laid great stress in the *Opificio*, such as the fact that Gen. 1:5 speaks of "one day," and not "first,"[64] or his insistence that the chronological references in the account of the creation must under no circumstances be understood in the sense of empirical time.[65]

---

[61] *Post.* 62.
[62] *Ibid.*, 63; cf. Ex. 4:22.
[63] *Post.* 64.
[64] *Opif.* 15, 35.
[65] *Opif.* 26–28. In the *Legum Allegoriae* Philo presents a completely different inter-

Philo performs a similar exegetical feat in his comments on 1 Sam. 2:5, where in the Song of Hannah he finds the following line: στεῖρα ἔτεκεν ἑπτά, ἡ δὲ πολλὴ ἐν τέκνοις ἠσθένητε. He now takes the *Sitz im Leben* of the song literally and places it after the birth of Samuel, but before the birth of his three brothers and two sisters mentioned in 1 Sam. 2:21. This leads him to ask how Hannah, at that time the mother of one, can boast of having borne seven children. Surely, this would not be possible, unless she μονάδα ἑβδομάδι τὴν αὐτὴν φυσικώτατα νομίζει, οὐ μόνον ἐν ἀριθμοῖς, ἀλλὰ καὶ ἐν τῇ τοῦ παντὸς ἁρμονίᾳ καὶ ἐν τοῖς τῆς ἐναρέτου λόγοις ψυχῆς.[66] Hannah, therefore, understands the cosmic truth of the unity of one and seven. The seemingly nonsensical text [seven children after the report of only one birth], taken literally, not only allows Philo to make his arithmological statement about the special relationship existing between the monad and the hebdomad, he is now also able to add a statement about the unique ("monadic") position of Samuel: "For Samuel who is appointed to God alone and holds no company with any other has his being ordered in accordance with the One and the Monad, the truly existent [κατὰ τὸ ἓν καὶ τὴν μονάδα, τὸ ὄντως ὄν].[67]

But the monad implies the hebdomad, and thus Samuel's involvement with the One implies the Seven, here expressed in language reminiscent of that applied to God in *Leg.* 1:2:16: "...a soul which rests in God and toils no more at any mortal task, and has thus left behind the Six, which God has assigned to those who could not win the first place ..."

Philo then uses etymology in order to clear up another difficulty in the biblical text: how can a "barren" woman give birth? He (probably correctly) relates στεῖρα, "barren," with στερρά, "firm" or "solid," and actually equates the two. Thus he can read 1 Sam. 2:5 as saying that the "firm" or "solid" woman, "who still abounds in power, bore ἑβδομάδι τὴν ἰσότιμον μονάδα."

In this discussion of 1 Sam. 2:5, in itself no more than an illustration of the nature of the soul, Philo uses:

1. a literal reading of the context of the biblical narrative,
2. the arithmological equation of one and seven,
3. an allegorical interpretation of the hebdomad as referring to "things divine,"
4. etymology,

---

pretation of Gen. 2:2f. In *Leg.* 1:5 he denies that God would ever stop creating, because it is ἴδιον for God to create. On the seventh day God, having brought to an end the formation of mortal things, begins the shaping of others more divine. Seven as the number of "things divine" plays an important role in Philo.

[66] *Deus* 10–13, esp. 11.
[67] Gen. 15:10; the birds listed there are irrelevant in the present context.

in order to produce the type of allegorical interpretation of one biblical passage that would make it useful for the discussion of the topic at hand.

Not all cases, however, in which Philo combines one and seven are quite so elaborately constructed. In Ex. 25:36 we find a description of the menorah which Philo uses in order to interpret a passage in Genesis; the connecting link is provided by the number seven:

1. Abram, at God's behest, takes a heifer, a she-goat, and a ram, cuts them into two and lays each half over against the other.

2. This makes six pieces of carcass, plus the severer, "the Logos, who separates the two sets of three and stations himself in the midst" and thus becomes the seventh.

3. Philo now introduces another illustration of the relationship of three plus three plus one. The menorah has three branches on either side with the central stem dividing the two sets of threes. In itself, it is made "of one piece of pure gold."[68]

4. Philo is now ready to explain the meaning of the form of the menorah, one of the most important symbols of the Jewish cult: "The One, alone and absolutely pure, has begotten the Seven, whom no other bore, begotten her by himself alone, and employing no other medium whatsoever."[69] Thus the menorah finds its explanation through the Greek myth of the birth of Athena by Zeus alone, without the interference of any mother.

Philo applies the identification of one and seven also to the Jewish liturgical year, which, in his view, reflects cosmic patterns. In *Spec.* 2:156f. he discusses the celebration of Passover, a festival lasting seven days. Here the number seven is viewed as the source of good things. The number seven and its character are primary; the festival is observed to celebrate the sacred character of the hebdomad: the feast lasts seven days

> to mark the precedence and honour which the number holds in the universe, indicating that nothing which tends to cheerfulness and public mirth and thankfulness to God should fail to be accompanied with memories of the sacred seven which he intended to be the source and fountain to men of all good things.

Although the festival lasts for seven days, the first and seventh days are declared holy, thus giving a natural precedence to the beginning and

---

[68] Quoted from Ex. 25:36. If in this passage Abram is identified with the *Logos*, in *Heres* 218 it is the center arm of the menorah which divided the other six. It is one of the few instances where Philo quotes at length from the biblical text (Ex. 38:15–17) and then slips in his interpretation in an almost off-handed fashion: "Thus by many proofs it is now established that the six is divided into two threes ὑπὸ μέσου τοῦ ἑβδόμου λόγου. Within the present context, Philo is mainly concerned with the question of division, and yet the identification of seven and logos is significant.

[69] *Her.* 216.

end. This allows Philo once again to illustrate the special relationship between one and seven, both of them understood as standing at the same time for beginning and end. The past adjoins the first day of the festival, and the future adjoins its last day. As a result, "the first and the last have each other's properties in addition to their own." The first is the "beginning of the feast and the end of the preceding past"; and the seventh is the "end of the feast and beginning of the coming future."[70]

The same connection between one and the beginning, and seven and the end, is made in *Spec.* 1:187, where Philo is commenting on Nu. 29:7–11. The following burnt offering is prescribed: one young bull, one ram, seven male lambs a year old. The total number of sacrificial animals is nine, but that is of no concern to Philo. He concentrates on the presence of both "one" and "seven" and comments:

> Treating it as a festival day, he made the sacrifices of the same number as those of the sacred-month days, namely a calf and a ram and seven lambs, thus blending the one with the seven and putting the completion in line with the beginning. For to seven belongs the completion of actions, to one their beginning.

This blending of one and seven, or even their identification, represents an interesting example of Philo's use of numbers and their relationships. Since only a fraction of the Hellenistic Pythagorean literature has survived,[71] it is impossible to make any firm claims for originality in this field. We do not know whether the equation of one and seven is original with Philo or not. We are able to state, however, that the use of biblical prooftexts to buttress an arithmological relationship is probably the work of Philo. He may have been forced into this equation by the need to harmonize seemingly contradictory, or at least conflicting, accounts in the biblical text. One of the most obvious problems of this type would be seen in the juxtaposition of Gen. 1:1 and 2:4. Since Philo could not admit the use of multiple sources in the Pentateuch which, to him, was the work of Moses, and since, for this same reason, he could not allow any inconsistencies in the text, he found the solution to the problem in the identification of the numbers one and seven, so that the seventh day is the same as day one—and that, indeed, is the day on which God created heaven and earth.

But such exegetical sleights-of-hand were not the only means by which Philo could establish the identity of one and seven. We observe the

---

[70] *Spec.* 157.

[71] See Helger Thesleff, *An Introduction to the Pythagorean Writings of the Hellenistic Period,* Acta Academiae Aboensis. Humanoria XXIV (Abo: Abo Akademi, 1961); and *The Pythagorean Texts of the Hellenistic Period,* XXX.1 (1965); also Walter Burkert, "Hellenistische Pseudopythagorica," and the other references given in note 31.

application of a different method when we read that each of the equinoxes occurs in a seventh month, "and during them there is enjoined by law the keeping of the greatest national festivals."[72] Such a statement is possible only because the Jewish calendar system had two different dates for the beginning of the new year and because Philo chose to ignore the historical development of the system. In the pre-exilic agricultural calendar the beginning of the new year occurred in the spring, in the post-exilic ecclesiastical calendar it fell into the autumn. As a result we get the following pattern.

spring equinox is in the first month	(old style)
spring equinox is in the seventh month	(new style)
autumn equinox is in the first month	(new style)
autumn equinox is in the seventh month	(old style)

Thus it is possible to say that both equinoxes occur in the seventh month, but also to state that both occur in the first month.

Philo was aided in the development of this pattern by another habit of his. On many occasions he equates the "seventh day" with the number "seven," thus transferring characteristics of the one to the other.[73]

In *Her.* 169–173 Philo gives a brief summary of the ten commandments, without quoting any of them *verbatim*. In 170 he makes the startling statement that the fourth commandment is ὁ περὶ τῆς ἀειπαρθένου καὶ ἀμήτορος ἑβδομάδος. The peculiarly Jewish character of the sabbath is replaced by an allusion to a Greek myth: the fourth commandment has as its subject the motherless birth of the virgin Athena by Zeus. When discussing the fourth commandment in *Decal.* 158–164, Philo again says that it deals περὶ τῆς ἑβδομάδος.

Sabbath

The close connection that Philo establishes between the sabbath and the number seven which, as we have seen, can go as far as complete identification, is merely a part of his consistent interpretation of the sabbath in a universalistic sense, thus depriving it of any specifically Jewish features. The sabbath [a term rarely used by Philo] is a universal

---

[72] *Opif.* 116.

[73] Colson translates, "of the seventh day." He discusses similar instances in Philo and also gives one reference to Josephus (*C. Ap.* 2:282). He chides the editors of the revised edition of Liddell & Scott for having expunged the entry of older editions, "The seventh day, *Eccl.*" Colson also points out that Philo sometimes has ἑβδόμη in the sense of ἑβδομάς (e.g., *Opif.* 116; *Post.* 64), but he does not venture an explanation of the phenomenon. (LCL Philo VII, p. 613, note on § 158.)

holiday, not merely the festival of a single city or country; it is the birthday of the world.[74] As a result, the purpose of the sabbath is universal in character: Those who would be citizens in ταύτῃ τῇ πολιτείᾳ, in the cosmos created by God, should follow God in this as in other matters:

rest on the seventh day,
turn to the study of wisdom,
> while they had leisure for the contemplation of the truths of nature,
>> they should also consider whether any offense against purity had been committed [εἴ τι μὴ καθαρῶς ἐν ταῖς προτέπαις ἐπράχθη] in the preceding days.[75]

A different reason for the keeping of the sabbath is given in *Abr.* 28:f. The reason is not, as a literal interpretation would have it, that after six days the multitude abstained from their usual tasks, but rather that, both in the world and in ourselves, "the number seven is always free from factions and war and quarreling and is of all numbers the most peaceful." Such a sweeping claim requires proof, and Philo promptly supplies it with the help for his arithmological psychology: our six senses[76] are always at war against each other, but the seventh [ἡ ἑβδόμη δύναμις ἡ περὶ τὸν ἡγεμόνα νοῦν] overcomes the six "and welcomes solitude and its own society, feeling that it needs no other and is completely sufficient for itself." Here the number seven, because it is the number of things divine, and because of its lordship over the six and its self-sufficiency, allows the universalistic explanation of the sabbath (a term avoided by Philo also in this passage).[77]

The character of seven as a leader is brought out in another discussion of the seventh day, in *Spec.* 2:56. Note the shift from "day" to "number": "The second [feast] to be observed is the sacred seventh day... Some have given to it the name of virgin, having before their eyes its surpassing chastity." Seven is then explained as:

motherless, begotten by the father of the universe alone,
the ideal form of the male sex with nothing of the female,
the manliest and doughtiest of all numbers,
well gifted by nature [εὖ πεφυκῶς] for sovereignty and leadership.

---

[74] *Opif.* 89: ἑορτὴ γὰρ οὐ μιᾶς πόλεως ἢ χώρας ἐστὶν ἀλλὰ τοῦ παντός, ... τοῦ κόσμου γενέθλιον. See also *Mos.* 1:207; 2:210; *Spec.* 1:170 [the seventh day is not only the birthday of the whole world (τοῦ κόσμου παντός), but it is of equal value to eternity (ἰσότιμον ἡγούμενος αἰῶνι τὴν ἑβδόμην)]; 2:59, 70.

[75] *Decal.* 98; in the following paragraph rest on the seventh day is prescribed as useful for man who has to labor for his living on six days every week.

[76] The line of argument at this point requires Philo to omit the organ of reproduction, usually counted as the seventh component of the irrational part of the soul.

[77] Philo's desire to avoid the use of the term sabbath is clearly demonstrated, e.g., by his changing the biblical text. Lev. 24:8 reads τῇ ἡμέρᾳ τῶν σαββάτων, and Philo changes this to ταῖς ἑβδόμαις.

But the most sweeping *interpretatio Graeca* of the sabbath is probably the one found in *Mos.* 2:209f. Again we notice the shift from day to number and, in this case, back to day.

1. Moses magnified τὴν ἱερὰν ἑβδόμην [the holy seventh day],
2. because its marvelous beauty is found in heaven, the entire cosmos, and in nature itself:
    a. it is motherless, exempt from female parentage, begotten by the father alone, without begetting, brought to birth, yet not carried in the womb;
    b. ever virgin,[78] neither born of a mother nor a mother herself, neither bred from corruption, nor doomed to corruption;
    c. the birthday of the world
        a feast celebrated by heaven
        a feast celebrated by earth and on earth—
        as they exult in the full harmony of the sacred number

The account of the people of Israel wandering in the wilderness for forty years contains the report of the miraculous provision of food for the people. Since on the seventh day they were not allowed to do any work, special provisions were made on the previous day to spare them any severe hardships. But the supply of a double ration of manna on the preceding day and its failure to appear on the sabbath had an unexpected side effect. The people, for many generations, had longed to know "what was the birthday of the world on which the universe was completed," and now they found the answer in the miracle of the double provision of food for the sabbath.[79] Philo here interprets what he sees as an historical event as a revelation of a cosmic fact.

The Hebdomad as a Cosmic Factor

Philo's often repeated statement that the seventh day is the birth of the cosmos is based upon one of his interpretations of Gen. 2:2f. The only passages in which he actually gives a reason for calling the seventh day "birthday of the cosmos" is *Spec.* 2:58f., where he interprets Gen. 2:2f. in a progressive manner: six is the number under which the parts of the universe were brought into being, seven that under which they were perfected, so that "from a higher point of view" Moses could call seven συντέλεια and παντέλεια. "Seven reveals as completed what six has

---

[78] "Ever Virgin" – in *Opif.* 100 this epithet is ascribed to philosophers other than Pythagorean; in *Leg.* 1:15 to the Pythagoreans themselves. The second view is supported by the statement in Stobaeus, *Ecl.* 1.1.10, that Pythagoras, likening the numbers to the God, called seven Athena. Cf. Philo LCL VI, 609, note on § 210.
[79] *Mos.* 1:205–207.

produced,[80] and therefore it may be quite rightly entitled the birthday of the cosmos, on which the Father's perfect work, compounded of perfect parts, was revealed as what it was."[81] Seven thus is not only the number of perfection, it is also the means through which this perfection is revealed.[82]

The most common symbol used by Philo to express the cosmic significance of the hebdomad, and at the same time to demonstrate the harmony existing between the cosmos and the Jewish cult as ordained by God and instituted by Moses, is the menorah. In *QE* 2:78 Philo refers to Ex. 25:37a and asks: "Why are there seven lamps on the lampstand?" The answer: the seven lamps are symbols of the planets, because the hebdomad "belongs to those things reckoned as divine." At this point Philo comes close to an astrological interpretation of the significance of the movement of the planets:

> And the movement and revolution of these through the zodiacal signs, are the causes, for sublunary beings, of all those things which are wont to take place in the embrace of concord, in the air, in the water, on the earth, and in all mixtures from animals to plants.

Without any specific biblical reference, Philo in *Mos.* 2:102f. describes the arrangement of the sacred furniture in the tabernacle.[83] He has Moses place the menorah at the south, "for the sun and the moon and the others run their courses in the south far away from the north." After a description of the arrangement of the branches of the menorah (three-one-three), Philo draws the analogy between the lampstand and the planetary system. Although he is aware that the exact sequence of the planets is a matter of dispute among astronomers, Philo accepts that theory which places the sun in the middle position, with three planets each above the

---

[80] See E.A. Speiser, *Genesis*, The Anchor Bible 1 (Garden City, N.Y., Doubleday, 1964) 7 *ad loc.*, and his translation, "God brought to a close the work that he had been doing," or A. Heidel, *The Babylonian Genesis* (Chicago U.P., 2nd ed., 1951) 127, who renders the verse as "and on the seventh day God declared his work finished." In view of the statement in the two preceding verses that God had completed his work on the sixth day, Heidel sees in the verb form "a declarative piᶜel."

[81] For a different line of interpretation of Gen. 2:3f., see *Leg.* 1:5f., where God on the seventh day starts with the creation of things "happy and blessed." There it is flatly denied that God ever ceases making: οὐ παύεται δε ποιῶν αὐτός.

[82] For another statement on seven as a means of revelation, see *Decal.* 105: "Nothing so much assures its (seven's) predominance as that through it is best given the revelation of the father and maker of all, for in it, as in a mirror, the mind has a vision of God as acting and creating the world and controlling all that is." It would be hasty to adduce this passage as a prooftext for number "mysticism" in Philo.

[83] The implied reference is to Ex. 25:31–40, where it is not stated, however, that the lampstand is placed in the south part of the tabernacle. Josephus, *Ant.* 3:146, says that the seven lamps faced southeast.

sun and below.[84] The reason adduced by Philo indicates that he has some knowledge of astronomical theory: the sun is in the middle position because "it gives light to the three above and the three below it." In *Her.* 221–225, Philo offers the same explanation, without indicating the biblical passage in which the menorah is described. In this treatise he makes explicit the reason for the shape of the lampstand: "The τεχνίτης, wishing that we should possess a copy of the archetypal celestial sphere with its seven lights, commanded this splendid work, the lampstand, to be wrought." The menorah is a copy of the planetary system.[85]

But not only liturgical instruments like the menorah reflect the harmony that exists between the cosmos and the Jewish cult, this is done also by the Jewish liturgical calendar. In *Spec.* 1:118f. Philo, without quoting the biblical reference at Num. 28:16, refers to the law concerning the festival of unleavened bread. During the first month, in this case at the time of the spring equinox, the festival shall be kept for seven days: "because the seven days of the feast bore the same relation to the equinox which falls in the seventh month as the new moon does to the month.... The seven days of the feast, which being of the same number as the new moons represented them collectively."

Even the number of sacrificial animals prescribed for the burnt offering at the new moons reflects the harmony existing between the cosmos and the ritual. In *Spec.* 1:177f. Philo, without specific reference to Nu. 28:11–14, states that the burnt offering calls for ten victims: two calves, one ram, and seven lambs. The offering is presented at the time of the new moon at the beginning of every month. The month, in turn, is a "complete or perfect whole," and for this reason the number of sacrificial animals should be perfect: ten is a perfect number.[86] This perfect number is divided according to a perfect pattern:

the two calves represent the waning and waxing [two motions]
the one ram represents the one law that governs the changes of the moon
the seven lambs represent the complete cycle of the changes in the forms of
    the moon, which is measured in units of seven days each:

---

[84] On the scientific uncertainty, see *Her.* 224. In the system adopted by Philo, the three planets above the sun are Saturn, Jupiter, and Mars, and those below are Mercury, Venus, and the moon [*ibid.*].

[85] The same explanation for the menorah is given by Josephus, *Ant.* 3:146.

[86] This is not true in a strictly mathematical sense, but reflects the extremely high esteem in which the decad was held by the Pythagoreans.

1. waxing crescent   - 7 days
2. full moon   - 7 days
3. waning crescent   - 7 days
4. new moon   - 7 days

28 days of the month

But the most dramatic and elaborate structure to indicate the cosmic importance of the hebdomad is developed by Philo in *QE* 2:68. The passage is instructive also as an illustration of the arbitrary manner in which Philo is willing to proceed whenever he wants to establish a specific point.

In the pattern usual for *Quaestiones et Solutiones*, Philo starts with a biblical quotation and a question relating to it. He abbreviates Ex. 25:21b [Heb. 22b] and asks: "What is the meaning of the words, 'I will speak to thee above from the mercy-seat, between the two cherubim'?" The reader would now expect an allegorical interpretation of the cherubim, but that Philo had already offered in the preceding chapters of this treatise. What we get now is a picture of the structure of the world above the intelligible world. We find the following pattern:

1.   He who is elder than the one and the monad and the beginning;
2.   the Logos of the Existent One, the truly seminal substance of existing things;
3/4.   two powers: creative ("God") royal ("Lord");
5/6.   two powers: propitious ("beneficial") legislative ("punitive");
7.   the ark (symbol of the intelligible world—symbolically contains all things established in the innermost sanctuary).

Philo considers this pattern so important that he repeats it twice in reverse sequence. First he states that "the number of things here enumerated amounts to seven." Then he gives the list in ascending order:

1.   the intelligible world;
2/3.   the two related powers: punitive beneficent
4/5.   the two preceding powers: creative royal
6.   the Logos
7.   the Speaker

And finally the descending order:

1.   the Speaker
2.   the Logos
3.   the creative power
4.   the ruling power
5.   the beneficent power
6.   the punitive power
7.   the world of ideas

The lowest of the seven is the world of ideas. There is no room in this system for any form of "number mysticism" through which man would be enabled to have a vision of God, much less to enter into union with the One. At the same time it is worth noting that Philo in this passage remains faithful to one of the basic principles of the Hebrew understanding of God and his people: God speaks and the people hear. God is the Speaker, and it is important to see that Philo has chosen a biblical text in which God appears as the Speaker to develop his elaborate system of the divine court—which, once again, reflects the importance and sanctity of the number seven.

Microcosmos

One of the underlying assumptions of Philo's understanding of the universe and all its parts, is the affinity, perhaps even identity, between the macrocosmos and the microcosmos represented by man. The concept itself is Stoic, but Philo can accept it without difficulty, provided he disregards the type of pantheism implied in the Stoic notion. Philo can see the unity of all creation because behind it all he recognizes one creator. Thus we should not be surprised if Philo recognizes parallels between the make-up of the world and that of man.

Her. 232f. can serve as a good example of Philo's procedure and exegetical method in this connection. The entire treatise is a detailed commentary on Gen. 15:2–18, but as usual Philo feels free to draw illustrative materials from other passages. The starting point for this pericope is Gen. 15:10: "He did not divide the birds" (230). The allegorical interpretation of the birds understands them as "two words or forms of reason." One is the archetypal reason above us, the other the copy which we possess.

Our psychic make-up represents an exact parallel to the structure of the heavens:
1. a.   Our νοῦς is indivisible by nature.
   b.   The sphere of the fixed stars is kept unsevered.
2. a.   The irrational part of our souls, through a sixfold division, has been formed into seven parts.[87]
   b.   The inner sphere of the heavens, by a sixfold division, produces the seven circles of the planets.[88]
This allows Philo to state: "I regard the soul as being in man what the

---

[87] The division of the irrational part of the soul into seven parts is the more common one in Philo; if occasion requires, he can also ignore one part (the organ of reproduction) and speak of only six components.

[88] Philo's astronomy is based upon Plato's *Timaeus* 35D.

heaven is in the universe." More than that: the two reasoning and intellectual natures, the cosmic and the human one, "are integral and undivided." And this, lest we forget, is the reason for the scriptural text: "The birds he did not divide."

The analogy between the starry heavens and the psychic make-up of man was made possible for Philo because he recognized the number seven as an element common to both. But he was also able to use his theories concerning the relationships between the monad and the hebdomad, the one corresponding to the fixed stars and the "reasoning and intellectual power," the other to the planets and the "irrational" part of our soul. The connection between this elaborate scheme and the biblical text supposedly under discussion is tenuous.

In *Her.* 225 Philo offers a different explanation of the structure of the human soul; unfortunately this passage is far from clear. Without any reference to a biblical passage, Philo states that the soul is tripartite, and each of the parts, "as has been shown," is divided into two, resulting in six parts, to which the ἱερὸς καὶ θεῖος λόγος, the "All-severer," makes a fitting seventh. Philo is alluding in this passage to *Her.* 132:[89] the soul consists of ψυχή, λόγος (understood as speech) and αἴσθησις, with the following subdivisions:

1. ψυχή a. rational
   b. irrational
2. λόγος a. true
   b. false
3. αἴσθησις a. presentations where the object is real and apprehended.
   b. presentations where it is not.

The whole section in which this passage occurs speaks of various forms of division being performed by the "Severer of all things," that is his world [τῷ τομεῖ τῶν συμπάντων ἑαυτοῦ λόγῳ] and in *Her.* 225 Philo finds himself able to add up the six parts and now, by adding the τομεὺς ἁπάντων ὁ ἱερὸς καὶ θεῖος λόγος, comes up with the hebdomad, as is "fitting" [εἰκότως].

The fact that Philo can divide an entity like the human soul into different numbers of components indicates what his priority really is: he wants to make a specific point; he wants to illustrate that point through the arithmological significance of a number, and he will then find (or produce) an appropriate number which will provide the example wanted. Any concrete connection with a scriptural text is practically nonexistent or, at best, strictly secondary.

---

[89] The soul is also given a tripartite division at *Conf* 21 [νοῦς, θυμός, ἐπιθυμία], but there we find no further subdivision.

Historical use of the hebdomad

Philo even insists that historical events reveal some of their significance by falling on certain dates or occurring after a specific interval of time. Again, a few examples involving the hebdomad may serve to illustrate this point.

In *QG* 1:77 Philo discusses Gen. 4:23, and in the process we can observe how he takes liberties with the literal meaning of the text.

Philo asks the kind of question usually found in this part of the corpus: "If sevenfold punishment shall be enacted for Cain, then for Lamech seventy times seven?" The question still follows the line of thought found in Genesis: the sevenfold punishment is threatened against anyone who would kill Cain; it is not the punishment inflicted upon the first fratricide.

Philo now proceeds in two steps: first he discusses the arithmological values of seven and seventy times seven, respectively, and then he demonstrates the moral justification for this kind of arrangement.

1. Philo follows the basic Pythagorean understanding of numbers when he states that "the ones are prior to the tens both in order and in power."[90] The Pythagoreans based their speculations on the numbers within the decade. Thus "seven is more archetypal and elder than seventy," while seventy is younger and derivative. These are the arithmological facts, the basis which determines the course of events.[91] Then Philo shifts in his interpretation: instead of following the text of Genesis, where the punishment is threatened as a revenge which is meant to protect the life of Cain, he now speaks of punishment exacted from Cain for his murder of Abel.[92] Cain, because he did not really know what he was doing, received the lesser punishment. But Lamech, having Cain as a warning example before him, had no excuse, was guilty of voluntary sin, and received punishment, both in the units and in the tens.

2. But what is the function of seven in this process? "According to the law," a sevenfold judgment is given.[93] The pattern adduced by Philo reads like a late version of the *lex talionis*: the judgment is inflicted upon each part of the irrational part of the soul:

---

90   Ralph Marcus, *ad loc.* in LCL XI, gives τάξει καὶ δυνάμει as the Greek equivalent.

91   Philo actually says "These things being determined ..."

92   According to Philo, Cain is "more simply punished in accordance with the first and doubtful number, I mean one." The "one" instead of "units" may be based upon an error in the Armenian translation or in the transmission of the Armenian text. But why a number within the decade should be called "doubtful" remains unclear.

93   Lev. 24:17: "He who kills a man shall be put to death." Similarly Gen. 9:6; Nu. 35:30; the penalty inflicted upon Cain: "when you till the ground, it shall no longer yield to you its strength; you shall be a fugitive and a wanderer on the earth" (Gen. 4:12). "Law" here may simply refer to the book of Genesis as part of Torah.

the eyes, because they saw what was not fitting;

the ears, because they heard what was not proper;

the nose, because it was deceived by smoke and steam;

the [organ of] taste, which was a servant of the belly's pleasure;

the [organ of] touch, to which the collaboration of the former senses in over-coming the soul are also brought in addition other separate acts, such as conquest and destruction of cities;

the tongue and the organs of speech for being silent about things that should be said and for saying things that should be kept silent;

the lower belly, which with lawlessness sets the senses on fire.

This, then, is the reason why "a sevenfold vengeance is taken on Cain."

This passage has hardly anything to do with the biblical text. Philo gives the story of Cain and Lamech a moralistic interpretation and starts, not from the text, but from his prior conviction that sin results from letting the components of the irrational part of the soul remain unchecked. In order to get this point across, Philo does not hesitate to alter the meaning of what to him was an historical narrative. Once again the number seven is the trigger which sets Philo's interpretation into motion.

In *QG* 2:13 Philo presents a long arithmological interpretation of the various time elements involved in the great flood. Here, too, the hebdomad plays an important role. The delay of the flood for seven days after Noah entered the ark is a representative example of the allegorical type of interpretation Philo can apply. The number seven itself is mentioned in the biblical text, and Philo merely adds his exegetical comments:

1. The seven days are a reminder of the genesis of the world, of which the birthday is celebrated on the seventh day.[94]

2. Whereas the creation was an expression of God's goodness, the destruction by flood was caused by "the ingratitude and impiety of those who have experienced good."

3. The delay presents an opportunity for repentance.

Philo recognizes the working of the hebdomad not only at the beginning of the flood, but also at its end. The situation is difficult to analyze, since the narrative in Genesis distinguishes two different stages (first the end of the increase in water and the beginning of its recession, and then, in chapter 8, the time when the earth was once again dry). Both of these stages are mentioned in the two different strands of the narrative, the

---

[94] The relationship between the destructive element of the flood and the birthday, either of the cosmos or of Noah, the righteous man, forms an important secondary motif in Philo's interpretation of the flood narrative. In *QG* 2:31, he flatly states that "the beginning of the flood fell in the seventh month on the birthday of the righteous man at the vernal equinox."

Priestly and the Yahwist.[95] In addition, there are differences between the Hebrew and the Greek texts.[96] But for Philo's purposes, this is not sufficient: in order to be able to impose his scheme upon the narrative, he has to read Gen. 8:14 as "in the seventh month," not, with the Hebrew text and most manuscripts of the LXX, "in the second month."

Philo then develops the following pattern:

1. The beginning of the flood and its diminution[97] both fell in the seventh month on the twenty-seventh day. But in reality these events were separated by seven months: the beginning of the flood occurred on Noah's birthday at the vernal equinox, the diminution began at the autumnal equinox.

2. This kind of schematization is possible because of the identity existing between one and seven: the seventh month of the equinox is potentially also the first, since the creation of the world took place in this month because all things were full at this time. Similarly (the month of) the autumnal equinox, (which) is the seventh in time, is the first in honor, the seventh having its beginning from the air.[98]

Philo, once again, takes advantage of the two different dates for the beginning of the year in Jewish tradition. He further postulates that both equinoxes occur on the twenty-seventh day of the seventh month, the source of this idea being unknown.

Philo is disturbed by the different dates he finds in Gen. 8:13 and 14. In *QG* 2:47 he asks: "Why was the earth dried up in the seventh month, on the twenty-seventh day?" Neither the Hebrew text, nor most manuscripts of the LXX mention a "seventh" month in this context at all. The standard readings in v. 13 is τοῦ πρώτου μηνός, in v. 14 τῷ μηνὶ τῷ δευτέρῳ. Philo, instead, keeps "first" in v. 13 and reads "seventh" in v. 14. This allows him to apply an arithmological interpretation to the passage. Instead of seeing in v. 13 the beginning of a process [ἐξέλιπεν τὸ ὕδωρ] in the first month, and in the second month the end result of this process [ἐξηράνθη],

---

95 Stage I, J: "the fountains of the deep were closed, and the waters receded from the earth continually" (Gen. 8:2a, 3); P: "at the end of a hundred and fifty days the waters had abated, and in the seventh month, the seventeenth day of the month, the ark came to rest on the mountains of Ararat" (Gen. 8:3b–4).

Stage II, J: "At the end of forty days Noah opened the window of the ark ... and the dove did not return to him any more ... and Noah ... looked,... and the face of the ground was dry" (Gen. 8:6–12, 13b); P: "in the six hundred and first year, in the first month, the first day of the month, the waters were dried from off the earth; ... in the second month, on the twenty-seventh day of the month, the earth was dry" (Gen. 8:13a, 14).

96 In Gen. 8:3, LXX, "on the twenty-seventh day."

97 "When the ark rested on the summits of the mountains" (*QG* 2:31).

98 *Ibid.* No reasonable explanation for the last clause seems to be possible (see R. Marcus in his note *ad loc.*).

he replaces the developmental interpretation with a static identification of the numbers one and seven, repeating in this process many of the things he had said on this topic in the earlier sections.

Here we have one of the clearest examples of forced exegesis in the writings of Philo. His preconceived notions about the harmony in the cosmos and the orderly development of historical events, based upon Neopythagorean arithmological speculations, take priority over any straightforward reading of the text.

If it is possible to observe arithmological patterns in the account of the creation and in the primeval history of man, we should expect Philo to apply the same system to the life of the man who composed the record which contains all these marvelous observations. And, indeed, Moses is associated with the number seven in its character as the number of "things divine."[99] In *Post.* 173 Philo states that the seven generations from Abraham to Moses are more perfect than the preceding twice ten generations. But it is also worth noting how Philo applies the language of the Greek mysteries to the Hebrew legislator. Moses is not only πάντα σοφός, he represents the seventh generation from Abraham, and that means that he does not, like those before him, "haunt the outer court of the Holy Place as one seeking initiation [οἷα μύστης], but as a sacred guide [ὥσπερ ἱεροφάντης][100] he has his abode in the sanctuary." Once again, the hebdomad is employed as a means to indicate Moses' superiority over the patriarchs and his closeness to things divine, all this expressed in Greek sacred terms.

Conclusion

This partial yet, it is hoped, representative survey of the arithmological use of the number seven by Philo has concentrated on trying to demonstrate the connection which he attempts to establish between the text of the Torah and the cosmos, the process of creation, the furniture and calendar of the Jewish liturgical life, and certain historical events. In many instances, the biblical text presents Philo with all the data required by him, but in many others the link between the biblical text and Philo's arithmological interpretation is, at best, tenuous. In some instances, he simply alters the reading in order to be able to develop his arithmological pattern.

Firm conclusions about the function of Philo's arithmology within the whole pattern of his exegesis can be drawn only when all the evidence

---

[99] Gen. 2:3.
[100] Cf. *Leg.* 3:219; *Cher.* 48, 49; *Sacr.* 60; *Gig.* 54; *Fug.* 85; *Somn.* 78; *Spec.* 1:319; *Praem.* 121.

has been collected and analyzed. But it is possible, even now, to make a few preliminary observations:

1. Arithmology is a frequently used exegetical tool of Philo's, but it is only one among several and must be judged as an integral part of his entire exegetical approach.

2. In his arithmology, Philo makes heavy uses of Greek myths and symbols, which he applies to purely Jewish concepts.

3. Arithmology allows Philo to stress two points:

   a. the cosmic and human order described by Moses is of universal validity, as is made most obvious in Philo's universalistic interpretation of the sabbath;

   b. this order is represented most clearly and purely in Jewish law, liturgy, and tradition; the Jewish religion is, therefore, the most "natural" religion.

4. The superiority of the Jewish tradition is not esoteric in character: as can be shown through arithmology, it is reasonable and demonstrably so.

Arithmology, then, is a tool valuable for Philo's intentions. It is an exegetical method alien to us, but certainly no more forced than most other aspects of allegorical interpretation. It deserves more careful study.

LIST OF CONTRIBUTORS

ROBERT M. BERCHMAN is Assistant Professor of Philosophy, Dowling College, Oakdale, New York 11769-1999.

JACQUES CAZEAUX is Director of Research, Centre National de la Recherche Scientifique, Lyon. His postal address is Maison de l'Orient, 7 Rue Raulin, 69007 Lyon, France.

EARLE HILGERT is Professor Emeritus of New Testament, McCormick Theological Seminary, Chicago, Illinois. His postal address is 3840 West Drive, Charlottesville, Virginia 22901-9223.

JOHN PETER KENNEY is Professor of Religion and Humanities, Reed College, Portland, Oregon 97202-8199.

KAREN L. KING is Professor of Religious Studies, Occidental College, Los Angeles, California 90041.

BURTON MACK is John Wesley Professor of New Testament, Claremont School of Theology, Claremont, California 91711.

DAVID WINSTON is Professor of Hellenistic and Jewish Studies, Graduate Theological Union, Berkeley, California 94709.

INDICES

Biblical Citations

Philonic Citations

ANCIENT AUTHORS AND TEXTS

Brown Judaic Studies

Brown Studies on Jews and Their Societies

Brown Studies in Religion